MILITARY PERSONNEL MEASUREMENT

MILITARY PERSONNEL MEASUREMENT

Testing, Assignment, Evaluation _____

Edited by
MARTIN F. WISKOFF
and
GLENN M. RAMPTON

PRAEGER

New York
Westport, Connecticut
London

123468

Library of Congress Cataloging-in-Publication Data

Military personnel measurement : testing, assignment, evaluation /
  edited by Martin F. Wiskoff and Glenn M. Rampton.
    p. cm.
  Includes index.
  ISBN 0-275-92924-8 (alk. paper)
  1. United States—Armed Forces—Personnel management.
2. Soldiers—United States—Examinations. 3. Soldiers—United
States—Classification. I. Wiskoff, Martin F. II. Rampton, Glenn
M.
UB337.M55   1989
355.6'1'0973—dc19   89-3691

Library of Congress Catalog Card Number: 89-3691
ISBN: 0-275-92924-8

First published in 1989

Praeger Publishers, One Madison Avenue, New York, NY 10010
A division of Greenwood Press, Inc.

Printed in the United States of America

The paper used in this book complies with the Permanent Paper Standard issued by
the National Information Standards Organization (Z39.48—1984).

10 9 8 7 6 5 4 3 2 1

Contents

TABLES AND FIGURES   ix

ACRONYMS   xi

ACKNOWLEDGMENTS   xv

INTRODUCTION   xvii
Martin F. Wiskoff and Glenn M. Rampton

1   ENLISTED SELECTION AND CLASSIFICATION:
   ADVANCES IN TESTING   1
   Mary K. Schratz and Malcolm James Ree

    Introduction   1

    History of Enlisted Testing   2

    Item Response Theory   8

    CAT in the Military   18

    Expanding the Testing Domain   28

    Conclusion   33

    References   34

2   PERSONNEL CLASSIFICATION/ASSIGNMENT MODELS   41
   Leonard P. Kroeker

    Introduction   41

    Military Accessioning Procedures   44

    Military Classification Models   50

    Other Allocation Systems   57

    Algorithms   60

     Person-Job Matching   61
     New Developments   64
     Summary   65
     References   66

3   COMPUTERIZED VOCATIONAL GUIDANCE SYSTEMS   75
    Herbert George Baker and Reginald T. Ellis

     Introduction   75
     Requirements for Vocational Information and Guidance   75
     Civilian Approximations of CVG Systems   76
     Components of a CVG System   78
     Military Approximations of CVG Systems   80
     Current U.S. Navy Programs   90
     Conclusion   91
     References   92

4   OFFICER APTITUDE SELECTION MEASURES   97
    Dianne C. Brown

     Introduction   97
     Officer Candidate Programs   98
     Officer Aptitude Selection Measures   100
     Brief Historical Review of Officer Selection Tests   115
     Summary and Conclusions   122
     References   125

5   AVIATOR SELECTION   129
    David R. Hunter

     Introduction   129
     Paper-and-Pencil Cognitive Ability Tests   131
     Personality, Interest, and Background Information Tests   137
     Psychomotor and Information-Processing Tests   145
     Light-Plane and Job-Sample Tests   154
     Discussion and Conclusions   158
     References   161

6   EVALUATION OF INDIVIDUAL ENLISTED
    PERFORMANCE   169
    Robert Vineberg and John N. Joyner

     Introduction   169
     Peacetime Criteria for Combat Performance   170

Types of Military Evaluation   172
Evaluation Systems of the Military Services   174
Research in Individual Evaluation   180
Notes   195
References   196

INDEX   201

ABOUT THE EDITORS AND CONTRIBUTORS   207

Tables and Figures

TABLES

1.1	Tests of ASVAB Forms 5, 6, 7	5
1.2	Tests of ASVAB Forms 8, 9, and 10	6
2.1	Hierarchy of Assignment Objectives	45
2.2	Military Accessioning Systems	50
4.1	Number and Percent of FY 1986 Active Duty Officer Accessions by Service and Source of Commission	101
4.2	Officer Selection Battery Forms 3 and 4 Validities for Subgroups	105
4.3	Officer Selection Battery Forms 1 and 2 Subtests and Content Description	106
4.4	Armed Services Vocational Aptitude Battery Subtests	107
4.5	U.S. Navy and Marine Corps Aviation Selection Test Battery	110
4.6	Construction of AFOQT Form 0 Composites	114
4.7	Aptitude Measures Used in the Selection of Officer Candidates by Service and Source of Commission, 1987	123
5.1	Summary of Paper-and-Pencil Cognitive Ability Tests	135
5.2	Summary of Personality, Interest, and Background Information Tests	144
5.3	Summary of Psychomotor and Information Processing Tests	152
5.4	Summary of Light-Plane and Job-Sample Tests	159

6.1   Measurement Techniques Categorized by Amount of
      Inference from Intervention to Job Performance   182
6.2   Intervention Alternatives for Inferring Task Performance
      on the Job   183

FIGURES

2.1   Payoff Value Matrix   62
3.1   Computerized Vocational Guidance Elements   79
3.2   AGENA Guidance Process Flow   83
3.3   AGENA Guidance Session in Progress   84

Acronyms

ACAP	Accelerated CAT-ASVAB Project
ACB	Aircrew Classification Battery
ACES	Army Continuing Education Service
ACT	American College Test
ADP	automated data processing
AFHRL	Air Force Human Resources Laboratory
AFOQT	Air Force Officer Qualifying Test
AFQT	Armed Forces Qualification Test
AFROTC	Air Force Reserve Officer Training Corps
AFSC	Air Force Specialty Code
AGCT	Army General Classification Test
AGENA	Automated Guidance for Enlisted Navy Applicants
AOCS	Aviation Officer Candidate School
APAMS	Automated Pilot Aptitude Measurement System
AQT	Aviation Qualification Test
AREIS	Army Education Information System
ARI	Army Research Institute for the Behavioral and Social Sciences
ASAP	Armed Services Applicant Profile
ASVAB	Armed Services Vocational Aptitude Battery
AVF	All Volunteer Force
BAT	Basic Abilities Test
BTB	Basic Test Battery

BUMED	Bureau of Medicine and Surgery
CAI	computer-assisted instruction
CAPS	Career Advisement and Personnel System
CAST	Computerized Adaptive Screening Test
CAT	computerized adaptive testing
CEEB	College Entrance Examination Board
CF	Canadian Forces
CFCIS	Canadian Forces Career Information System
CLASP	Classification and Assignment Within PRIDE
CNATRA	Chief of Naval Air Training
COBRA	Computer Based Recruit Assignment
CODAP	Comprehensive Occupational Data Analysis Program
COMPASS	Computer Assisted Assignment System
CVG	computerized vocational guidance
CVIS	Computerized Vocational Information System
CVT	Control of Velocity Test
DI	Decision Index
DMT	Defense Mechanism Test
DOB	Differential Officer Battery
DOD	Department of Defense
EER	Enlisted Efficiency Report
EPAS	Enlisted Personnel Allocation System
EPI	Eysenck Personality Inventory
EST	Enlistment Screening Test
FAR	Flight Aptitude Rating
FAST	Flight Aptitude Selection Test
GPA	grade point average
GRIP	Graphic Information Processing Tests
HP	Hewlett Packard
IRT	item response theory
JOIN	U.S. Army Joint Optical Information Network System
MCT	Mechanical Comprehension Test
MEDCOM	Naval Medical Command
MEPS	Military Entrance Processing Station
MMPI	Minnesota Multiphasic Personality Inventory
MOS	military occupational speciality

MTA	Military Testing Association
NGCT	Navy General Classification Test
NORC	National Opinion Research Center
NOTAP	Navy Occupational Task Analysis Program
NPRDC	Navy Personnel Research and Development Center
NROTC	Navy Reserve Officer Training Corps
NVIS	Navy Vocational Information System
OAR	Officer Aptitude Rating
OCS	Officer Candidate School (Army)
OSB	Officer Selection Battery
OTS	Officer Training School
PAE	Physical Aptitude Examination
PJM	person-job match
PQS	Personnel Qualification Standards
PRIDE	Personalized Reservation for Immediate and Delayed Enlistment
PROMIS	Procurement Management Information System
RAAF	Royal Australian Air Force
RAF	Royal Air Force
RCAF	Royal Canadian Air Force
ROTC	Reserve Officer Training Corps (Army)
RTC	Recruit Training Center
SAT	Scholastic Aptitude Test
SCM	Sequential Classification Module
SKT	Specialty Knowledge Test
SMA	Sensory Motor Apparatus
SQT	Skill Qualification Test
SVIB	Strong Vocational Interest Blank
TLV	Trade and Lifestyle Videotape
UPT	Undergraduate Pilot Training
USAF	United States Air Force
USAFA	United States Air Force Academy
USMA	United States Military Academy
USNA	United States Naval Academy
VOICE	Vocational Interest for Career Enhancement
WAPS	Weighted Airman Promotion System
WCS	whole candidate score
WPS	whole person score

Acknowledgments

Acknowledgments should be made to the many individuals who contributed to the generation of this book. The major credit, of course, must go to the authors who persevered through long and often frustrating delays. Credit is due to David Atwater, M. A. Fischl, Paul Foley, and Randolph Park who participated in the early stages of chapter development. Chapter reviews that improved the clarity and technical accuracy of the material were provided by Bruce Bloxom, John Ellis, Arthur Gilbert, Jackie James, Gerald Laabs, Richard Sorenson, Lonnie Valentine, and Joe Ward. The editors are indebted to Mary Schratz for her hard work and cheerful spirit in integrating material from diverse sources to produce a fine chapter and to Herb Baker for his tenacity in motivating us to complete the book. Special thanks to Suzanne Wood who splendidly performed the tasks of manuscript editing and coordinating the myriad details necessary to produce a final publication.

Introduction

MARTIN F. WISKOFF and GLENN M. RAMPTON

Military manpower and personnel research has been in the forefront of technological development ever since the innovative work in World War I to design tests and procedures to assess military conscripts. In instances such as the World Wars, the work was driven by the necessity to address severe military operational problems rapidly. However, researchers have also been motivated by the push of technology and its potential for application within a military milieu. This book encapsulates innovation and technology that owe their creation to both sources of inspiration.

In their emphasis on preparedness, military forces in the West have undoubtedly devoted more resources to personnel research and development than has any other segment of their society. Much of this work has been published as unclassified agency technical reports and, as such, has been generally available to military researchers through automated scientific information retrieval systems. The work has also been disseminated at governmental meetings, such as NATO panels, the Military Testing Association (MTA) and The Technical Cooperation Program. Very little of this information, however, has appeared in refereed, academically oriented journals, making it relatively inaccessible to the scientific community at large.

Recognizing this, Raymond Waldkoetter, at an MTA meeting several years ago, proposed development of a series of books documenting military advances in personnel technology and practice. One volume, *Military Contributions to Instructional Technology*, edited by John Ellis, was published in 1986. The present book owes its inspiration to Ray Waldkoetter and to the 30 years of intellectual stimulation provided by the Military Testing Association.

In Chapter 1 the continuous line is drawn from World War I to the present in screening and selecting enlisted personnel for military service. This work has been the landmark accomplishment of military personnel research and has had major implications for the military of many nations and for the private sector. Mary K. Schratz and Malcolm James Ree also portray the future era of personnel testing through their discussions of the technological breakthrough known as item response theory and its practical application via computerized adaptive testing and anticipated developments in new types of computerized tests.

The very significant contribution that the computer has already made to personnel decision making is described in Chapter 2 by Leonard P. Kroeker. The military is faced with classification decisions aimed at making best placement of the available manpower into training courses and jobs. Kroeker explicates how the military services have designed systems to address the complex issue of "person-job match"—that is, to optimize utility of the pool of talent, by matching individuals with specific attributes to jobs with specific requirements.

It is a truism in a free society that the vocational interests and motivation of personnel must be considered in making occupational assignments. Herbert George Baker and Reginald T. Ellis in Chapter 3 propose computerized vocational guidance (CVG) as the next wave of occupational exploration and person-job matching in the military. They clarify the terms of reference of CVG, the past difficulties in operational implementation, and the potential for the future.

Chapter 4 focuses on the officer community. The military service academies are unique institutions in that, in addition to providing quality college-level education, they also produce our future military leaders. Officers are also developed through special programs within our nation's universities or at military schools for college graduates. Dianne C. Brown describes the various officer candidate programs, presents the measures used for applicant selection, and provides a brief historical overview of three officer selection programs.

The special case of aviator selection is documented by David R. Hunter in Chapter 5. Emphasis is placed on the worldwide concern for ensuring that only the best-qualified personnel are allowed into the expensive training that is required to enter this demanding fraternity. He details the variety of instruments that have been investigated, their predictive value and utility, and their crossnational usage.

In Chapter 6, Robert Vineberg and John N. Joyner tackle the thorny issue of the criteria that are available within a military setting against which one can document the efficacy of our selection instruments. Drawing upon years of military research, they describe the variety of methods used to assess individuals in the Armed Forces. They evaluate the different performance testing and rating systems, describe their history and current status, and appraise their utility for various military settings.

MILITARY PERSONNEL MEASUREMENT

1

Enlisted Selection and Classification: Advances in Testing

MARY K. SCHRATZ AND MALCOLM JAMES REE

INTRODUCTION

The selection of personnel suited for military service, and their classification for entry into military occupational specialties, is a crucial problem for all branches of the military. Psychological tests have served as a critical tool in the selection and classification process. In this chapter, the history of enlisted testing is described—from the development of the first large-scale intelligence testing program in World War I through the use of the modern Armed Services Vocational Aptitude Battery in the assessment of more than a million applicants to the services annually in the 1980s.

Developments in test theory and in computer technology during recent years have encouraged research on new testing techniques and predictors of successful performance in the military. In this chapter, a brief introduction to item response theory and new techniques such as computerized adaptive testing (CAT) is provided, and practical testing problems for which item response theory can be useful are discussed. The concept of CAT, whereby interactive microcomputers serve as the testing vehicle, is introduced, along with the motivation for using CAT in military personnel selection. Current CAT programs in the military are also described. Finally, the chapter concludes with a description of the work under way by the military services to expand the testing domain, by including new predictors enabling improved selection and classification of military personnel.

HISTORY OF ENLISTED TESTING

World War I and World War II

The military has been in the forefront of psychological testing for more than 70 years. The first group test of mental ability was developed in response to the need to assess a large number of men for the military mobilization of World War I (WWI). DuBois (1970) reports that Robert M. Yerkes, president of the American Psychological Association in 1917, organized committees to offer service to the war effort. One committee on the assessment of recruits was instrumental in bringing forth group psychological testing for the war effort. In just seven months, this committee produced the Army Alpha, a battery comprised of eight ability tests. By the end of the hostilities of WWI, more than 1.25 million men were tested with one of the five forms of the Army Alpha. In addition, a nonverbal form, the Army Beta, was also developed and administered. The impact of the Army Alpha was far-reaching and led to the acceptance and use of psychological testing for military personnel selection.

By the outbreak of World War II, the Army, Navy, and Air Force each had a testing research and development effort. The Department of the Army designed the first in a series of measures of general trainability beginning with the Army General Classification Test (AGCT) and continuing with the Armed Forces Qualification Test (AFQT) series. The AGCT included the four subtest areas of Reading and Vocabulary, Arithmetic Computation, Arithmetic Reasoning, and Spatial Relations. The AFQT continues to be important today in modified form and will be discussed in further detail.

The Navy developed a Navy General Classification Test (NGCT) comprised of verbal questions, and a Basic Test Battery (BTB) which contained not only measures of general ability but also tests of special knowledge such as Mechanical Aptitude, Clerical Aptitude, Spelling, and Radio Code (Stuit, 1947).

The Army Air Force embarked upon a program to build paper-and-pencil selection and classification tests (Guilford & Lacey, 1947) for aircrew members such as pilots, bombardiers, and navigators, and psychomotor tests (Melton, 1947) for aircrew specialties.

The 1944 Metric—A Common Scale

During WWI and WWII, there was no consistent metric for reporting scores on the military tests. This created problems for military manpower planners because they could not answer questions about the aptitudes of potential recruits. A stable reference metric was sought, which led to the collection of data on a standardization sample representing the nearly 12 million men who served in WWII. This reference population was defined as all men in the armed services as of December 31, 1944, and included all enlisted men, officer candidates, and both direct and risen-through-the ranks commissioned officers. Both the AGCT (Uhlaner & Bolanovich, 1952) and the NGCT (Stuit, 1947) batteries were standardized on this reference population.

Technical wisdom has grown in the last 40 years and a number of shortcomings of this effort to develop a common metric can be identified. First, while scores on the AGCT and NGCT were "equated" via equipercentile methods, the content of the two batteries was quite different. The "equating" of nonequivalent tests is now commonly called calibration (Angoff, 1971). Calibration of nonequivalent tests is considered to be sample-dependent and, therefore, not widely generalizable. This means that the resulting "equated" scores may not provide as dependable a metric as originally intended. Second, inspection of only the verbal questions of both the AGCT and the NGCT batteries reveals a substantial difference in the level of difficulty of the content, and this can present problems when determining "equivalent" scores. Third, an ogive was manually fit to the equating data, requiring a series of subjective judgments. In summary, while the 1944 metric was implemented in the first form of the AFQT in 1950, this metric and its subsequent application is rife with ambiguity.

The AFQT

The AFQT was developed and implemented to provide equitable distribution of military personnel to the various services (United States Military Entrance Processing Command, 1984). The AFQT Form 1 consisted of verbal, quantitative, and space perceptual tests, containing 90 questions and requiring a total of 45 minutes to complete. Form 3, implemented in 1953, added tool knowledge questions that continued to be included in several subsequent forms. Each of these tests was "equated" to the AGCT either directly or through chains of other tests. However, it is difficult to determine the extent to which the 1944 metric was maintained, owing to changes in test length, test content, and scoring method over the years.

To this day, the AFQT continues to serve as the mental ability qualification standard for the armed services. In 1966 the Department of Defense (DOD) directed the services to work together on the development of a common test battery for use in recruiting (United States Military Entrance Processing Command, 1984). The new tests were intended to determine mental qualification of applicants (providing a measure similar to the AFQT) and to be used in recruit classification and assignment. As a result, the Armed

Services Vocational Aptitude Battery (ASVAB) was developed, which includes the AFQT as an index of trainability. The present AFQT also serves as a valuable tool in comparing the distribution of recruit ability in the various services (United States Military Entrance Processing Command, 1984).

The ASVAB

The first form of the ASVAB was used only for testing students in high schools from 1968 to 1974. The battery included tests with counterparts in the service selection and classification batteries, although testing time was limited to 2.5 hours (United States Military Entrance Processing Command, 1984). During this period, the Air Force was developing and using the Airman Qualifying Examination (a descendant of the 1948 Airman Classification Battery) for classifying recruits into occupational specialties, whereas the Navy continued to employ the BTB. For a while, both of these service-specific instruments were also used for selection purposes in lieu of the AFQT.

Form 2 of ASVAB was also used strictly in the high schools (1973–76). Form 3, however, was implemented by the Air Force for selection and classification beginning in 1973, and by the Marine Corps beginning in 1975 (United States Military Entrance Processing Command, 1984). The effectiveness of ASVAB Forms 2 and 3 led DOD to task the services to develop and use a single battery in both the high schools and the Military Entrance Processing Stations (United States Military Entrance Processing Command, 1984). ASVAB Forms 6 and 7 were implemented for joint service use on January 1, 1976, while Form 5 was administered in the high schools. Table 1.1 shows the tests included in Forms 5, 6, and 7 of ASVAB, number of items, and testing time.

By aggregating the individual tests included in ASVAB Forms 6 and 7, the services formed composite scores that supplemented general aptitude data provided by the AFQT (consisting of Word Knowledge, Arithmetic Reasoning, and Space Perception, at this time). All of the composites of ASVAB Forms 5, 6, and 7, including the AFQT, were calibrated via equipercentile methods to the Army Classification Battery, or to the AFQT portion of ASVAB Form 3.

The joint service implementation of ASVAB has not been without growing pains. By the spring of 1976, scores on ASVAB Forms 5, 6, and 7 were found to be too high when compared with the expected distribution of scores for ASVAB. Maier and Truss (1982) suggest three causes for this "norming error." First, they speculate that the correction for guessing of the reference test used for Air Force and Navy recruits was never applied to the scores. Second, they suggest that there was coaching on the test used

Table 1.1
Tests of ASVAB Forms 5, 6, 7

Tests	Number of Items	Testing Time(Minutes)
Arithmetic Reasoning (AR)	20	20
Attention to Detail (AD)	30	5
Automotive Information (AI)	20	10
Electronics Information (EI)	30	15
General Information (GI)	15	7
General Science (GS)	20	10
Mathematics Knowledge (MK)	20	20
Mechanical Comprehension (MC)	20	15
Numerical Operations (NO)	50	3
Shop Information (SI)	20	8
Space Perception (SP)	20	12
Word Knowledge (WK)	30	10

with Army recruits. Finally, they fault the use of operational test scores as the reference for Army examinees, and the exclusion of all examinees not qualifying for enlistment. In order to correct the problems, the original sample data were reconstructed from archives and proper scoring procedures applied to the tests. The equating tables built from these analyses were approved for operational use and implemented in 1980.

While problems with Forms 6 and 7 were being rectified, an improved battery (ASVAB Forms 8, 9, and 10) was being developed. DOD, in cooperation with the U.S. Department of Labor, collected data for a new normative sample for use with future versions of ASVAB. This national sample of 9,173 subjects was representative of the 25 million young men and women between the ages of 18 and 23 who were potential enlistees in the armed services. The sample was collected by the National Opinion Research Center (NORC) at the University of Chicago, and is documented in a series of reports (See Department of Defense, 1982).

Before the new norms established on reference form ASVAB Form 8a could be implemented, anomalies in the speeded test scores were detected (Sims & Maier, 1983). Air Force researchers (Earles et al., 1983) conducted an investigation with basic recruits, which revealed that the type of answer sheet used by NORC largely accounted for the problem. Wegner and Ree (1985) conducted an equating study to adjust for the use of the nonoperational answer sheet. This study led to the implementation of the new metric in 1984, providing ASVAB scores referenced to a recent population of American youth (Ree, Valentine, & Earles, 1985).

To this day, ASVAB Form 8a serves as the reference form for the development of new ASVAB tests. Table 1.2 shows the tests included in Forms 8, 9, and 10, number of items, and testing times.

Comparing Tables 1.1 and 1.2, it is evident that ASVAB Forms 8, 9, and 10 differ from Forms 5, 6, and 7 in several ways: in the tests comprising the battery, the numbers of items included for individual tests, and in the testing times. Conversion tables were prepared, based on a study involving 8,000 subjects (applicants and recruits), for the AFQT portion of Form 7 and Forms 8, 9, and 10. For the first time, verification of this equating study also took place, by conducting another study based on about 15,000 applicants for the military enlistment (Ree et al., 1982). The verification study yielded the following results: (1) the original equating was shown to be correct; (2) factor structure and item characteristics were thoroughly analyzed; and (3) item parameters and test characteristic curves were generated using the new methods of item response theory.

Table 1.2
Tests of ASVAB Forms 8, 9, and 10

Tests	Number of Items	Testing Time(Minutes)
Arithmetic Reasoning (AR)	30	36
Auto & Shop Information (AS)	25	11
Coding Speed (CS)	84	7
Electronics Information (EI)	20	9
General Science (GS)	25	11
Mathematics Knowledge (MK)	25	24
Mechanical Comprehension (MC)	25	19
Numerical Operations (NO)	50	3
Paragraph Comprehension (PC)	15	13
Word Knowledge (WK)	35	11

Subsequent forms of ASVAB have been identical in content to Forms 8, 9, and 10. ASVAB Forms 11, 12, and 13 were implemented by DOD for use by the services in 1984. These forms were equated to Form 8a in a study involving both applicants for enlistment and recruits, which revealed that resulting equatings conducted in these two populations were identical. Subsequently a small problem with the equating was found, caused by an error in printing the test booklets; this problem was later corrected in the verification of the equating. Benefiting from the knowledge obtained during the equating of Forms, 11, 12, and 13, it was possible to equate the next set of ASVAB Forms (15, 16, and 17) directly to Form 8a (the reference form) using service recruits. A subsequent verification of the equating was conducted, however, using military applicants. Forms 15, 16, and 17 were implemented by the services in late 1988.

An Era of Progress

The ASVAB era can be characterized as a time of learning and progress. The AFQT remains a good indicator of training potential (United States Military Entrance Processing Command, 1984), though there have been many changes of tests and format over the years. It is likely that the efficacy of general ability as a predictor accounts for the continuity of the AFQT as a measure of learning ability.

Service-specific composites have also undergone many changes over the years. Most of the services build composites on the basis of maximum predictability rather than with the goal of differential prediction, which may be a chimera undiscovered in aptitude testing. Frequently, the same test is found in more than one composite. Even when tests are not used in multiple composites, however, the intercomposite correlations are high, probably owing to general ability. While this situation does not facilitate differential prediction, it increases validity for all composites.

ASVAB test scores are converted to standard scores based on norms established through equating. This process serves to eliminate or to reduce differences in the forms of the battery and ensures equity, so that it is a matter of indifference as to which form of the battery the examinee takes. Conversion to standard scores has been a consistent practice for all ASVAB composites, except the AFQT, which (prior to the introduction of Forms 15, 16, and 17) has been required in raw score form for possible hand scoring in an emergency.

There is always a risk when using a battery such as ASVAB, because of sometimes intense pressures by applicants and recruiters, that the administration is affected by compromise. Service researchers have devised procedures to detect compromise by comparing the percentile score of the

AFQT composite with a composite formed of subtests not included in the AFQT, but that correlate highly with the AFQT (Sims & Truss, 1982). In addition, deliberate failure detection procedures, to detect those instances when an examinee feigns a poor score, have been constructed to be used during mobilization for armed conflict (Ree & Valentine, 1987).

The joint-service nature of the ASVAB program requires extensive coordination among representatives of the service personnel laboratories, the service policy sections, the Office of the Assistant Secretary of Defense, and the United States Military Entrance Processing Command. These parties form the Joint-Services Selection and Classification Working Group and meet quarterly to guide the development and operation of the ASVAB program. In addition, the Manpower Accession Policy Steering Committee, composed of high-ranking military officials, meets to set policy as the issues require. Advising the Steering Committee is a blue-ribbon committee, called the Defense Advisory Committee, comprised of experts in the field of personnel testing.

New Directions

The armed services continue to forge the history of testing by establishing the most ambitious and heavily funded research and development agenda in this country. Recent developments in test theory and computer technology have precipitated research on new testing techniques and the development of new predictors for use in the military enlistment and classification process. The remainder of this chapter focuses on these areas of interest to the military. The next section presents a brief introduction to item response theory and the application of this new methodology to current testing problems. In the following section, the concept of computerized adaptive testing, the motivation for CAT in enlisted personnel screening and selection, and current CAT programs in the military are addressed. Finally, the last section provides a description of ongoing military work on expanding the testing domain to include new predictors designed to improve applicant selection and classification.

ITEM RESPONSE THEORY

What is item response theory? This topic was introduced to measurement specialists more than 30 years ago (Lord, 1952), yet practical applications in large-scale testing programs are very recent, coinciding with increased availability of computers for use in research. Item response theory (IRT) is a complex area in test theory. Models underlying practical applications of IRT techniques carry strong assumptions, and sophisticated computer programs are required for estimating the parameters of these models. Practical applications of item response theory do offer significant advantages for testing programs, however, particularly for those administered by microcomputer. Some of the advantages and assumptions of IRT methods are described below. A discussion of IRT calibration procedures is provided, and some practical applications of item response theory for large-scale testing programs are also discussed.

Advantages of Item Response Theory

An important practical advantage of item response theory is that, once a set of test items has been fitted to an item response model, one can obtain an estimate of an examinee's ability from any subset of items (Bock & Wood, 1971; Wright, 1968). Thus, examinee ability estimates can be determined on the basis of one item or responses to many items (Weiss & Kingsbury, 1984).

IRT models can be used to obtain ability estimates for individuals taking different (and often more appropriate) subsets of items *and* provide a basis for comparing examinees (Bock & Wood, 1971; Hambleton & Cook, 1977). An illustration of this property is provided by "computerized adaptive testing." A computerized adaptive test is one for which examinees are administered test items on a microcomputer and the items administered are matched or tailored to the examinee's estimated ability level. Test items are selected from a large bank of questions calibrated by IRT methods. Thus, while two different examinees may take an easy and a difficult subset of test items, respectively, their test scores will be on the same scale and can be used in making comparisons. Using an adaptive testing strategy, fewer test items need be administered, resulting in efficient testing. Testing can be continued to a fixed error criterion, resulting in precise measures *at all ability levels*. Many of the functions typically performed by a test administrator are carried out by the microcomputer in computerized testing, reducing human error and providing for better standardization. Computerized testing also allows for dynamic scoring and reporting of examinee test data. The development of computerized adaptive tests is discussed in more detail in the next section.

A second illustration of how IRT methods can be used to obtain comparable ability estimates for those examinees taking different subsets of test items can be seen in test equating. In many practical testing applications, examinees will take different tests. While they may be designed to be parallel, it is often necessary in practice to determine comparable or "equivalent" scores on the two tests. IRT equating methods (Lord, 1980) may be used to meet this objective (e.g., Marco, Petersen, & Stewart, 1979). Practical needs for multiple versions of tests may thus be served by IRT methods (Hambleton & Cook, 1977).

It is often claimed that IRT techniques provide sample-free estimates of parameters (Hambleton & Cook, 1977; Wright, 1968). Thus, while traditional item statistics such as difficulty and discrimination are known to vary from one group to another depending on the average ability level of the group being tested, IRT parameters should in theory remain the same. Once placed on a common scale, IRT parameters are predicted to be invariant for different groups of examinees. Thus, in item response theory, test questions are estimated to be of a particular difficulty level, requiring a certain level of ability (proficiency) to answer correctly, regardless of the average level of ability of the particular group with whom the examinee responding to the question is tested. This property of invariance facilitates the construction of modern tests, where test items calibrated to a common scale can be drawn from a computerized item bank, to match test specifications for different ability or grade groups. The development of item banks is discussed in more detail later in this chapter.

Practical advantages of item response theory for large-scale testing programs are substantial. Present microcomputer technology will support test administration and scoring in a dynamic and interactive fashion, as in computerized adaptive testing. In addition, the microcomputer can serve as a powerful tool to support the test-construction process, particularly in building item-response theory-based tests. As an example, the Navy Personnel Research and Development Center implemented an integrated microcomputer-based system to support test-construction functions in the context of a large-scale computerized adaptive testing program (Schratz, Carroll & Hurrell, 1988). Authoring test questions and subsequent revision and review can be performed on the microcomputer; this system can also be used to assemble new tests and bank new test items using IRT procedures (Swanson, 1986; Wild, 1986). Analytic functions integral to the test construction process can be performed from the local microcomputer work station, with microcomputer to mainframe computer data communication procedures. Pioneering efforts are under way involving practical applications of the computer in IRT-based test construction in this country (Assessment Systems Corporation, 1984; Yen, 1983) and overseas (Van der Linden, 1987).

Assumptions of Item Response Theory

Models underlying item response theory require that certain conditions be met to ensure proper application. In practical applications of IRT models, the mathematical form of an "item characteristic curve" is specified by the practitioner and estimates of the item parameters are obtained to describe the curves; an item characteristic curve, or an item trace line, is a mathematical function that relates "probability of success on an item to the ability measured by the item set or test that contains it" (Hambleton & Cook, 1977, p. 78). A chief difference (Hambleton & Cook, 1977) among IRT models is in the mathematical forms of the corresponding item characteristic curves: the number of parameters required to describe an item characteristic curve will depend on the IRT model used. Common forms of item characteristic curves include the one-, two-, and three-parameter logistic models for application to dichotomously scored test items, and nominal and graded response models applied to available item options (for example, as described by Hambleton & Cook, 1977).

The model that has thus far gained prominence in its application to ability tests composed of multiple-choice items is the three-parameter logistic model. For this model, the logistic item response curve (Lord, 1980) indicating the probability that a person with ability V responds correctly to item j, can be written as (Green et al., 1984b):

$$P_j(V) = c_j + \frac{1 - c_j}{1 + \exp(-1.7a_j(V_j - b_j))}$$

The probability rises from c to 1 as V increases. The rise is gentler for low a, and sharp for high values of a. The a parameter can be interpreted as item discriminability, b as item difficulty, and c as pseudochance level (Green et al., 1984b).

A condition of critical concern in practical applications of IRT models is the fit of the model used to the item response data. According to Lord (1980), item response theory will not hold for every test item and for every examinee. When test items are ambiguous, have more than one correct answer, or have no correct answer, the model will not fit. If examinees skip back and forth through a test, omit some items, or mark unfinished items at random, the model will not apply. For large sets of well-written test items and large numbers of examinees, few items should be found where use of IRT methods is inappropriate because of fit. Lord (1980, p. 15) discusses IRT models as being used "with confidence only after repeated and extensive checking of their applicability"; the usual procedures involve substituting estimated item parameters for true parameters and examining fit to observed data. The extent to which poor fit to the data can be tolerated cannot be stated exactly; however, Lord (1980, p. 15) states one should have confidence in the "practical value of the model for predicting observable results" if such checks are found to be satisfactory on frequent occasions.

IRT models used in ability testing also require the condition of local independence among test item responses. What this means is that performance on one item should not affect an individual's performance on other items in the test. Formally, local independence requires that any two items are uncorrelated when Θ is fixed (Lord, 1980). The condition of local independence follows from an assumption that the test items are homogeneous and measure a single ability. If all of the items measure a single ability, which can be thought of as the common factor of test items measuring one dimension, the local independence assumption should be satisfied.

Recent work by Ackerman (1987) has focused on examining the robustness of IRT estimation programs to violations of the local independence assumption. Item response data with varying degrees of response dependency were generated in this study and results suggest that violation of local independence, as defined by the dependency model employed, has an effect on item parameter calibration for the two-parameter logistic model. The implication of this finding is that, if test items are calibrated in a dependent sequence and then separated (e.g., in an adaptive test), misestimation of parameters can affect ability estimation. Ackerman (1987) recommends that calibration of item parameters be conducted jointly with study of the response processes required by each item on a calibrated test. If violations of the condition of local independence are suspected, calibration results should be handled carefully.

Current methods of item response theory used in practical applications are based on the condition of unidimensionality—that is, items in a given test measure the same construct. Green et al. (1982, 1984a, 1984b) point out, however, that empirical results have shown the model to be suitable when the test items simply have one dominant dimension. According to Green et al. (1982, 1984a, 1984b), there are several possible ways of obtaining evidence of unidimensionality, including: (1) showing fit of the IRT model to the item response data (a necessary but not sufficient condition); (2) factor analysis of the item intercorrelations; and (3) sorting items into clusters on the basis of item type or item content, obtaining scores on separate clusters, and intercorrelating these scores to see if they are sufficiently high to consider the test unitary. In a recent review of the literature, Hattie (1984) noted 87 indices of dimensionality. In another recent study, Hambleton and Rovinelli (1986) focused on three promising methods: (1) nonlinear factor analysis, which does not require linear relationships among the variables and between variables and underlying traits; (2) residual analysis, involving an assessment of the overall fit of a unidimensional model to a set of data through the analysis of residuals; and (3) the Bejar analysis method, providing a check on whether the subset of items in which an item is calibrated affects the estimated parameters. A fourth method, linear factor analysis, was included in this study for comparison. Results showed nonlinear factor analysis to be the most promising of those methods studied, although more experience in applying this procedure was encouraged before a recommendation could be made (Hambleton & Rovinelli, 1986).

A recent development among techniques to explore dimensionality is "full-information" factor analysis. This procedure uses marginal maximum-likelihood estimation procedures in performing an item-factor analysis for the purpose of identifying relationships among test items. The approach has been used in several recent studies (Bock, Gibbons, & Muraki, 1985, 1986; Kingston, 1986; Schratz, 1985; Zimowski & Bock, 1987; Zwick, 1986).

In short, while IRT holds much promise with respect to practical applications for large-scale testing programs, the conditions to be met for appropriate use of these methods are strict. Further knowledge with respect to the robustness of these models when underlying conditions are not met will undoubtedly emerge in the future, as will new models designed to fit common measurement problems.

Item Response Theory Calibration Methods

IRT parameters are of two types: (1) those pertaining to test items; and (2) those pertaining to examinees. These are commonly referred to as item parameters and ability parameters, respectively. There are a number of computer programs currently available for estimating item and ability parameters. Some of the more commonly used programs are described below.

LOGIST

The LOGIST program has been developed at Educational Testing Service by Marilyn Wingersky and others, under the direction of Frederic Lord (Wingersky, Barton, & Lord, 1982; Wingersky, Patrick, & Lord, 1987). The current version of LOGIST is known as LOGIST 6. This Fortran program is used to estimate item parameters for binary scored multiple-choice items and examinee ability via the three-parameter logistic item-response model (or the one- and two-parameter models) by maximizing a criterion function. The criterion function is the maximum-likelihood function. To use LOGIST, it is essential that the user prepare a scored item-by-person response matrix. LOGIST estimation typically occurs in several steps and each step contains several stages with multiple iterations; abilities are estimated while certain item parameters are held fixed, and item parameters are estimated while abilities are held fixed. End products of a successful LOGIST run include a summary report and a detailed report of the run.

BILOG

The BILOG computer program (Mislevy & Bock, 1984) was developed by Robert Mislevy of Educational Testing Service and Darrell Bock of University of Chicago. This program is used to score *and* analyze binary test items and provides item parameters for the one-, two-, and three-parameter logistic models. A file of scored item responses is prepared from an original item-by-person response matrix by this program. Item parameters are then estimated by the marginal maximum-likelihood procedure (Bock & Aitkin, 1981). Ability estimates can be otained for examinees by maximum likelihood or by Bayesian estimation. Prior distributions of ability may be selected by the user or may be estimated from the data. Tests of model fit and plots of individual item trace lines are provided.

ASCAL

The ASCAL computer program (Assessment Systems Corporation, 1986) was developed by David Vale and others of Assessment Systems Corporation. This program uses Bayesian modal and maximum-likelihood procedures in estimating item parameters for the three-parameter logistic model. A model fit statistic for each item is also provided. The ASCAL program has been found to provide accurate item parameter estimates economically and simply (Vale & Gialluca, 1985).

MULTILOG

The MULTILOG program (Thissen, 1986) was developed by David Thissen of the University of Kansas. MULTILOG uses item response theory to analyze *and* score multiple category items. Four different multiple category logistic models can be used in MULTILOG: (1) Samejima logistic model for graded responses; (2) Bock multinomial logit model for multiple nominal categories; (3) Bock-Samejima-Thissen model for multiple-choice items with guessing; and (4) Masters' partial credit model. The MULTILOG program permits estimation via marginal maximum likelihood, and maximum likelihood to a manifest ability criterion. The MULTILOG program also allows the user to mix continuous variables with categorical item responses and estimates a continuous latent trait from both qualitative data and quantitative measurements.

Many current applications of item response theory require the use of large numbers of calibrated test items forming an "item bank." The parameters of these items are determined by administering them to many examinees. For the purpose of calibrating test items via the three-parameter logistic model, a sample of 1,000 examinees responding to each item is minimal and 2,000 examinees adequate (Green et al., 1984b). Since these banks of test questions contain many more questions than can be administered to a single examinee group, parameters are usually estimated from several groups and then linked to a common scale.

A recent review of different approaches to linking item parameters onto a common scale is provided by Vale (1986). For the purpose of linking and calibrating, data are collected in accordance with an anchor design. Tests can be calibrated and a linking transformation used to place parameters on a common scale. Vale points out that the linking transformation must yield an "equivalent" transformation, regardless of which scale is chosen for the common score scale (Test X, Test Y, or another). While several methods are available for determining the linking transformation, a linear transformation is often used to express one ability scale or one item difficulty scale in terms of another (Vale, 1986). An alternative for calibration followed by a linking is the process of joint, or simultaneous, calibration. Here, anchoring designs can be accommodated in a single calibration run; some of the well-known calibration programs described above readily support this alternative.

Vale (1986) reports the results of a simulation study involving three calibration and linking designs: (1) a *separate design*, in which two tests are calibrated separately and the items linked by a transformation involving the difficulty parameters; (2) a *standard design*, in which two tests are calibrated simultaneously in a single run; and (3) an *interlaced design*, in which a test is formed (of any length) beginning with each sequential item in a complete set of items and all tests are calibrated in a single run of the ASCAL program. Results of the Vale study suggest that the anchor design to use when practically feasible is the jointly calibrated interlaced design. If groups of examinees are large random samples from a common population, however, the design is largely irrelevant. Results also suggest that calibration and linking be done with tests as long as possible.

The Department of Defense is currently exploring alternative ways of implementing item response theory for the purpose of calibrating test items "on-line" in a large-scale computerized adaptive testing program. The next section of this chapter briefly describes the development of a computerized adaptive testing version of the Armed Services Vocational Aptitude Battery (CAT-ASVAB); greater detail can be found in Wiskoff and Schratz (1989). Data for calibrating new CAT-ASVAB test items will be obtained on-line, by administering a few new test items to each examinee in addition to the adaptive test. In an adaptive test, the item-by-person matrix contains little data (i.e., there are few test items administered to examinees and the responses are scattered rather than occurring in fixed blocks). New calibration methods are thus needed (McBride & Sympson, 1985). The overall objective of this work is to implement IRT methods effectively so as to ensure the comparability of the CAT-ASVAB scores for the duration of the program. Preliminary work suggests that changes in item difficulty, which can occur for a variety of reasons, may dictate adjustments.

Recent work by Mislevy (1986) suggests that auxiliary information about examinees can be helpful in estimating item parameters. The precision of item parameter estimates may be enhanced by capitalizing on dependencies between the latent variable (ability) and variables associated with the examinee, such as age, courses taken, and years of schooling. According to Mislevy (1986), an increase in information on item parameters of about two to six items can be expected in typical applications; a numerical example presented by Mislevy also suggests that the increase will vary by item parameter type. While it is possible to use auxiliary information to improve estimates of examinee ability, Mislevy (1986) does not recommend this, as these scores will be used to compare examinees. Practical applications for which using auxiliary information are most promising in parameter estimation are those where few items are administered to each examinee, as in adaptive testing.

In summary, recent work on new item response theory calibration techniques has pointed to new directions for future theoretical developments and practical applications.

Item Response Theory Applications

Practical applications of item response theory in large-scale testing programs are very recent, occurring mainly within the last decade. Applications of item response theory can be found with respect to both conventional paper-and-pencil tests and adaptive tests. For conventional tests, early applications (e.g., Rentz & Bashaw, 1975) of item response theory were motivated by the potential benefits afforded by the score scales developed via IRT methods. Work in this area has yielded promising findings and, as a consequence, some current conventional paper-and-pencil test series use IRT methods to determine scales for scoring and reporting. Notable examples of this are the Stanford Achievement Test (Lenke, 1981; Lenke & Canner, 1980, Lenke & Rentz, 1982; Schratz 1983, 1984a, 1984b; Schratz & Lenke, 1980) and the Comprehensive Tests of Basic Skills, Form U (Yen, 1983). "Customized" tests, designed to assess specific objectives identified as important by the state or by the local education agency, have also capitalized on IRT methods for determining score scales, frequently obtaining norm-referenced information about student performance in the process (Keene & Holmes, 1987; Yen, Green, & Burket, 1987).

In addition to applications in test scoring and reporting, item response theory can be useful in many other stages of test construction. Yen (1983) discusses the application of item response theory methods in the development of the Comprehensive Tests of Basic Skills. An automated test selection program was used to produce a statistically "ideal" test as a starting point for further refinement by test developers. Test developers would then refine the test using an interactive program, and receive immediate feedback on statistical properties of the test. Using this program, it was possible to display standard error curves for up to four versions of a test simultaneously and to compare them. Yen (1983, p. 137) reports that using the IRT approach resulted in a "clearer picture of the relative contribution of each item to the test's statistical characteristics, particularly in terms of difficulty and measurement accuracy." Wild (1986) provides an account of the use of item response theory methods in assembling a portion of the Graduate Records Examination and the Graduate Management Admissions Test, with the assistance of a microcomputer-based system. According to Wild, early reports from test developers have been encouraging. Positive comments include satisfaction with being able to see the impact of choosing a single test question on test characteristics, and with viewing the results of preliminary selections in relation to target curves showing conditional standard errors of measurement.

IRT methods are, of course, integral to the development of computerized adaptive tests. In adaptive testing, IRT methods serve as the basis for selection of test questions for tailored administration to examinees *and* as the basis for dynamic scoring of responses to test questions. Specifically, IRT parameters associated with individual test items are utilized to select the most appropriate test questions for administering, and to determine an examinee's estimated ability level. IRT methods are utilized in all stages of adaptive test construction, including developing calibrated item banks, specifying and evaluating adaptive testing strategies, scoring the tests, and determining test reliability and validity. Applications of computerized adaptive testing for use in the selection and classification of military personnel are discussed in detail in the following section of this chapter. It is important to note here that computerized adaptive tests have recently been commercially developed for use in other settings, notably educational and vocational counseling (McBride & Moe, 1986; Ward, Kline, & Flaugher, 1985).

In summary, while practical applications of item response theory in large-scale testing programs are very recent, well-established examples of both paper-and-pencil tests and computerized adaptive tests using these methods exist, developed for use in diverse settings. Many of the potential advantages of item response theory described earlier in this chapter have been realized in several phases of the test construction process and in test delivery. Further discussion of the use of IRT methods in the construction and delivery of computerized adaptive tests for military selection and classification purposes follows.

CAT IN THE MILITARY

Current applications of computerized adaptive testing methodology can be found in military personnel testing. A brief discussion of the concept of CAT is presented below and the motivation for CAT in enlisted personnel screening and selection is described. Current CAT programs in military personnel testing are discussed in some detail.

The Concept of CAT

Computerized adaptive testing is a relatively new method of testing involving three major components: (1) the interactive computer administration of tests; (2) the application of item response theory methods; and (3) the application of adaptive testing strategies (Weiss & Kingsbury, 1984). While the availability of computers has enabled the development and refinement of IRT techniques, it is the microcomputer, serving as a testing tool, that has furthered recent research on computerized adaptive testing.

Current adaptive testing procedures implemented on microcomputers utilize IRT methods in determining an initial estimate of examinee ability; selecting a test item for administration to an examinee; scoring the response to the item; determining a revised ability estimate; and selecting a new test item for administration. Thus, through the application of IRT methods, examinee ability is estimated immediately after a response is given to a test item during the course of adaptive testing. Use of IRT methods in adaptive testing provides test scores on a single scale that can then be used in making comparisons, *even though the microcomputer has designed a different test for each examinee.*

Adaptive testing strategies will differ depending on the measurement goals required for particular applications. Basic components of the adaptive testing procedure are an item pool, an initial ability estimate, an item selection algorithm, a scoring method, and a termination criterion (Weiss & Kingsbury, 1984). Since examinees are administered only those test items suited to their ability level in adaptive testing, large "pools" of test questions must be developed, containing many more items than are needed for a paper-and-pencil test and spanning a wide range of difficulty (Prestwood et al., 1985; Wiskoff & Schratz, 1989). These pools of test questions must be calibrated via one of the common IRT models, with all test items in a given testing area calibrated to a common scale. It is important to note that certain conditions must be met in the development of item banks for use in adaptive tests; this is largely due to the application of IRT models carrying strong assumptions, as discussed earlier, and to the use of the microcomputer as a presentation medium (Wiskoff & Schratz, 1989).

In implementing CAT procedures, choice of an initial ability estimate at the start of testing must be made. In the CAT-ASVAB battery, the mean of the latent ability distribution ($\Theta = 0$) is assigned to the examinee as an initial ability estimate for the aptitude area tested. An argument in favor of this procedure is that, when tests are used—as they are in the selection of military personnel—as contests, an attempt should be made to ensure equity. However, it is possible, and in some cases it may be desirable, to begin testing with different ability estimates for different examinees. In a recent discussion of the application of CAT to educational problems, Weiss and Kingsbury (1984) illustrate this point: if a student's achievement level is thought to be high, testing can begin with a relatively difficult item, rather than an item of average difficulty for every examinee. Weiss and Kingsbury (1984) note that, because the level of difficulty of the items that are selected for administration will gradually move to the examinee's estimated ability level as the test progresses, an inaccurate starting point should not seriously affect the results. However, an accurate initial ability estimate can result in the need for reduced numbers of items administered to examinees to achieve precise measurement.

Choice of an item selection algorithm must be made in implementing a computerized adaptive test. An "infotable" is used in CAT-ASVAB to select the most informative item for administration to the examinee at his or her ability level. This technique is used in conjunction with a procedure for controlling the rate of item usage (Sympson & Hetter, 1985) and, in special cases, a procedure to ensure that test content is covered. An alternative to maximum-information item selection is Owen's Bayesian procedure, whereby items are selected to minimize the expected posterior variance of the ability estimate (Owen, 1975; Jensema, 1977).

A choice among scoring methods must also be made in implementing computerized adaptive tests. During the course of adaptive testing, an examinee's response to the last item administered is scored, and the examinee's estimated ability level is determined based on the responses to previous questions in that aptitude area. Owen's (1969) procedure can be used to determine interim and/or final ability estimates; other Bayesian methods can also be used. A second popular choice for the estimation of examinee ability is maximum-likelihood procedures. These estimation procedures can also be used to determine interim and/or final ability estimates. The maximum-likelihood approach can also be very useful when used in conjunction with the Bayesian approach. Weiss and Kingsbury (1984) point out that Bayesian ability estimates are regressed toward the prior ability estimate. On the other hand, Lord (1980) notes that the maximum-likelihood estimate of an examinee's ability will be infinite when all questions are answered correct or incorrect, which, of course, causes difficulty in the early stages of adaptive testing where few items have been administered. Taking this into account, Weiss and Kingsbury (1984) recommend using the Bayesian scoring procedure during the course of testing, until it becomes possible to obtain maximum-likelihood estimates. This practical approach enables all examinee response patterns to be scored and should result in relatively unbiased ability estimates at most test lengths (Weiss & Kingsbury, 1984).

In implementing adaptive testing procedures, a choice must also be made as to the termination criterion for the test. Current procedures for CAT-ASVAB involve administering a prespecified number of items to each examinee in the aptitude area tested adaptively. In this case, measurement error must be determined for various levels of ability in the metric of the reported score. The range of standard errors for these ability levels must also be determined since the standard error varies not only as a function of ability but also as a function of the particular adaptive test to which the examinee responds. An alternative to this procedure, which is practical for many applications, is to continue testing in an area only as long as is necessary for each examinee. Using this approach, testing will continue until each examinee is measured to a predetermined level of precision. This approach ensures that assessment is equally precise for all examinees.

While computerized adaptive testing is a relatively new method of testing, guidelines (American Psychological Association, 1985, 1986; Green et al., 1982, 1984a, 1984b) have recently emerged with respect to appropriate measurement properties for this method of testing and alternative procedures for adaptive testing are known, as described above. Choices among alternative procedures to be implemented in adaptive tests must be made with respect to measurement goals. As Lord (1980) has noted, it is likely that in the future many mental tests will be administered and scored by computer.

The Motivation for CAT in Enlisted Personnel Screening and Selection

Much of the research on computerized adaptive testing has been sponsored by military research organizations such as the Office of Naval Research, the Navy Personnel Research and Development Center, the Army Research Institute, and the Air Force Human Resources Laboratory. Motivation for research on computerized adaptive testing by the military is described below.

First, computerized adaptive testing can be expected to provide more efficient test administration and test scoring than is possible for some paper-and-pencil testing programs. Military research on the Computerized Adaptive Screening Test (CAST) has shown that testing time can be dramatically reduced. Knapp and Pliske (1986) report the average administration time for CAST to be about one-fourth the amount of time required to administer the paper-and-pencil counterpart. In addition to efficiency in test administration, a computerized adaptive testing system also provides for computerized scoring and recording, during and at the completion of the testing session. The potential benefits of computerized adaptive tests in these areas have served to motivate the development of CAST (Baker, Rafacz, & Sands, 1984) and the development of CAT-ASVAB (Wiskoff & Schratz, 1989).

Better test security provides a second motivation for the use of computerized adaptive tests by the military. While paper-and-pencil tests are especially susceptible to breaches of security via theft, compromise, and coaching, using electronic media reduces the possibility of theft. As an example, the CAT-ASVAB local network of microcomputers has an entire test item bank stored in the random access memory of the examinee test station. One rationale for choosing this network design was that test items are erased when power is removed, in contrast to designs where item banks are stored on removable media or on a central file server (Tiggle & Rafacz, 1985). This approach, implemented in the Accelerated CAT-ASVAB Project (ACAP), is expected to better protect test items against theft and compromise than is possible using printed material. In addition, a basic component of any computerized adaptive testing system is a test item bank, and this can also serve to deter test compromise and coaching. Examinees are administered different tests selected from the item bank, and an item-exposure control procedure (Sympson & Hetter, 1985) can be implemented to further reduce compromise by controlling the rate of item usage from the bank.

A third motivation for the use of computerized adaptive tests by the military is the capability to produce more frequent test revisions and to deliver them to the field. As Wiskoff and Schratz (1989) have pointed out, the development of replacement ASVAB tests is a lengthy and expensive process that is time-consuming for military personnel. The CAT-ASVAB system, using methodology for item calibration described earlier in this chapter, is expected to allow for on-line administration of experimental replacement test questions to examinees. This approach has the potential to reduce the time required for the preparation of new tests and to cause less disruption of operational testing. Use of an integrated and fully automated microcomputer-based system to support IRT-based test construction, as described previously in this chapter, is also expected to reduce lead time for the preparation of new tests. A particularly promising feature of this system is the capacity for central item banking, including item text and associated diagrams, charts, and figures. Transfer of test item files, including scoring information directly to the CAT-ASVAB delivery system, is also a decided advantage.

A fourth motivation for use of computerized adaptive tests by the military is the potential for increased measurement precision. The ASVAB battery includes a limited number of items comprising each test, and these items have been selected to provide the best measurement near the center of the ability distribution. Thus, high- and low-ability military applicants are often assessed with less precision than those of average ability (Wiskoff & Schratz, 1989). The CAT strategy provides dynamic tailoring of test difficulty to the ability level of the examinee and thus can improve measurement precision, particularly for those examinees at the extremes of ability. As described in the third section of this chapter, it is possible to implement present adaptive testing methodology to continue testing only until a predetermined level of error remains; in this way, precision of measurement is equal for all applicants tested.

The potential for providing new types of cognitive measures is a fifth motivation for use of computerized adaptive tests by the military. Wiskoff and Schratz (1989) point out that the content of ASVAB, and hence CAT-ASVAB, has evolved from earlier versions of the paper-and-pencil battery and from instruments like the service classification batteries. The ASVAB battery currently includes those aptitudes that have shown validity through prediction of training success for each of the services (United States Military Entrance Processing Command, 1984). New predictors of success in training or in "on-the-job" performance are expected to be introduced to CAT-ASVAB and to ASVAB as validity is established; research undertaken by all branches of the military services on the development of these new predictors is presented later in this chapter. A description of current CAT programs in the military follows.

Current CAT Programs

Computerized Adaptive Screening Test. The first application of computerized adaptive testing in the military appears in the Army's Joint Optical Information Network (JOIN) System. According to Sands and Gade (1983), the JOIN System was developed to assist army recruiters in the following areas: sales presentation, aptitude screening, vocational guidance, classification/assignment, personnel training, and management support. Development of the JOIN system was sponsored by the U.S. Army

Recruiting Command, with the Army Research Institute and the Navy Personnel Research and Development Center providing research and technical advisory services via an interlaboratory agreement initiated in 1982 (Sands & Rafacz, 1983).

The JOIN system includes CAST, designed to predict performance on a qualifying test for entry to all military services. Because recruiters need a vehicle for identifying those applicants who will pass the qualifying test, a paper-and-pencil test known as the Enlistment Screening Test (EST) was developed and has been used to predict performance on the AFQT portion of the ASVAB (Mathews & Ree, 1982). CAST was subsequently developed to replace the EST in Army recruiting (Sands & Rafacz, 1983).

CAST consists of a system designed to deliver a screening test in Word Knowledge and in Arithmetic Reasoning. CAST software was developed to administer and score test items, and to compute and record examinee ability estimates after a response has been given to each test question. Software was developed to run on the following hardware comprising an examinee testing station: an Apple-II Plus microcomputer, two mini-floppy disk drives, a numeric keypad, and a video display monitor (Sands & Gade, 1983; Sands & Rafacz, 1983).

Sands and Rafacz (1983) describe the field test of the CAST microcomputer system involving administration of the adaptive tests to 364 Army applicants at a single military entrance processing station, where 20 Word Knowledge test items and 15 Arithmetic Reasoning test items were administered adaptively. Subsequent to data collection, the predictive validity of CAST was evaluated. Individual subtest validities and combined subtest validities were determined for various test lengths defined post hoc. A recommendation was made that CAST be implemented to administer ten Word Knowledge test items and five Arithmetic Reasoning test items. This combination of Word Knowledge and Arithmetic Reasoning test lengths yielded predictive validity as high as the EST and also held administration time to a minimum. The recommended CAST testing procedure has been implemented on 1,200 operational JOIN systems (Sands & Gade, 1983).

Pliske, Gade, and Johnson (1984) describe a cross-validation study of CAST. In this study, Army applicants in the midwestern region of the United States were tested with CAST and their scores were matched to the AFQT scores obtained at the military entrance processing stations. For this sample, the correlation between CAST and AFQT scores was found to be very high (.80). It was concluded on the basis of this data that CAST is a good predictor of performance on the AFQT and is a reasonable alternative to the EST.

Knapp and Pliske (1986) describe further cross-validation of CAST conducted in 60 Army recruiting stations nationwide; results of the first six

months of data collection were described. In this study, both CAST and
EST data were matched to AFQT scores when possible, although difficulties were encountered in retrieving scores because a large number of
prospects did not appear for further testing with the AFQT. The resulting
CAST sample was only about one-third its original size. Some of the findings of this study were that: (1) CAST is a good predictor of AFQT scores
($r = .82$); (2) the current length of the test (ten Word Knowledge items and
five Arithmetic Reasoning items) is appropriate; and (3) race and sex
subgroup differences in AFQT predictions exist, but their magnitude is not
large. Some recommendations are made by Knapp and Pliske (1986) pertaining to modifications to the CAST software to provide recruiters with
probabilistic information concerning classification into different qualifying
categories. Knapp and Wise (1987) discuss possible plans for further refinement of CAST.

*Computerized Adaptive Testing Version of the Armed Services Voca-
tional Aptitude Battery.* A joint services effort is under way to develop a
CAT version of the ASVAB. The Department of Defense officially recognized the potential of CAT for improving the process of accessioning personnel into the armed services and initiated the CAT-ASVAB program in
1979 (Wiskoff, 1981). Plans for operational implementation of the CAT-
ASVAB battery have involved developing adaptive tests for interactive
computer administration in all power test aptitude areas presently covered
by the ASVAB battery. A comprehensive account of the major components
of the CAT-ASVAB program can be found in Wiskoff and Schratz (1989).
A brief description follows.

The CAT-ASVAB program is currently being conducted in multiple stages
(as described by Wiskoff & Schratz, 1989). The first stage involved an experimental CAT-ASVAB system, developed on Apple III computers, for
research conducted with military subjects. The second stage is known as
ACAP and is intended to evaluate the feasibility of CAT technology in a
limited number of military entrance processing stations and mobile examining team sites. The third stage of the CAT-ASVAB program is intended to
utilize lessons learned from the earlier stages to decide upon the best method
of introducing CAT-ASVAB to the military entrance processing environment on a larger scale.

CAT-ASVAB psychometric developments include item banks; procedures for test administration, scoring, scaling, and equating; determining
reliability and validity; and developing a technical manual. With respect to
item banks, Wiskoff and Schratz (1989) emphasize the importance of the
following steps in development: (1) the content of each aptitude area must
be clearly specified; (2) item reviews by expert judges to evaluate the content, format, clarity, and appropriateness of test items; (3) when sufficient

numbers of items covering measurement objectives have been written, reviewed, and modified, they should be pretested to obtain preliminary information on their difficulty and validity; (4) the item parameter estimates necessary for the computerized adaptive testing process must be determined.

With respect to test administration and scoring, paper-and-pencil tests require that a test proctor track the time for administering each test and communicate test instructions to a group of examinees in a clear and consistent manner. In contrast, these functions are part of the role of the microcomputer delivery system in computerized testing. Answer sheets for paper-and-pencil tests must be scored once the test has been completed; however, for a computerized adaptive test, the microcomputer delivery system dynamically selects and scores each test item administered and, through IRT methods, the examinee's ability is estimated. Administering the CAT-ASVAB tests includes providing sample items in each aptitude area for practice purposes. The CAT-ASVAB test administration procedures (described by Wiskoff & Schratz, 1989) differ for power tests, speeded tests, and test items included for experimental purposes. The power tests are administered adaptively and scored by IRT methods. The speeded tests are administered by computer, though not as adaptive tests, and IRT methods are not appropriate for scoring. Recent research (Greaud & Green, 1986; Wolfe, 1985) has resulted in consideration of the following speeded test procedures subsequently adopted for ACAP: (1) maintaining similarity in format to the paper-and-pencil test in terms of number of items displayed on a computer screen; (2) maintaining the same time limit as for the paper-and-pencil test, and the same number of items, although responding in a computerized mode is much quicker; and (3) employing a rate score, the geometric mean response time across computer screens, for each test. Items included in ACAP for experimental research purposes are computer-administered and scored as right or wrong, but are not used in determining an ability estimate for operational use by item response theory or other methods; instead these items are being used to further research on calibration procedures.

In the development of the CAT-ASVAB program, it has been planned that the CAT/ASVAB battery will be gradually introduced to the military accessioning environment and for some time military applicants will be tested with either the ASVAB or the CAT-ASVAB battery. ACAP test data are being collected (beginning in 1988) on examinees of the intended test-taking population, in the military entrance processing environment, for the purpose of calibrating CAT-ASVAB. It is planned that equipercentile equating methods, used to place new forms of the ASVAB on the same scale as a reference form of the battery, be used to determine "equivalent" scores for ACAP and ASVAB. A major goal of this work is to place ACAP scores on the same scale as scores determined in a reference population of American youth (Department of Defense, 1982). The equating of ACAP and ASVAB scores will be cross-validated during a Score Equating Verification, and scores earned on ACAP will be operational scores of record. The psychometric recommendations of the CAT-ASVAB Technical Committee leading to the ACAP field test are being documented in a Psychometric Decision List.

The evaluation of a computerized adaptive test must rely on an examination of the estimated measurement error associated with resulting test scores and the validity of test scores for their intended purpose. For an adaptive test, measurement error depends on the stopping rule used. The experimental CAT-ASVAB system and the ACAP system have been developed to administer a fixed number of items. Ranges of standard errors must be determined for all subtests of the battery and for composite scores (combinations of subtest scores) reported for selection and classification purposes. Preliminary empirical information of CAT-ASVAB reliability comes from a study conducted among military recruits using the experimental CAT-ASVAB system; test-retest reliabilities compared favorably with the paper-and-pencil ASVAB battery (Moreno, 1985).

Studies conducted with the experimental CAT-ASVAB system have shown similar predictive validity to ASVAB (Day, Kieckhaefer, & Segall, 1986; Moreno, Segall, & Kieckhaefer, 1985). From the training schools of 23 occupational specialties across the four military services, individual performance data were collected for more than 7,500 recruits. These preliminary studies have shown that experimental CAT-ASVAB subtests and selector composites are as valid as those for ASVAB. Further evidence for the validity of the CAT-ASVAB battery comes from study of the content of the item pool for each subtest; in the development of CAT-ASVAB, reviews were conducted by expert judges, providing a verification of item-level content specifications and a comparison, at the test level, of the content of an initial CAT-ASVAB item bank and that of an ASVAB reference test (described in Schratz, 1986). Preliminary investigations of the underlying factor structure of ASVAB and the experimental CAT-ASVAB system have provided evidence that the CAT-ASVAB battery measures the same traits or constructs as ASVAB (Day et al., 1986; Green, 1988; Martin, Park & Boorum, 1986; Moreno et al., 1984, 1985). While some work has been done on potential differences in measures under alternate modes of administration (Cudeck, 1985; Greaud & Green, 1986; Martin et al., 1986), additional studies are needed.

The development of a comprehensive CAT-ASVAB Technical Manual, documenting psychometric and system development progress to support operational use of the test battery, is also under way. This Manual is envisioned as a "living document that will continue to grow as the program advances, more technical data is accumulated, and psychometric/systems advances are made" (Wiskoff & Schratz, 1989).

The implementation of a computer system to support administration of the CAT-ASVAB battery on a national level entails decisions regarding computer system functional requirements, system design and evaluation, and data flow and management. Nine systems criteria for CAT-ASVAB have evolved over time and have been described elsewhere (McBride & Sympson 1985; Rafacz & Tiggle, 1985; Sands, 1985; Wiskoff & Schratz, 1989). Alternate system designs were considered for implementing ACAP (Tiggle & Rafacz, 1985). This effort resulted in the selection of the Hewlett Packard Integral Personal Computer (HPIPC) as the basic building block upon which to develop the ACAP computer network for CAT-ASVAB. Each HPIPC consists of the following computer hardware: (1) a central processing unit with 512 kilobytes of main random access memory (RAM); (2) an ambient light independent electroluminescent screen; (3) a full-size keyboard; (4) an integrated (quiet) ink-jet printer; and (5) a power cord and two network cables. There are three hardware components of the ACAP computer network that use the HPIPC: (1) examinee testing stations, (2) test administrator stations, and (3) data handling computers.

Each examinee testing station consists of the basic HPIPC, but is currently configured with 1.5 megabytes of total RAM (expandable to 7.5 megabytes), and an examinee input device developed from the standard HPIPC keyboard. The printer is not used by the examinee station, but is available in the event an examinee station must serve as the backup to the test administrator station (Rafacz, 1986). The weight of this station is 25 pounds. Jones-James (1986) discusses the CAT-ASVAB psychometric functional requirements supported by an examinee testing station.

The test administrator station is in every respect identical to the examinee station but is configured with 2.5 megabytes of total RAM, a standard keyboard, and a functional printer for the generation of recruiter reports. Rafacz (1986) describes in more detail the operation of the test administrator station, including the failure recovery operations that make the ACAP system highly reliable. At a testing site, an HPIPC local area network could consist of as many as 30 examinee stations monitored by a test administrator station. This local area network can operate in either a "networking," the predominant mode, or "standalone," the backup (failure-recovery) mode. Once a CAT-ASVAB testing session is completed, examinee testing performance data would be stored onto a microfloppy disk and sent by registered mail to a parent Military Entrance Processing Station (MEPS). At the MEPS, a data-handling computer would compile disks received from the testing sites (including the MEPS itself as a testing site) and store all collected data onto cartridge tapes for transmission to the United

States Military Entrance Processing Command Headquarters (USMEP-COM HQ). At USMEPCOM HQ these cartridge tapes are further compiled by a data handling computer that in turn generates a single cartridge tape for transmission to the CAT-ASVAB Maintenance and Psychometric (CAMP) Facility at the Navy Personnel Research and Development Center. Each data-handling computer is identical to an examinee station, but is configured with a standard keyboard, a 55 megabyte mass storage device, and a tape drive unit. Folchi (1986) discusses the operation and functions of the data-handling computer that support the ACAP network.

Software for the computer sytem developed for ACAP is written in the "C" programming language. System designers selected this language because it is native to the UNIX 5.02 operating system installed in read only memory of the HPIPC, and it has certain characteristics that are important in software development, performance, and testing (Rafacz, 1986). These considerations, coupled with the multitasking features of the UNIX operating system, make the HPIPC a very powerful software development system.

Additional studies are being conducted to assess the impact of introduction of CAT-ASVAB to the military accessioning environment. Wiskoff and Schratz (1989) describe recent work in the following areas: (1) examinee attitudes toward taking tests via computers; (2) public information and education, involving an assessment of concerns of special interest groups and the preparation of tailored information programs to meet them; (3) program evaluation, involving systematic evaluation of examination results, quality assurance testing, and future computerized test design and related psychometric research; and (4) concept of operations, involving an assessment of alternative siting strategies for components of the CAT-ASVAB system and associated benefits and economic consequences.

The investigation of CAT as a replacement for existing military test batteries is in reality a cooperative pursuit among different nations. A brief description of the international efforts in Germany, Belgium, Israel, Australia, Canada, and Great Britain is provided by Wiskoff and Schratz (1989).

EXPANDING THE TESTING DOMAIN

In recent years, all branches of the military have been actively pursuing the development of new predictors for potential use in the selection and classification of personnel. Progress has been made in developing these new predictors, and many studies are currently under way to assess their validity and, in particular, their incremental validity in comparison to the measurements made using the ASVAB alone.

As indicated in previous sections of this chapter, the ASVAB has served as a valid predictor of trainees' success in the military services (United States Military Entrance Processing Command, 1984). The content of the ASVAB, and hence CAT-ASVAB, has evolved from earlier forms of the paper-and-pencil battery and from the service classification batteries. There is a strong feeling among service researchers that more extensive information on the suitability of applicants for specific training programs, and for specific occupations in the military, may be gained from the introduction of additional cognitive and noncognitive tests to the selection and classification process.

The potential use of computers in the accessions testing process opens the door to development of new types of tests, measuring new and different skills and characteristics of examinees. Moreover, computerized adaptive administration of the ASVAB has the potential for reducing testing time, thereby allowing for the introduction of new measures to the test session without increasing the length of the session.

While a comprehensive presentation of the service research efforts is not possible, the diversity of the work will be apparent in the selected examples presented below. As the merits of these new tests are established, it can be expected that they will be introduced to the selection and classification process.

Army Efforts

The work of the U.S. Army in the development of new predictors is embodied in a multifaceted program known as "Project A." Operational goals of Project A include: (1) developing new measures of job performance as criteria against which to validate selection/classification measures; (2) validating existing selection measures against both existing and project-developed criteria; (3) developing and validating new selection and classification measures; (4) developing a utility scale for different performance levels across military occupational specialties; and (5) estimating the relative effectiveness of alternative selection and classification procedures in terms of their validity and utility (Campbell, 1986).

Campbell (1986) and others (for example, McHenry et al, 1987; Peterson et al., 1987) have reported evaluations of a trial predictor battery, based on data collected for military occupational specialties ranging from tank crewmen to military police, in relation to five job performance constructs. The trial predictor battery includes: paper-and-pencil cognitive tests of spatial ability; computerized measures of psychomotor skills, perceptual speed and accuracy, memory, and reaction time; and noncognitive measures of temperament, interest, and biodata. Peterson et al.

(1987, p. 2) point out that ASVAB serves as an "excellent predictor" of "can-do" job performance criteria, such as core technical proficiency (representing the capability to perform tasks central to the military occupational specialty [Campbell, McHenry, & Wise, 1987]), and general soldiering proficiency (representing the ability to perform a variety of tasks as a soldier). ASVAB appears not to be as strong a predictor of "will-do" job performance criteria, involving effort and leadership, personal discipline, physical fitness, and military bearing (Peterson et al., 1987).

Spatial and perceptual/psychomotor measures of the trial battery are equally poor predictors of the "will-do" job performance criteria (Peterson et al., 1987). Peterson et al. note, however, that predictive validities for the computer-administered perceptual/psychomotor battery for "can-do" criteria were .49 and .56, as compared to .60 and .66 for ASVAB, while the computerized battery can be administered in less than half the time required for ASVAB. The spatial tests, also requiring less testing time than ASVAB, did nearly as well (.54 and .64) on "can-do" criteria as ASVAB. Noncognitive measures appear to be poorer predictors of "can-do" job performance criteria than ASVAB, spatial, and perceptual/psychomotor measures of the new trial battery (Peterson et al., 1987). These data also indicate, however, that temperament and biodata measures included in the trial battery are more effective predictors of "will-do" criteria.

A preliminary look at the incremental validity of the Project A predictors by Peterson et al. (1987) found that adding the trial battery to the ASVAB increased prediction of all job performance criteria, especially for the "will-do" criteria. Results presented by McHenry et al. (1987) indicate that while addition of either cognitive or noncognitive measures from the trial battery improve prediction of all job performance criteria from ASVAB alone, the introduction of noncognitive measures accounts for the largest gains in measuring "will-do" factors of performance. Peterson et al. (1987) indicate that, since the results of this study have indicated that the new predictors make meaningful increments to validity over ASVAB prediction for important elements of job performance, future plans include refinement of the trial battery.

Air Force Efforts

The U.S. Air Force is conducting a multiyear basic-research program on new assessment techniques known as the Learning Abilities Measurement Program (LAMP). The goals of this program are to: (1) specify the basic parameters of learning ability; (2) develop techniques for assessing knowledge and skill levels of individuals; and (3) study the feasibility of a model-based system of psychological assessment (Kyllonen, 1986). According to Christal (1985), advances in cognitive psychology and the availability of microcomputers have provided the opportunity to study new abilities, to measure response latencies, and to assess learning efficiency under laboratory conditions. Christal (1985) has described the activities of an ability measurement laboratory that utilizes microcomputers in the assessment of information processing speed, using Air Force basic trainees in studies such as those described below.

As part of the LAMP program, Kyllonen (1985) reports results of studies applying different methods in examining the dimensionality of information processing speed. A whole-task analysis procedure was used in one study, involving the administration of a variety of cognitive tasks tapping verbal, quantitative, reasoning, and memory skills. Factor analysis (and other multivariate procedures) applied to performance data revealed separate verbal, quantitative, and reasoning accuracy factors, and also separate verbal, quantitative, and reasoning speed factors. General speed and general accuracy factors were identified at the second level.

A second study was conducted by Kyllonen (1985) to determine the information processing stage that best explains the locus of individual difference variation in task proficiency. A series of tasks was administered on microcomputers that could be ordered from simple to complex in terms of processing requirements, and an attempt was made to determine estimates of encoding, comparison, decision, and response-execution speed. Results of a factor analysis and two-dimensional scaling solution provided evidence for a general speed factor, and for specific speed factors ordered by process and by content.

In a third study, a coding analysis approach designed to address how various kinds of information in memory are accessed was followed (Kyllonen, 1985). Response latency was found to increase as a function of depth of memory search. A multidimensional scaling of the data revealed two-ordered dimensions, depicting amount of perceptual processing and amount or depth of memory search required. Projections of simple reaction time, choice reaction time, and physical identity matching tasks on the memory search dimension were identical, indicating that these tasks require the same minimal amount of memory search.

On the basis of the results of these three studies, Kyllonen (1985) concluded that information processing is multidimensional, and that cognitive behavior results from interaction among different processes. He points to the need for a theory-based taxonomy of information processing speed variables before assessment applications can be pursued systematically. In a review of traditional validation studies for psychological tests, and studies that have utilized testing methods based on cognitive psychology, Kyllonen (1986) discusses ways in which development in cognitive psychology might enhance current cognitive testing practices. He suggests that, in addition to serving as supplements to current selection and classification procedures in providing performance prediction for specialized occupations, cognitive tasks may be useful measures of changes in processing efficiency as a result of practice and enable cognitive diagnosis and prescription.

Navy Efforts

The U.S. Navy has embarked on research designed to develop a new battery of computerized tests of spatial ability, cognitive speed, reasoning, and memory (Wolfe et al., 1987). This research has addressed the reliability, construct validity, and predictive validity of this new battery against school and hands-on job performance criteria.

The Navy work has focused on the use of computers in assessing performance. Among the reasons (Wolfe et al., 1987) for this are the following: (1) computers can measure response latency for individual test questions; (2) computers can be used to generate test questions that involve dealing with moving stimuli; (3) computers enable controlled exposure of stimuli, useful in testing memory; and (4) simulations of tasks involved in job performance can be generated using computers. The two approaches followed in the development of the new battery have been measurement of general abilities (critical to a number of military jobs), and measurement of job-specific skills.

Wolfe et al. (1987) report that, in relation to job-specific skills, a computerized battery of tests known as the Graphic Information Processing Tests (GRIP) has been under development and validation. A recent version of the battery, including tests of memory, perceptual speed, flexibility of closure, and vigilance, has been specially designed to predict job performance for Navy Sonar technicians.

Measurement of general abilities has been undertaken through the development of new measures of spatial ability. Wolfe et al. (1987) contend that, while a spatial test was included in earlier forms of ASVAB, computerized testing offers promise for measuring important dimensions of spatial ability not previously measured by ASVAB. Evidence for this was found by Hunt et al. (1987) working with college students: (1) computer-controlled analogs can capture the individual variation in spatial-visual reasoning measured by conventional paper-and-pencil tests: (2) computer-controlled analogs are preferable because they provide measures of both speed and accuracy within a single task and allow for study of individual difference in speed-accuracy trade-offs; and (3) the ability to work with moving elements in a spatial display is distinct from the ability to work with static visual displays.

Based on these findings, three spatial tests were selected for validation on Navy personnel: (1) Integrating Details, a complex spatial problem-solving task involving correctly connecting puzzle pieces to form a unitary object and examining its match to a completed puzzle; (2) Rotation, a simple spatial problem-solving task, involving the ability to mentally rotate a geometric figure and decide if it is the same or different from a test figure; and (3) Intercept, a dynamic test of spatial ability involving the ability to intercept moving stimuli. Wolfe et al. (1987) report that preliminary studies involving Navy machinist mates have yielded promising predictive and incremental validity evidence for the Integrating Details test, and in particular for a "decision latency" measure, with respect to hands-on job performance criteria.

Future work with the Navy computerized cognitive tests is expected to include studies of reliability and validity for a large set of job categories (Wolfe et al., 1987). Cognitive speed and psychomotor tests are also receiving attention. A recent review of military and civilian psychomotor literature (Bosshardt, 1988) suggests that several types of psychomotor abilities (including multilimb coordination, wrist-finger speed, manual dexterity, and control precision) may be useful to measure in the selection process.

Navy work has also focused on the development and validation of a background questionnaire known as the Armed Services Applicant Profile (ASAP), for potential use as a supplemental military applicant screening instrument (Trent, 1988). The ASAP contains 130 biodata items related to personal, school, and work experiences. Validation of the ASAP instrument involved testing about 120,000 applicants to the military during a three-month period (approximately 88 percent of those applying for service). Approximately 56,000 of the applicants entered the military and were tracked to identify those completing one year of service and those who left the military. Scoring keys were developed based on responding differences between the two criterion groups and cross-validated. ASAP scores were found to be good predictors (rbis = .27) of service completion in the cross-validation samples (Trent, 1988). In addition, ASAP was found to improve prediction of service completion significantly when used in conjunction with current operational screening measures (the AFQT and high school diploma attainment).

CONCLUSION

The work of the military services in developing and implementing personnel selection and classification instruments has been fruitful and extensive. The work described in this chapter has spanned cognitive and noncognitive domains, as well as various modes of test administration. With the introduction of computers to the testing process, we can look forward to many exciting developments in the future. Continued progress on enlisted selection and classification procedures will undoubtedly enrich the history of psychological testing at large.

REFERENCES

Ackerman, T. A. (1987, April). The robustness of LOGIST and BILOG IRT estimation programs of violations of local independence. Paper presented at the annual meeting of the American Educational Research Association, Washington, DC.

American Psychological Association. (1985). *Standards for educational and psychological testing*. Washington, DC: Author.

_____ . (1986) *Guidelines for computer-based tests and interpretations*. Washington, DC: Author.

Angoff, W. H. (1971). Scales, norms, and equivalent scores. In R. L. Thorndike (Ed.), *Educational measurement* (pp. 508-600). Washington, DC: American Council on Education.

Assessment Systems Corporation. (1984). *User's manual for the MicroCAT testing system* (Research Report ONR-85-1). St. Paul: Author.

_____ . (1986). *User's manual for ITEMAN, RASCAL, and ASCAL*. St. Paul: Author.

Baker, H. G., Rafacz, B. A. & Sands, W. A. (1984). *Computerized Adaptive Screening Test (CAST): Development for use in military recruiting stations* (Report No. NPRDC TR 84-17). San Diego: Navy Personnel Research and Development Center.

Bock, R. D., & Aitkin, M. (1981). Marginal maximum likelihood estimation of item parameters: Application of an EM algorithm. *Psychometrika, 46*, 443-459.

Bock, R. D., Gibbons, R., & Muraki, E. (1985). *Full-information item factor analysis* (MRC Report 85-1). Chicago: Methodology Research Center/NORC.

_____ . (1986). *Full-information item factor analysis* (MRC Report 85-1, revised). Chicago: Methodology Research Center/NORC.

Bock, R. D., & Wood, R. (1971). Test theory. In P. H. Mussen and M. E. Rosenzweig (Eds.), *Annual review of psychology* (pp. 193-224)). Palo Alto, CA: Annual Review, Inc.

Bosshardt, M. J. (1988). *Utility of psychomotor tests for prediction of Navy enlisted performance* (Report No. NPRDC TN-88-44). San Diego: Navy Personnel Research and Development Center.

Campbell, J. P. (1986, August). *When the textbook goes operational*. Paper presented at the annual meeting of the American Psychological Association, Washington, DC.

Campbell, J. P., McHenry, J. J., & Wise, L. L. (1987, April). *Analysis of criterion measures: The modeling of performance*. Paper presented at the mid-year conference of the Society of Industrial and Organizational Psychology, Atlanta.

Christal, R. E. (1985, September). Learning Abilities Measurement Program (Project LAMP). Paper presented to the Defense Advisory Committee on Military Personnel Testing, San Diego.

Cudeck, R. (1985). A structural comparison of conventional and adaptive versions of the ASVAB. *Multivariate Behavioral Research, 20*, 305–322.

Day, L. E., Kieckhaefer, W. F., & Segall, D. O. (1986). *Predictive utility evaluation of computerized adaptive testing in the armed services* (Contract No. N66001–83–D–0343). San Diego: Navy Personnel Research and Development Center.

Department of Defense. (1982). *Profile of American youth: 1980 nationwide administration of the Armed Services Vocational Aptitude Battery.* Washington, DC: Office of the Assistant Secretary of Defense, Manpower, Reserve Affairs and Logistics.

DuBois, P. H. (1970). *A history of psychological testing.* Boston: Allyn and Bacon.

Earles, J. A., Guiliano, T., Ree, M. J., & Valentine, L. D. (1983). The 1980 youth population: An investigation of speeded subtests. Unpublished manuscript, Air Force Human Resources Laboratory, Manpower and Personnel Division, Brooks AFB, TX.

Folchi, J. S. (1986). Communication of computerized adaptive testing results in support of ACAP. *Proceedings of the 28th Annual Conference of the Military Testing Association*, 618–623.

Greaud, V. A., & Green, B. F. (1986). Equivalence of conventional and computer presentation of speed tests. *Applied Psychological Measurement, 10*, 23–24.

Green, B. F. (1988). Construct validity of computer-based tests. In H. Wainer & H. Braun (Eds.), *Test validity* (pp. 77–86). Hillsdale, NJ: Lawrence Erlbaum Associates.

Green, B. F., Bock, R. D., Humphreys, L. G., Linn, R. L., & Reckase, M. D. (1982). *Evaluation plan for the computerized adaptive vocational aptitude battery* (Research Report 82–1). Baltimore: Department of Psychology, The Johns Hopkins University.

_____ . (1984a). *Evaluation plan for the computerized adaptive vocational aptitude battery* (Manpower and Personnel Laboratory Technical Note 85–1). San Diego: Navy Personnel Research and Development Center.

_____ . (1984b). Technical guidelines for assessing computerized adaptive tests. *Journal of Educational Measurement, 21*, 347–360.

Guilford, J. P., & Lacey, J. I. (Eds.). (1947). *Army Air Force's aviation psychology program research reports: Printed classification tests* (Report No. 5). Washington, DC: U.S. Government Printing Office.

Hambleton, R. K., & Cook, L. L. (1977). Latent trait models and their use in the analysis of educational test data. *Journal of Educational Measurement, 14*, 75–96.

Hambleton, R. K., & Rovinelli, R. J. (1986). Assessing the dimensionality of a set of test items. *Applied Psychological Measurement, 10*, 287–302.

Hattie, J. (1984). An empirical study of various indices for determining unidimensionality. *Multivariate Behavioral Research, 19*, 49–78.

Hunt, E., Pellegrino, J. W. Abate, R., Alderton, D. L., Farr, S. A., Frick, R. W., & McDonald, T. P. (1987). *Computer controlled testing of spatial-visual ability* (Report No. NPRDC-TR-87-31) San Diego: Navy Personnel Research and Development Center.

Jensema, C. J. (1977). Bayesian tailored testing and the influence of item bank characteristics. *Applied Psychological Measurement, 1*, 111-120.

Jones-James, G. (1986). Design and development of the ACAP test administration software. Proceedings of the 28th Annual Conference of the Military Testing Association, 612-617.

Keene, J. M., & Holmes, S. E. (1987, April). *Obtaining norm-referenced test information for local objective-referenced tests: Issues and challenges.* Paper presented at the annual meeting of the National Council on Measurement in Education, Washington, DC.

Kingston, N. (1986). *Assessing the dimensionality of GMAT verbal and quantitative measures using full information factor analysis* (Research Report RR-86-13). Princeton, NJ: Educational Testing Service.

Knapp, D. J., & Pliske, R. M. (1986). *Preliminary report on a national cross-validation of the Computerized Adaptive Screening Test (CAST)* (Research Report 1430). Alexandria, VA: Manpower and Personnel Research Laboratory.

Knapp, D. J., & Wise, L. L. (1987, August). *Refining the Computerized Adaptive Screening Test (CAST).* Paper presented at the annual meeting of the American Psychological Association, New York.

Kyllonen, P. C. (1985). *Dimensions of information processing speed* (Report No. AFHRL-TP-84-56). Brooks AFB, TX: Air Force Human Resources Laboratory.

_____ . (1986). *Theory-based cognitive assessment* (Report No. AFHRL-TP-85-30). Brooks AFB, TX: Air Force Human Resources Laboratory.

Lenke, J. M. (1981, April). *A look at the outcomes of test equating using Rasch Model procedures.* Paper presented at the annual meeting of the National Council on Measurement in Education, Los Angeles.

Lenke, J. M., & Canner, J. M. (1980, April). *A design for linking tests of a multi-level, multi-form achievement test.* Paper presented at the annual meeting of the National Council on Measurement in Education, Boston.

Lenke, J. M., & Rentz, R. R. (1982, April). *The use of the Rasch Model in the development of the Stanford Achievement Test.* Paper presented at the annual meeting of the National Council on Measurement in Education, New York.

Lord, F. M. (1952). A theory of test scores. *Psychometric Monograph*, No. 7.

_____ . (1980). *Applications of item response theory to practical testing problems.* Hillsdale, NJ: Lawrence Erlbaum Associates.

Maier, M. H., & Truss, A. R. (1982). *Original scaling of ASVAB forms 5, 6 and 7: What went wrong* (Research Contribution No. 457). Alexandria, VA: Center for Naval Analyses.

Marco, G., Petersen, N., & Stewart, E. (1979). A test of the adequacy of curvilinear score equating models. *Proceedings of the 1979 Computerized Adaptive Testing Conference*, 167-196.

Martin, C. J., Park, R. K., & Boorum, D. (1986, April). *Validating a computer adaptive testing system using structural analysis.* Paper presented at the annual meeting of the American Educational Research Association, San Francisco.

Mathews, J. J., & Ree, M. J. (1982). *Enlistment Screening Test Forms 81a and 81b: Development and calibration* (Report No. AFHLR-TR-81-54). Brooks AFB, TX: Manpower and Personnel Division.

McBride, J. R., & Moe, K. C. (1986, April). *Computerized adaptive achievement testing: A prototype.* Paper presented at the annual meeting of the National Council on Measurement in Education, San Francisco.

McBride, J. R., & Sympson, J. B. (1985). The computerized adaptive testing system development project. *Proceedings of the 1982 Item Response Theory and Computerized Adaptive Testing Conference,* 342-349.

McHenry, J. J., Hough, L. M., Toquam, J. L., Hanson, M. A., & Ashworth, S. (1987, April). *Project A validity results: The relationship between predictor and criterion domains.* Paper presented at the mid-year conference of the Society of Industrial and Organizational Psychology, Atlanta.

Melton, A. W. (Ed.) (1947). *Army Air Force's aviation psychology program research reports: Apparatus tests* (Report No. 4). Washington, DC: U.S. Government Printing Office.

Mislevy, R. J. (1986). *Exploiting auxiliary information about examinees in the estimation of item parameters* (Research Report No. RR-86-18-ONR. Princeton, NJ: Educational Testing Service.

Mislevy, R. J., & Bock, R. D. (1984). BILOG: *Item analysis and test scoring with binary logistic models.* Mooresville, IN: Scientific Software.

Moreno, K. E. (1985, September). *Reliability and validity of CAT-ASVAB.* Paper presented at the meeting of the Defense Advisory Committee on Military Personnel Testing, San Diego.

Moreno, K. E., Segall, D. O., & Kieckhaefer, W. F. (1985). A validity study of the Computerized Adaptive Testing Version of the Armed Services Vocational Aptitude Battery. *Proceedings of the 27th Annual Conference of the Military Testing Association, 1,* 29-33.

Moreno, K. E., Wetzel, D. C., McBride, J. R., & Weiss, D. J. (1984). Relationship between corresponding Armed Services Vocational Aptitude Battery (ASVAB) and computerized adaptive testing (CAT) subtests. *Applied Psychological Measurement, 8,* 155-163.

Owen, R. J. (1969). *A Bayesian approach to tailored testing* (Research Report 69-92). Princeton, NJ: Educational Testing Service.

———. (1975). A Bayesian sequential procedure for quantal response in the context of adaptive mental testing. *Journal of the American Statistical Association,˙ 70,* 351-356.

Peterson, N., Hough, L., Ashworth, S., & Toquam, J. (1987, April). *New predictors of soldier performance.* Paper presented at the mid-year conference of the Society of Industrial and Organizational Psychology, Atlanta.

Pliske, R. M., Gade, P. A., & Johnson, R. M. (1984). *Cross-validation of the Computerized Adaptive Screening Test (CAST)* (ARI Research Report 1372).

Alexandria, VA: U.S. Army Research Institute for the Behavioral and Social Sciences.

Prestwood, J. S., Vale, C. D., Massey, R. H., & Welsh, J. R. (1985). *Armed Services Vocational Aptitude Battery: Development of an adaptive item pool* (Report No. AFHRL-TR-85-19). Brooks AFB, TX: Air Force Systems Command.

Rafacz, B. A. (1986). Development of the test administrator's station in support of ACAP. *Proceedings of the 28th Annual Conference of the Military Testing Association*, 606-611.

Rafacz, B. A., & Tiggle, R. B. (1985). *Functional requirements for the Accelerated CAT-ASVAB Project (ACAP) development system.* Unpublished manuscript, Navy Personnel Research and Development Center, San Diego.

Ree, M. J., Mathews, J. J., Mullins, C. J., & Massey, R. H. (1982). *Calibration of Armed Services Vocational Aptitude Battery Forms 8, 9, and 10* (Report No. AFHRL-TP-81-49). Brooks AFB, TX: Air Force Human Resources Laboratory.

Ree, M. J., & Valentine, L. D. (1987). *Armed Services Vocational Aptitude Battery (ASVAB): Development of deliberate failure keys for Forms 11, 12, & 13* (Report No. AFHRL-TP-86-57). Brooks AFB, TX: Air Force Human Resources Laboratory.

Ree, M. J., Valentine, L. D., & Earles, J. A. (1985). *The 1980 youth population: A verification report* (Report No. AFHRL-TP-84-47, AD-A153-821). Brooks AFB, TX: Air Force Human Resources Laboratory.

Rentz, R. R., & Bashaw, W. L. (1975). Equating reading tests with the Rasch Model (Project OEC-0-72-5237). Washington, DC: U.S. Office of Education.

Sands, W. A. (1985). An overview of the Accelerated CAT-ASVAB Program. *Proceedings of the 27th Annual Conference of the Military Testing Association*, *1*, 19-22.

Sands, W. A., & Gade, P. A. (1983). An application of computerized adaptive testing in U.S. Army recruiting. *Journal of Computer-Based Instruction, 10*, 87-89.

Sands, W. A., & Rafacz, B. A. (1983). Field test evaluation of the Computerized Adaptive Screening Test (CAST). *Proceedings of the 25th Annual Conference of the Military Testing Association*, 112-117.

Schratz, M. K. (1983). An empirical study of the consistency of Thurstone and Rasch Model approaches to the vertical equating of a multi-form, multi-level achievement test series (Doctoral dissertation, Fordham Univeristy, 1983). *Dissertation Abstracts International, 44*, 1997B.

_____. (1984a, April). *Vertical equating: An empirical study of the consistency of Thurstone and Rasch Model approaches.* Paper presented at the annual meeting of the National Council on Measurement in Education, New Orleans.

_____. (1984b, August). *An empirical study of the consistency of Thurstone and Rasch Model approaches to vertical scaling.* Paper presented at the annual meeting of the American Psychological Association, Toronto.

_____ . (1985). Assessment of the unidimensionality of CAT-ASVAB subtests. *Proceedings of the 27th Annual Conference of the Military Testing Association, 1*, 34–37.

_____ . (1986, August). *Test content considerations in the development of adaptive item pools.* Paper presented at the annual convention of the American Psychological Association, Washington, DC.

Schratz, M. K., Carroll, L. K. & Hurrell, R. M. (1988). *Second-generation CAT-ASVAB tests: Advances in testing and testing technology.* Unpublished manuscript, Navy Personnel Research and Development Center, San Diego.

Schratz, M. K., & Lenke, J. M. (1980). *Equating a multi-level, multi-form achievement series through the Rasch Model.* Paper presented at the annual meeting of the Florida Educational Research Association, Ft. Lauderdale.

Sims, W. H., & Maier, M. H. (1983). *The appropriateness for military application of the ASVAB subtest and source scale in the new 1980 reference population* (Memorandum 83–3102). Alexandria, VA: Center for Naval Analyses.

Sims, W. H., & Truss, A. (1982). *Development and application of a Pseudo-AFQT for ASVAB 8/9/10* (Report No. 470). Alexandria, VA: Center for Naval Analyses.

Stuit, D. B. (1947). *Personnel research and test development in the bureau of naval personnel.* Princeton, NJ: Princeton University Press.

Swanson, L. (1986, August). *Technical software issues in IRT based test development.* Paper presented at the annual meeting of the American Psychological Association, Washington, DC.

Sympson, J. B., & Hetter, R. D. (1985, October). Controlling item-exposure rates in computerized adaptive testing. In W. A. Sands (Chair), *Computerized adaptive testing research at the Navy Personnel Research and Development Center.* Symposium conducted at the 27th annual conference of the Military Testing Association, San Diego.

Thissen, D. (1986). *Multilog: A user's guide.* Mooresville, IN: Scientific Software.

Tiggle, R. B., & Rafacz, B. A. (1985). Evaluation of three local CAT-ASVAB network designs. *Proceedings of the 27th Annual Conference of the Military Testing Association, 1*, 23–28.

Trent, T. (1988). *Joint service adaptability screening: Initial validation of the Armed Services Applicant Profile (ASAP)* (Report No. NPRDC–TR–88). San Diego: Navy Personnel Research and Development Center.

Uhlaner, J. E., & Bolanovich, D. J. (1952). *Development of Armed Forces Qualification Test and predecessor Army screening tests, 1946–1950* (Report No. 976). Washington, DC: The Adjutant General's Office.

United States Military Entrance Processing Command. (1984). *Test manual for the Armed Services Vocational Aptitude Battery* (DOD 1304.12AA). North Chicago: Author.

Vale, C. D. (1986). Linking item parameters onto a common scale. *Applied Psychological Measurement, 10*, 333–344.

Vale, C. D., & Gialluca, K. A. (1985). *ASCAL: A microcomputer program for estimating logistic IRT item parameters* (Research Report ONE–85–4). St. Paul: Assessment Systems Corporation.

Van der Linden, W. J. (Ed.). (1987). *IRT-based test construction* (Research Report 87-2). Netherlands: Department of Education, University of Twente.

Ward, W. C., Kline, R. G., & Flaugher, J. (1985, December). *College Board computerized placement tests: Summary of pilot testing results, 1984-1985.* Paper presented at the ETS/DOD conference on testing technology and applications, Princton, NJ.

Wegner, T. G., & Ree, M. J. (1985). *Armed Services Vocational Aptitude Battery: Correcting the speeded subtests for the 1980 youth population* (Report AFHRL-TR-85-14). Brooks AFB, TX: A.F. Human Resources Laboratory.

Weiss, D. J., & Kingsbury, G. G. (1984). Application of computerized adaptive testing to educational problems. *Journal of Educational Measurement, 21,* 361-375.

Wild, C. L. (1986, August). *Using an item response theory system to develop tests.* Paper presented at the annual meeting of the American Psychological Association, Washington, DC.

Wingersky, M. S., Barton, M. A., & Lord, F. M. (1982). *Logist user's guide: Logist 5, version 1.0.* Princeton, NJ: Educational Testing Service.

Wingersky, M. S., Patrick, R., & Lord, F. M. (1987). *Logist user's guide: Logist 6, version 1.0.* Princeton, NJ: Educational Testing Service.

Wiskoff, M. F. (1981). Computerized adaptive testing. *Proceedings of the National Security Industrial Association First Annual Conference on Personnel and Training Factors in System Effectiveness, 1,* 33-37.

Wiskoff, M. F., & Schratz, M. K. (1989). Computerized adaptive testing of a vocational aptitude battery. In R. F. Dillon & J. W Pellegrino (Eds.), *Testing: Theoretical and applied perspectives.* New York: Praeger.

Wolfe, J. H. (1985). Speeded tests—Can computers improve measurement? *Proceedings of the 27th Annual Conference of the Military Testing Association, 1,* 49-54.

Wolfe, J. H., Alderton, D. L., Cory, C. H., & Larson, G. E. (1987). Reliability, and validity of new computerized ability tests. *Proceedings of the Department of Defense/Educational Testing Service Conference on Job Performance Measurement Technologies,* 369-382.

Wright, B. D. (1968). Sample-free test calibration and person measurement. *Proceedings of the 1967 Invitational Conference on Testing Problems.* Princeton, NJ: Educational Testing Service.

Yen, W. M. (1983). Use of the three-parameter logistic model in the development of a standardized achievement test. In R. K. Hambleton (Ed.), *Applications of item response theory* (pp. 123-141). Vancouver, BC: Educational Research Institute of British Colombia.

Yen, W. M., Green, D. R., Burket, G. R. (1987). Valid normative information from customized achievement tests. *Educational Measurement Issues and Practice, 6,* 7-13.

Zimowski, M. F., & Bock, R. D. (1987). *Full-information item factor analysis of test forms from the ASVAB CAT pool* (MRC Report 87-1, revised. Chicago: Methodology Research Center/NORC.

Zwick, R. 1986. Assessment of the dimensionality of NAEP year 15 reading data (Research Report 86-4). Princeton, NJ: ETS.

2 _____

Personnel Classification/ Assignment Models

LEONARD P. KROEKER

INTRODUCTION

Each month the armed services take in thousands of persons who must be placed among a broad range of jobs. Each person inducted must be utilized somewhere within a particular service branch. The classification problem, which is the central question addressed in this chapter, consists of arranging assignment procedures so that a close match between human skills and job requirements is achieved.

A substantial portion of the following discussion will deal with the quality of matches resulting from various assignment procedures. An optimal* matching of persons and jobs is one that cannot be improved upon by any other allocation. The optimal assignment problem is of major interest to both military managers and civilian executives because of the costs associated with inappropriate matches. One need only examine the psychological journal literature devoted to topics such as increasing productivity and enhancing job satisfaction to appreciate the degree of importance attached to the effective utilization of personnel (Hunter & Schmidt, 1982).

Discussions of personnel classification and assignment problems are frequently overwhelmed by an emphasis on human resources (manpower) considerations, such as the allocation or movement of groups of people, as opposed to personnel concerns, such as person-job matching (Skinner & Jackson, 1977; Lee & Schniederjans, 1983). This chapter offers a view of the assignment problem that originates from within the domain of psychological concerns related

---

*Optimal assignment is defined as the matching of persons to jobs so that the sum of the assignment payoffs is a maximum. Dunnette (1966) has provided a succinct description and discussion of the optimal assignment problem.

to personnel selection and classification. The problem will, therefore, be presented from a perspective that focuses on the techniques developed within psychological research and supplements them with those developed within operations research and management science disciplines.

Objectives

The objectives of this chapter are to describe the historical development of person-job match research, and to discuss the nature of personnel assignment procedure changes brought about by policy controversies, computer technology advances, and measurement innovations. It will be primarily devoted to initial assignment concerns as opposed to reassignment, reenlistment, and other human resource distribution/employment issues.

Since World War II, personnel researchers have been responsible for various improvements in techniques for classifying and assigning military personnel. These innovations, along with discussions of related classification and assignment issues, form the basis of the chapter. Very little attention will be devoted to developing the underlying mathematical structure.

The principal focus of the chapter is the literature dealing with classification and assignment problems arising in military contexts. Model development has benefited greatly from the large amount of research aimed at meeting these military problems. Since the assignment of large numbers of people arises primarily in these settings, it is not surprising that the large body of research literature deals mainly with military applications. Research material will be drawn from various sources and no attempt will be made to separate it according to context.

In perusing the research literature one is led to conclude that many of the developments occurring in the 1960s depended upon concepts developed in response to problems that originated in the 1940s. Many of those concepts were refined in the 1970s (Ash & Kroeker, 1975; Dunnette & Borman, 1979) and yielded products of various kinds, many in the form of computer programs. Systems evolving in the 1980s also bear strong relationships to previous research, but in addition appear more responsive to pragmatic system requirements and individual psychological needs. Future trends suggest the development of more powerful and more efficient systems that also exhibit greater responsiveness to individual needs (Hakel, 1986).

Differential Classification History

The following paragraphs provide a brief overview of the historical development of the differential classification/assignment concept.

The earliest major efforts to address differential classification problems were made during World War II, when the U.S. military services attempted to maximize organizational effectiveness by manipulating training assignments (Dubois, 1947). These efforts required information on a person's probable success in a given specialty as well as the relative importance of the specialty, where it was assumed that relative importance would change as logistical and other conditions changed.

The procedures for obtaining maximum efficieny in selecting personnel by means of test scores when a single assignment is involved have been known for many years. Brodgen's *Psychometrika* paper (1946) was the first devoted to developing a procedure to maximize efficiency of selection and assignment when each person was eligible for several assignments.

Thorndike (1950) prepared a unique formulation of the classification problem that included a careful examination of the underlying concepts and yielded a thoughtful discussion of a number of issues, some of which remain unresolved today. Lord (1952) derived an analytical form of a solution that resembled Brogden's. A practical solution of both the Thorndike and Lord problem was unavailable until Votaw (1952) developed a rapidly converging successive approximation procedure. A demonstration of the application of this technology to the assignment of persons to Air Force jobs was provided by Votaw and Dailey (1952).

In an article describing the use of the optimal regions method to solve the classification problem, Dwyer (1954, 1957) noted the equivalence of Votaw's formulation and those found in other disciplines. In particular, he noted its resemblance to the Hitchcock transportation problem for which Dantzig (1951) and Flood (1953), among others, had provided solutions.

In a subsequent research paper, Votaw (1956) reviewed the early research on personnel classification problems and addressed several assignment issues. In addition, he described a useful mathematical linkage between classification and linear programming techniques and discussed a number of general methods for computing assignment solutions.

The most significant recent influence in furthering differential classification objectives has been Ward's research (1958, 1959, 1979, 1983). His formulation stipulated that payoffs were generated by a regression (or analysis of variance) model and that the benefit accruing from person-job assignments was measured by the magnitude of the model's interaction term (Ward & Jennings, 1983; Ward, 1983). In other words, the amount of interaction present in a given assignment problem was found to be directly related to the benefit obtainable through the use of a differential assignment procedure.

It is now possible to identify conditions under which differential classification is critical to human resources managers and also those under which the process is of marginal value (Ward & Sorenson, 1986). Further discussion of this issue is left to a later section.

MILITARY ACCESSIONING PROCEDURES

The following topics will be discussed in this section: the historical background of military accessioning systems; the influences on efforts to develop and improve them; and the characteristics of the procedures used by the various service branches.

Early personnel assignment (in the 1950s) in the armed services was accomplished monthly by large teams of classification technicians who sorted through cards containing recruit information (e.g., aptitude test scores, biographical data, etc.) and who used their best judgment as the basis for filling duty assignments and training school quotas. This manual procedure involved the human evaluation of trade-offs among multiple system objectives and often yielded person-job mismatches because of the difficulty of monitoring global system performance and meeting system constraints simultaneously. The mismatches resulted in considerable system turbulence as manifested by unacceptable training school failure rates, large numbers of personnel reassignments, and inefficient use of training school resources (Sorenson, 1968).

During the decade of the 1950s, a period of relative tranquility prevailed, and personnel system turbulence was tolerated by U.S. military leaders. In the following decade, however, rapidly changing social and political conditions motivated efforts to improve existing assignment systems (Harding & Richards, 1971). During this period, training school assignment and subsequent occupational classification consisted of screening an applicant by administering mental aptitude examinations to determine the training schools and, hence, the jobs for which the applicant qualified. Then the service selected an occupation for the recruit based on the service priorities and the recruit's aptitudes (Morgan & Roseen, 1974).

Assignment decisions were based on factors such as available positions, training school openings, previous commitments made by recruiters, transportation costs, aptitude examination scores, and staffing priorities. The hierarchy of assignment objectives underlying the decisions is displayed in Table 2.1

Table 2.1
Hierarchy of Assignment Objectives

---

1.   Honor recruiting commitments, then

2.   Fill schools in order of priority assigned by each service, then

3.   Whenever possible, fill each school without violating minimum qualification standards (physical, mental, etc.), then

4.   Minimize transportation costs of school assignments (Army and Navy systems only), then

5.   Maximize preferences and/or counselor recommendations, then

6.   Maximize aptitudes of those assigned to classes, then

7.   Assign remaining trainees to directed duty assignments in accordance with service priorities, transportation costs, preferences, recommendations, in that order.

Source: Morgan & Roseen (1974).

Major Influences

Within the last two decades several factors have altered the course of personnel assignment system development and refinement. Among them are the increasing availability and utilization of electronic computers and the decision to change from a draft-dependent human resources environment to the All Volunteer Force (AVF). Changes in the nation's economic climate and the changing structure of its demographic profile also play a part in modifying accessioning and assignment procedures.

The availability of highly efficient large-scale electronic computing systems has been a major force in stimulating the development of computer-based methods of personnel assignment. Management experts contended that more effective organizations could be constructed and maintained by harnessing available and relatively inexpensive computing capability and by focusing this technology on the person-job matching problem (Lawler, 1974).

Each of the armed services must operate within a large collection of constraints dictated by existing regulations, previous practices, and assumptions about the personnel required for various job assignments. The major purpose to be served by a computer-based assignment system thus becomes one of satisfying all mandatory requirements and as many of the desirable requirements as possible, while maximizing the overall utility for all assignments made. Early work to examine the feasibility of using automated procedures to accomplish the above objectives for enlisted personnel was conducted by Dow et al. (1964).

A second major factor influencing assignment system development was the shift of the armed services to the AVF concept. Morgan and Roseen (1974, p. 23) state that "just as the existence of the draft was the central factor underlying the operational characteristics of the pre-Volunteer recruiting, classification and assignment (RCA) process, the absence of a draft-guaranteed supply of quality accessions has been the dominant factor in shaping the adjustments and adaptations made in this area." Furthermore, they contend that the subsequent RCA process is considerably more complex and that the

relative complexity can be traced to two fundamental changes:

1. Decision-making authority has been diffused over a greater number of participants, including prospective recruits themselves; and

2. Elimination of the draft has underscored the importance of several major institutional influences and interrelationships affecting structure and operation of the RCA systems (Morgan & Roseen, 1974, p. 23).

An interesting and potentially useful utility approach to meet anticipated AVF problems involving personnel assignment was outlined by Watt (1973) in a brief preliminary report. Unfortunately, this research did not continue because of lack of funding.

Human resources projections for the remaining decades of this century signal a significantly lower applicant pool. For example, the model used by Borack and Govindan (1978) forecasts a decline from 1975 levels of approximately 28 percent by 1994. The projected reduction in size of the applicant pool may affect both the organizational structure of the armed services and the procedures used to allocate personnel. In fact, assignment efficiency promises to be an even greater concern in the future than it is today. Hence, the assignment systems of tomorrow will need to be designed to reflect this increased emphasis on person-job match efficiency.

In addition to the human resources supply issue, the personnel retention question surfaces as a policy concern within various services from time to time. A timely response to Navy concerns was that of Thomason and Rutledge (1981). Subsequently, an attrition/retention component was developed and implemented in the Navy's classification system (Kroeker & Folchi, 1984a).

In recent years opportunities for women in the armed services have increased significantly. The rapid increase in the number of women an active duty began after 1972. At that time women made up about 1.5 percent of the active force, and by the end of 1980 women constituted approximately 8.4 percent of the active duty force. The increased emphasis on the role played by women in the armed services will be reflected in the design of assignment systems currently under development. For example, it appears increasingly likely that person-job match functions dealing with physical strength capabilities will be included when existing assignment algorithms are revised.

Army Classification Procedures

Allocating Army personnel was initially accomplished manually by Basic Training Camp counselors who were given quotas for assignment of soldiers to school courses (Bolin & King, 1958). This procedure was replaced in 1958 by a mechanized assignment system that used more background information and that resulted in substantially improved assignments (Boldt et al., 1960; Boldt, 1964).

Despite the optimal allocation research contributions of Brogden (1946, 1954) and Dwyer (1953, 1954), computer-based algorithms were run only under experimental conditions by Army agencies. As the use of electronic computing machinery became more common, the utilization of this technology gained acceptance. The first operational Army assignment system containing an optimization model (ACT II) was implemented in 1967 (Hatch, 1971).

The ACT II model was designed to handle the allocation of large numbers of soldiers at one time. It was capable of determining the number of persons who could be assigned to their preferred military occupational specialty (MOS) at a minimum transportation cost when system constraints, such as those listed in Table 2.1, were relaxed in order of priority. It was also capable of optimally assigning the recruits to Advanced Individual Training schools in order to maximize the sum of predicted performance (Aptitude Area) scores (Sorenson, 1967).

The shift to the AVF concept undermined the usefulness of the ACT II system since the latter was designed to operate in a draft environment. Its successor, the Recruit Quota for Enlistment System (REQUEST) model, is in use today and assigns personnel to MOS categories in accordance with established Army policy requirements. It enables a recruiter to determine the availability of a training school opportunity and to reserve a school space for a given applicant.

Marine Corps Classification Procedures

The Marine Corps also began with a manual assignment system for allocating recruits to training school courses and other duty assignments following basic training. The procedure was revised periodically to reflect updated operational concerns and was finally replaced in 1965 by a computerized system known as the Computer Based Recruit Assignment (COBRA) model (Dunnette, 1966; Hatch, 1971).

The model used probability of success estimates that were obtained in the manner described below. The Army Area Aptitude Battery was administered to all recruits and eight Area Aptitude composite scores were computed from linear combinations of the basic tests in the battery. The composites were then used to estimate each recruit's success chances in each of the assignment categories.

The optimal assignment solution developed for use in the COBRA model depended on the acquisition of a feasible solution (Hatch, 1971). The computer programs FEASFIND and QUOTFIND constituted the central elements of the system and accomplished the following tasks:

1. They determined whether or not mandatory requirements could be met.
2. They assigned persons meeting the desirable requirements to the maximum extent possible.
3. They assigned persons failing to meet desirable requirements to as few different assignment categories as possible.
4. They reduced quotas to accomplish a feasible solution, that is, by reducing quotas less among high-priority assignments than among lower priority ones.

The process of classifying and assigning recruits occurred during the first week of the month when the data for recruits due for outposting during the following months were sent to Marine Corps headquarters. Recommended assignments were generated by the COBRA model and returned to the Recruit Depot for review. Any necessary changes were then made and the assignments were given to the recruits three or four days prior to completion of Recruit Training (Harding & Richards, 1971).

Air Force Classification Procedures

The earliest Air Force person-job match procedures consisted of a hand-sorting process in which career counselors reviewed test scores, discussed available job options, and completed the assignment process during the recruit's basic training phase.

In 1967 the Automated Assignment Process (AAP) was implemented at the Reception Center, an Air Force basic training facility. Job data consisting of weekly airmen quotas required by each Air Force Specialty Code (AFSC), mandatory and desired AFSC prerequisites, AFSC priority, and personal data were entered into the system. A qualification score, reflecting the extent to which the airman met all the desired AFSC prerequisites, was computed for each person-job combination. The procedure yielded a job assignment within the highest priority AFSCs of the airmen with the best qualification scores (Harding & Richards, 1971).

In 1976 the Air Force implemented a computer-based assignment system for new enlistees which was called the Procurement Management Information System (PROMIS) (Hendrix et al., 1979). It differed from its predecessor in that job reservations could be made at an earlier point in the accession process. Instead of awaiting assignment at the basic training facility, a recruit received a guaranteed assignment prior to entering basic training. Field recruiters were linked to the Recruiting Service's Accession Control Center (ACC) by means of Wide Area Telephone Service (WATS) lines and as a result reserved job vacancies as far as six months in advance.

Navy Classification Procedures

Before 1966, classification and assignment of Navy enlisted personnel were performed manually. According to Swanson and Dow (1965), this posed a particularly difficult problem because of the large number of Navy schools to which personnel were assigned. For example, in 1965, there were 1,000 or more men of differing abilities to be assigned to 70 categories each week, with up to 30 assignment constraints to be met. It became apparent that the small number of personnel specialists could not consider every person for every possible assignment.

Following the successful outcome of a feasibility study (Dow et al., 1964), Swanson and Dow (1965) developed the Computer Assisted Assignment System (COMPASS). The model was designed to optimize the outcome of the classification process and was impemented by the Navy in 1966.

Modifications of the allocation system resulted in the development of the COMPASS II model (Hatch et al., 1968), which was implemented in 1969. The design of the model was heavily influenced by issues such as the distribution of shortages and was only minimally responsive to personal needs.

In response to the recruiting problems generated by the introduction of the AVF, the Navy began offering training school guarantees to applicants during the intial stages of the accession process. The automated computer-based reservation system introduced in 1976 to accomplish the above task was called the Personalized Reservation for Immediate and Delayed Enlistment (PRIDE) system.

An overview of the various systems used by the services over the years is provided in Table 2.2.

A useful comparison of the models currently used by the services is provided by Stillwell (1983). The discussion is oriented toward the development

Table 2.2
Military Accessioning Systems

	ARMY	MARINE CORPS	AIR FORCE	NAVY
1950	Hand-sorting Procedure	Hand-sorting Procedure	Hand-sorting Procedure	Hand-sorting Procedure
1955				
1960				
1965	ACT II	COBRA	AAP	COMPASS COMPASS II
1970	REQUEST		PROMIS	
1975			APDS-PROMIS	PRIDE
1980		RDM		CLASP
1985	(EPAS)	(MC-RAS)	(PROMIS II)	(CLASP-RTC)

of a future Army model that will take into account numerous constraints arising from manpower force-structure requirements.

MILITARY CLASSIFICATION MODELS

The optimal utilization of personnel resources is a problem that has interested researchers for more than 35 years. In the psychological literature it is referred to as a classification or placement issue whereas in the operations research field it is known as the transportation problem (Wagner, 1975).

This section contains an outline of the assignment problem, a discussion of the optimization criterion problem, a review of existing large-scale allocation systems, and a description of optimal sequential assignment systems.

The personnel assignment problem may be stated as follows:

Let p_{ij} be the payoff resulting when person i is assigned to job j where:

$$i = 1, 2, \ldots, I;$$
$$j = 1, 2, \ldots, J;$$
$$I = \text{number of persons to be assigned;}$$
$$J = \text{number of job categories, and}$$

let x_{ij} be an indicator variable such that

$$x_{ij} = 1 \text{ if person } i \text{ is assigned to } j; \text{ and}$$
$$x_{ij} = 0 \text{ otherwise.}$$

The problem requires the assignment of I persons to J job categories so that the objective function

$$\sum_{i=1}^{I} \sum_{j=1}^{J} p_{ij} x_{ij} \tag{1}$$

assumes a maximum value under the following restrictions:

1. $\displaystyle\sum_{j=1}^{J} x_{ij} = 1$ for all i,

2. $\displaystyle\sum_{j=1}^{J} q_j = I$ where q_j is the quota of persons to be assigned to job category j and

3. $\displaystyle\sum_{i=1}^{I} x_{ij} = q_j$

The restrictions state that one person can be assigned to only one job, that the total number of persons in all job categories equals the number to be assigned, and that the number assigned to category j equal the quota q_j. The formulation of the assignment problem* is presented and discussed in Boldt (1964), Hatch et al. (1972), Pina (1974), and Ewashko et al. (1974).

In its simplest form, the problem assumes that each person is eligible for all possible jobs, that the number of persons to be assigned exactly equals the sum of the job quotas, and that the objective of the allocation process is the maximization of the payoff sum. A useful study of the consequences of relaxing some of these requirements† is provided by Votaw (1956). The more important deviations from the above formulation and the ensuing effects are discussed later.

---

*The problem as stated above is identical to the transportation problem when the payoff sum is maximized under the constraint that the number of persons assigned must equal the number of available jobs.

†Sometimes there is a question concerning the number of job categories, J, that ought to be used. Job clustering can be used to reduce J, without loss of differential classification effectiveness, when little or no person-job interaction is present (Ward, 1983).

The Criterion Problem

Assignment payoffs are usually expressed in terms of their contributions to an objective function. The latter represents the functional relationship between the criterion variable (e.g., utility or benefit to the military) and the assignment predictor variables (e.g., test scores). In our case, a payoff value p_{ij} is associated with a unit of activity, x_{ij}, and contributes to the objective function shown as equation 1.

Personnel assignment payoff values have frequently taken the form of success prediction estimates (Sorenson, 1965; Swanson & Dow, 1965; and Alf & Wolfe, 1968) and most have employed test scores to predict training school success. Other criterion estimates have been based on variables such as personnel shortages, system requirements, and training costs. For an example of a cost matrix approach, see Huber (1966).

Horst and Sorenson (1976) have noted that optimal use of human resources cannot be achieved merely by assigning personnel to job categories based on predictions of success or other similar estimates. They contend that such procedures do not necessarily yield distributions of personnel that fulfill system demands. It appears that payoff values used for assignment purposes should reflect a broad range of allocation objectives, some of which could include success prediction estimates.

Payoff values are occasionally restricted to numerical values of zero and one. By setting the payoff value to zero if a person is not eligible for a given job, and to one otherwise, all eligible persons are deemed equally eligible. Thus, no distinction is made as to whether it is better to assign a person to one job or another within the set of jobs for which he or she is eligible. Assignments made on this basis emphasize fill objectives at the expense of person-job matching. A more extensive discussion of the role of payoff values and the mechanisms used to generate them is located in a later section.

Two examples of allocation systems that depend on dichotomous payoff values will be described below. They are characterized by a fill assignment policy as opposed to a fit policy (Pina, 1974), where a fill policy is described as one in which job vacancies are filled from available resources under the constraint that each individual assigned meets minimum job requirements. A fit policy, on the other hand, is governed by an optimal person-job match criterion as it fills vacancies from the available resources.

Allocation Systems Driven by Fill Policies

Recruit Distribution Model (RDM). The RDM and its predecessor, the COBRA model, were developed in response to the following Marine Corps requirements: (1) recruits at the Recruit Training Center (RTC) were to be assigned to available job categories using an efficient batch process, (2) policies governing differential rates of filling the categories were to be accommodated, and (3) objectives concerning minority/majority group composition within categories were to be met.

The allocation problem was interpreted as one requiring a series of optimizations, each constrained by previous ones and each providing additional constraints for subsequent optimizations. In each solution phase all personnel were considered for assignment simultaneously (Hatch, 1971).

During the initial stage of the solution procedure, a feasible set of quotas was obtained and used in place of the original quotas whenever the latter proved to be infeasible. Job category priorities and share coefficients represented fill distribution policy under infeasibility conditions resulting from unique talent mixtures within the applicant pool.

At the next stage the minority distribution that most closely resembled specified minority target percentages was determined and in the third stage the model derived the distribution that minimized the length of waiting time for personnel awaiting training.

In the final stages of the process, two assignment objectives were addressed: (1) the number of recruits assigned to the highest prerequisite levels within each job category was maximized, and (2) the average probability of success in training was maximized under the solution constraints imposed by all previous stages.

COMPASS II Model. At present the Navy uses a computer-based system, COMPASS II, to assign recruits at the RTC. During their fifth week of recruit training the recruits are interviewed for classification purposes. The interviewer develops five occupational group recommendations based on ASVAB test scores, civilian job experience, educational background, and vocational objectives and preferences.

The objectives of the COMPASS II system are to maximize the utilization of training school vacancies, minimize transportation costs, maximize adherence to interviewer recommendations, and finally to maximize the probability of success in training schools (Hatch et al., 1968). The model closely resembles the COBRA model in that a series of optimizations is conducted, each constrained by previous optimization stages.

Clearly, fill policy overshadows all other considerations in the above models. Objectives such as probability of success in training school are addressed, but only in the latter optimization stages when their influence is minimal.

In both of the above models, persons are aggregated in groups for batch assignment. For example, all recruits engaged in the fifth week of training are considered for assignment at one time by the COMPASS II system.

Kuhn (1955, 1956), Ford and Fulkerson (1962), and others have described algorithms that can be used when batch optimization is required. Among the studies comparing the performance characteristics of various batch assignment algorithms are those of Munkres (1957), Florian and Klein (1969), McWilliams (1970), and O'Connell and Shore (1974).

At a later point in this chapter, systems capable of handling personnel one at a time will be described and discussed.

Sequential Assignment

Before the AVF was introduced, recruits were usually assigned to schools following basic training. Under these conditions, a batch allocation process was an economical and efficient procedure. However, at present the recruiting services of the various branches allocate many school/job guarantees at the time of enlistment.

As a consequence of this policy shift, the assignment problem has changed in a fundamental way. At any given time a recruiter has only a small number of applicants available for assignment to a large number of jobs. The process is one of assigning a single individual at a time to one of a number of available jobs and to do so in a way that fills all jobs and that approximates an optimal batch assignment solution. It is called a sequential assignment process (Rafacz & Halstead, 1977).

It is worth noting that under a sequential assignment process a recruit applicant usually has an opportunity to evaluate several job options, which are the ones that the service considers optimal or near optimal. The result is a decision to which both parties have contributed and a commitment that both will likely honor.

The shift to sequential assignment facilitated the development of allocation algorithms that included fit policies as well as fill objectives (Ward et al., 1978; Kroeker & Rafacz, 1983). Several examples of allocation systems that incorporate both policies are decribed below.

Systems Based on Fit/Fill Policies

In each of the following models the sequential nature of military assignment is recognized and accommodated in model formulation. Moreover, in each case job options ranging from optimal to least acceptable are identified, because there is no guarantee that applicants will accept the optimal job.

PROMIS Model. In the Air Force recruiting process, applicants for enlistment are handled sequentially on a first-in first-out basis. Following qualification screening, each applicant is offered a selection of jobs from which to choose an assignment classification. According to Hendrix et al. (1979, p. 14), "applicants arriving at the job reservation stage . . . represent a random process. It is the objective of APDS/PROMIS to optimally assign applicants to job classifications as they complete the qualification procedures. Since these completion times are random, applicants must be processed one at a time."

In order to achieve an allocation that was as good as one obtained under a batch assignment procedure, Ward (1958, 1959) produced an allocation index based on his Decision Index (DI) process. According to Hendrix et al. (1979, p. 14), "DI is an approximation technique for a batch assignment problem. It yields an allocation index with a range of numerical values. . . . The largest value represents the best approximation for the optimum assignment for a person."

The algorithm facilitates the determination of an optimal person-job match (PJM) by comparing an individual with all other competing individuals. Persons compete only for jobs available from the time of arrival at the assignment facility.

Jobs are made available as of specific dates that are distributed over the time horizon. For a given person, a job is considered only in the first month during which it is available following the person's stated availability date. The first available date procedure follows recruiting management policy, which requires filling jobs nearer the current date before those available at later dates.

The grouping of jobs by month provides a consistent, although arbitrary, justification for grouping applicants. While applicants would logically be considered for all jobs beyond their arrival date, limiting the search for a particular job to its first month of availability also limits the applicant pool in which the individuals compete. . . . The applicant is thought of as competing with those other individuals who arrive for job reservation during the same calender month" (Hendrix et al., 1979, p. 15).

Haltman (1974) provided a detailed account of the evolution of the Air Force sequential assignment model. Details of the operational model are found in Ward et al. (1978) and Hendrix et al. (1979).

CLASP Model. The Navy's recruiting process, similar in some respects to that of the Air Force, also includes a mechanism to distribute job guarantees before enlistment. A sequential assignment procedure is, therefore, essential. The Classification and Asssignment Within PRIDE (CLASP) model accomplishes this task by generating job options that are discussed by both the applicant and the Navy classifier before reaching the classification decision.

The algorithm underlying the procedure is based on the DI process (Ward, 1959). As in the Air Force model, an applicant is considered as a competitor among those persons who arrive for reservation during the same calender month. The procedure considers each applicant as a potential candidate for every Navy rating (job category) and assigns a numerical utility score to each rating for that person. This is acomplished by evaluating and weighting five utility functions and applying transformations to yield DI scores for ratings.

The resulting scores facilitate the ordering of ratings from highest to lowest, where the highest is the optimal one for the individual. The resulting list length is reduced by removing all ratings for which the person does not qualify or for which there are no openings within the month under consideration.

The top five jobs on the amended list are discussed with the applicant and, when a selection is agreed upon, the job is reserved for the applicant. A detailed discussion of the model is provided in Kroeker and Rafacz (1983).

EPAS Model. The Army enlistment process also involves mental and physical examinations before job assignment is considered. The signing of the enlistment contract is a key decision point because it identifies a recruit's immediate work area and because it obligates the Army to a training commitment. At this point, each applicant is sequentially assigned to an MOS (Eaton & Goer, 1983).

Only one of the four Enlisted Personnel Allocation System (EPAS) modules will be considered here, namely, the Sequential Classification Module (SCM). The other three modules are employed before the SCM is used and involve factors such as training requirements, manpower availability, and manpower distribution characteristics. Within the constraints determined by the three modules, the SCM identifies ordered lists of MOS recommendations for each prospective enlistee (Schmitz et al., 1984).

The EPAS system yields an optimization of several objective functions simultaneously as opposed to the traditional optimization of a single measure. The model maximizes expected job performance, expected service time, and reenlistment potential and fills jobs according to set priorities (Schmitz et al., 1984). The SCM integrates the results from the previous stages, determines applicant eligibility, assesses an applicant's potential, and presents the resulting recommendations.

Each of the three systems described above addresses the concerns of the respective recruiting services to fill job categories. However, they differ from previous systems in an important way: namely, that they either stem from fit policies (e.g. PROMIS, CLASP) or they accommodate them. Both the PROMIS and CLASP models are directly dependent on differential classification considerations such as the person-job interaction concept (Ward, 1983). It is not clear to what extent the SCM will employ this concept.

Over the years a variety of allocation systems have been proposed and tested, including both military and nonmilitary systems. It is the purpose of the following section to examine these systems briefly and describe the methodology employed, the results achieved, and the conclusions reached.

OTHER ALLOCATION SYSTEMS

First, several systems depending on the maximization of a univariate criterion function will be described. Next, an innovative approach involving multiattribute models will be explored. Finally, models based on discriminant analysis methodology will be examined and discussed.

Single Criterion Models

An early assignment model developed by Army researchers (Boldt & Johnson, 1963) explored the use of several objective functions in order to accommodate recruit preferences in the allocation process. In each case a single criterion value described the merit of placing a given person in a designated MOS category. The system was capable of handling large numbers of enlistees at one time and was prepared for use in allocating recruits to Army billets on a weekly basis.*

An assignment system that received considerable attention and that was extensively tested in a research environment was one developed to provide career counseling for Army officers (Eastman, 1978). Research results indicated that assignment policies and practices of career branch personnel could be captured in an effective way and that optimal assignments could be generated efficiently using a procedure developed by Ford and Fulkerson (1962).

The development of the Personnel Assignment, Distribution, and Rotation (PADRO) model by Thorpe and Connor (1966) and the Computer Assisted Distribution and Assignment (CADA) model by Whitehead, Suiter, and Thorpe (1969) represented important steps in the evolution of Navy assignment systems. The research activities constituted the first attempt to formulate a comprehensive systems model that could simulate Navy enlisted personnel distribution and assignment functions.

Multiple Criterion Models

The assignment of persons to jobs becomes much more complex when the match is described in terms of more than one criterion measure. Pierskalla

---

*The system formed the basis of the computerized assignment program (CAP) used by the Army about a decade later.

(1968) and Charnes et al. (1969), among others, have developed approaches that permit higher dimensional optimizations and that allow alternative allocation strategies to be explored. For example, Charnes et al. have questioned the usefulness of conventional practices that assume fixed job descriptions along with static organization charts and other arrangements that are prescribed almost independently of the available personnel. They suggest that different mixes of personnel might be used to determine how jobs might best be arranged so that lack of skills on the part of some may be overcome by others who possess the requisite skills. In general, the models proposed are designed explicitly to deal with organizational dynamics. Further elaboration of this early work is found in Pollatschek (1972), Charnes et al. (1973), Srinivasen and Thompson (1973), and Charnes et al. (1975).

The static multiattribute assignment model developed by Moore and Scholtz (1974) was based on the work of Charnes et al. (1969, 1973). The purpose of the model was to assign persons so that the discrepancies between assignees' multiple attributes and desired performance levels for various jobs was simultaneously minimized. Various attribute measures were obtained using the Navy Occupational Task Analysis Program (NOTAP), and the model's performance was evaluated.

Recent research efforts involving the multicriterion problem have led to the development and use of generalized goal programming models (Lee & Schniederjans, 1983) and preemptive multicriterion approaches (Klingman & Phillips, 1982). Network formulations (Liang, 1984; Liang & Thompson, 1986) represent attempts to improve the efficiency of the distribution process using a preemptive ordering of multiple allocation criteria.

Discriminant Analysis Models

Discriminant analytic methodology has been applied to personnel classification problems for several decades. Its appeal was due in part to the nature of the classification problem, namely, that discrete groups of persons were to be identified (Creager, 1957). For example, in the broader context of improving decision-making accuracy, Cronbach and Gleser (1965) described a number of situations in which decisions involving discrete groups should be made and in which the use of discrete payoff functions was appropriate.

Early work by Alf and Dorfman (1967) resulted in the production of an analytic method to classify individuals optimally into two subgroups on the basis of a psychological test cutting score. The cutting score was chosen so as to maximize the expected value of the decision procedure.

King (1965) noted that personnel assignment decisions were often made in a state of limited information, since the persons to be assigned usually had never performed the vacant jobs. For that reason, he argued, the decision maker should solve a two-stage problem involving the prediction of individual's performances in unfamiliar environments and the determination of an optimal allocation of individuals to jobs on the basis of those predictions. The stochastic assignment model that resulted from this research allowed the decision maker to integrate the prediction and allocation phases.

Profile Matching Models

Cardinet (1959) provided a clear introduction to the differential classification concept and to the use of a profile matching technique to accomplish differential classification. It was an extension of Brogden's (1954) research and in its simplest form consisted of the comparison of an applicant's profile with a standard profile. Cardinet reported that the French Air Force had used the technique and declared it highly satisfactory for classifying personnel.

Ward and Hook (1961) developed a clustering approach to facilitate the grouping of applicant test score profiles. A unique feature of this technique was that the grouping was accomplished in stages, with allocation payoff maximized at each stage. Later research resulting in the development of an assessment-classification model (Schoenfeldt, 1974) was based directly on the Ward and Hook methodology.

Statistical clustering of job profiles was also a fundamental step taken by Cleff and Hecht (1971) in developing a person-job profile matching system. An adaptation of the Pearson product-moment correlation coefficient was used to determine profile similarity and a sum of squared differences measure was employed as an auxiliary index (Cleff, 1979).

Several profile matching systems have been introduced and evaluated in business environments. The Jobmatch system, a procedure to match candidate and job profiles, was recently implemented by Citibank Corporation for its nonprofessional employees (Sheibar, 1979). A sales job-matching system developed by Cleff (1980) was implemented in various college division sales regions of a large publishing corporation. Satisfactory results were reported in both evaluations.

Miscellaneous Models

The Human Resources Information System (HRIS) was developed for use by the State Department to provide an ongoing assessment of human resource utilization in pursuit of management objectives (Whitman & Hyde, 1978). The personnel placement and classification functions are among its major components.

Several methods of position-person matching were considered in developing HRIS—namely, career pattern modeling, hit-or-miss screening, and degree-of-fit scoring. In career pattern modeling each functional specialty was surveyed to determine the kinds of positions it encompassed, and a logical path was constructed to delineate for employees what experience, training, and supervisory responsibilities should be acquired at each grade level. In the hit-or-miss screening approach, employee skills, backgrounds, and preferences were examined in order to produce lists of potential candidates who satisfied the requirements. The most flexible approach was the degree-of-fit scoring method, which compared position requirements against personal qualifications and resulted in a score that described the quality of the match.

ALGORITHMS

A variety of algorithms have been developed and used to achieve optimal assignment over the years. Depending upon the circumstances under which the allocation was to be achieved, a unique formulation might be required.

Optimal Assignment Algorithms

Early solutions dedicated to the solution of assignment and transportation problems, when all objects/persons were to be assigned at the same time, were derived and published in the mathematical literature by Kuhn (1955, 1956) and Munkres (1957). Hatch (1971) developed a similar formulation of the problem in terms of more recent methodological developments—namely, the use of linear programming constraints.

Near Optimal Solutions

The work of Horst and Sorenson (1976) represented one of the first attempts to address the sequential nature of personnel assignment in the military. The methodology used matrix transformations to achieve optimal differential assignment. Subsequent work (Horst, 1981) attempted to adapt and refine the earlier procedures.

Other attempts to achieve optimal personnel allocations within the constraints of the military recruiting procedures (i.e., sequential treatment of applicants) yielded a variety of solutions (Hendrix, 1976; Rafacz & Halstead, 1977; Ward, 1958, 1959).

The algorithm that has had the most impact on current military classification procedures is the Decision Index algorithm (Ward, 1959; Ward et al., 1978, Kroeker & Rafacz, 1983). It is used by both the PROMIS and CLASP systems and it has significantly influenced the development of EPAS.

Discriminant Function Approaches

Other approaches to the same problem, based on discriminant function methodology, were also attempted. The models proposed by Alf and Dorfman (1967), Creager (1957), and Guilford and Michael (1949) are illustrations of these approaches. Other algorithms, based on methodology related to the discriminant function approach have been proposed by Cardinet (1959), Cleff (1979), King (1965), Schoenfeldt (1974), and Ward and Hook (1961).

Algorithm Performance

Algorithm performance characteristics have been among the foremost concerns of assignment system managers. For example, before the PROMIS system was introduced, McWilliams (1970) evaluated a number of algorithms and Beatty (1977) examined a number of procedures to improve the computational efficiency.

A more extensive discussion of computational aspects and specific algorithm characteristics is beyond the scope of this present chapter and will not be attempted here.

PERSON-JOB MATCHING

The desirability of developing techniques to accomplish matching has been addressed by researchers in various disciplines (Fine, 1958; Gale & Shapley, 1962; Weil, 1967; Greenberg & Greenberg, 1980; Roth, 1982). However, the unique requirements and various practical and research problems encountered within each discipline shape the procedures developed to meet those problems. For example, within military differential classification, methodologies have been adapted to address the special problems raised by service enlistment procedures and by the sequential nature of military accessioning.

In the first part of this section, the matching process and its constituent parts are examined from a military accessioning perspective. In the second part, more general matching processes are discussed.

Goodness of Fit

When applicants were assigned to jobs largely on the basis of minimum qualifying scores and intuitive judgments, there was room for improvement in matching. In today's military environment, with its emphasis on technological sophistication and extensive training requirements, and its expensive recruitment and retention costs, a close correspondence between person and job is a highly valued outcome and goodness of fit a most important concept.

Close correspondence is particularly difficult to achieve without the assistance of the computer. For example, a good person-job match requires that a classifier/recruiter be able to synthesize a complex mixture of service requirements and applicant strengths, weaknesses, and interests. Computer models enable such synthesis to be accomplished in standardized ways so that a close correspondence is more likely to occur for each candidate (Roberts & Ward, 1982).

Person-Job Interaction

Various informational elements about persons and jobs may be combined to yield a measure of future expected performance or payoff for each person on every job. The payoff values may be placed in a matrix as shown in Figure 2.1.

Employing analysis of variance (ANOVA) concepts and using ANOVA terminology in this example yields the following expression for the degree of interaction, Q_{IJKL}, between persons I and K, and jobs J and L:

$$Q_{IJKL} = (P_{IJ} - P_{IL}) - (P_{KJ} - P_{KL}) \qquad (2)$$

Figure 2.1
Payoff Value Matrix

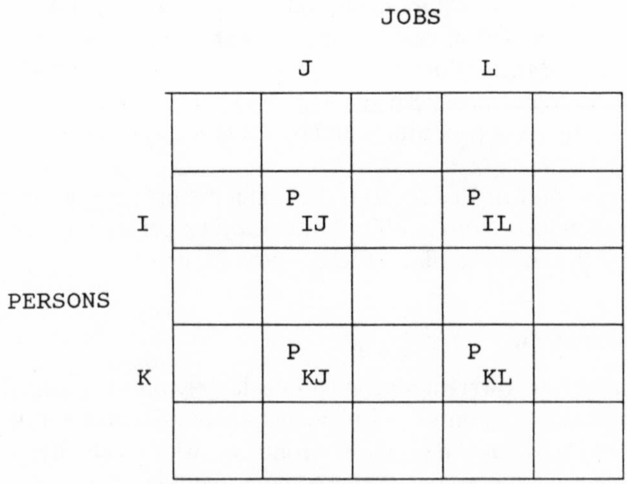

JOBS

		J		L	
I		P_{IJ}		P_{IL}	
PERSONS					
K		P_{KJ}		P_{KL}	

Ward (1983) noted an important relationship between the optimal assignment problem and the person-job interaction term, based on Q. An optimality index*, O_{IJ}, was found to be a useful indicator of the extent to which assigning person I to job J could be expected to increase or decrease the overall objective function, Z. Equations 3 and 4 summarize the relationships among the O (optimality index) variance, the Z (objective function) variance, and S, the interaction sum of squares.

For N persons assigned to N jobs,

$$\sigma_o^2 = \frac{S}{N^2} \tag{3}$$

$$\sigma_Z^2 = \frac{S}{N-1} \tag{4}$$

The three indicators shown in equations 2, 3, and 4 are all measures of potential improvement in personnel assignment. In fact, all related to the differential prediction index first developed by Horst (1954). In summary, it makes sense to design interactive payoff functions and to use interaction-producing predictor variables to improve differential assignment.

Payoff Functions

For many years, classification and assignment policies were adhered to in general, but the mathematical representations of those policies were never explicitly formulated and detailed evaluation of policy execution could not be undertaken. However, the availability of computers made possible such representation without the need for exceedingly burdensome calculations on the part of the recruiter or classifier.

The payoff functions integrate information about persons (attributes) and jobs (properties) according to the requirements specified by military manpower managers (Ward, 1977; Kroeker, 1979). Examples of Marine Corps payoff functions are found in Kroeker and Folchi (1984b, 1985). Examples of payoff functions for other services are found in Ward et al. (1978) and Kroeker and Folchi (1984a). Determination of the functional form of payoff functions may be accomplished through the use of a variety of policy-capturing or policy-specifying techniques (e.g., Ward, 1977).

The identification of input variables needed by particular payoff functions and the development of measures of these variables generates a unique set of new problems. Such problems vary in the complexity of the measurement

---

*In simplest form the optimality index is the payoff value minus person (row) and job (column) means plus the grand mean (Ward, 1958, 1959, 1983).

issues involved, range from basic to applied research settings (Kroeker, 1982; Thomas et al., 1984; Hetter and Abrahams, 1981), and employ results from related areas (Folchi, Foley & Kroeker, 1984).

Other Matching Processes

A variety of matching processes within other disciplines have been proposed (Crawford & Knoer, 1981; Heflich, 1981; Moore, 1977; Schoenna, 1972). Typically, the methodologies employed to achieve matching differ from those used by most of the military models (e.g., Ross & Zoltners, 1979).

NEW DEVELOPMENTS

Current Research

This section presents a brief overview of current research efforts. It addresses both continuing developmental efforts of existing models such as PROMIS, CLASP, and CAPS as well as future models such as EPAS.

U.S. Services. Work is currently under way to improve the Air Force's PROMIS system by including one new component and upgrading another. Inclusion of the Vocational Interest For Career Enhancement (VOICE) inventory will permit integration of personal work interest information into the assignment decision process (Alley, 1978). The technical school success component is being improved by the use of ASVAB subtest scores as opposed to area composite scores (Pina, 1986).

The Army Research Institute has recently undertaken a project to modernize and improve the process of identifying the MOS for which a recruit ought to be trained. Parts of the Enlisted Personnel Allocation System are still under development while others are being tested under a variety of conditions (Schmitz & McWhite, 1986). One of the most significant innovations of this system will be its use of the interaction concept to accomplish differential classification. For example, EPAS will provide a mixture of job options richer for a high-quality applicant whose contribution to the interaction term is substantial than for a low-quality applicant whose contribution is minimal.

The Navy's current research emphasis is focused on: (1) improving the CLASP model by including one or more job-performance-based components (Kroeker, Bearden, & Laabs, 1985), and (2) developing a classification model for use at the RTCs. One of the most useful auxiliary measures obtained from CLASP operational data is one showing a job's presentation frequency—that is, the number of times the job has been offered to different qualified candidates. The sales effectiveness statistic derived from the measure is being used by Navy managers to identify and diagnose potential recruiting and future marketing problems.

Other research projects (Ward & Sorenson, 1986), still in varying stages of completion, involve the development of procedures to increase the differential classification potential (i.e., person-job interaction) of an operational set of predictor variables.

Other Services. Research activities related to the development of the Career Advisement and Personnel System are continuing within the Naval section of the British Ministry of Defense. The system has two functions: the first is to help the careers advisor to decide whether to accept a recruit or wait for one of better quality; and the second is to assist the advisor in making a reservation (Dodd, 1980). Improving manpower quality within each of the service branches is the primary objective of the CAPS system.

Related Research

Several research areas have yielded products that may be very useful for the further development and elaboration of future generations of classification and assignment models. These are the computerized testing, computerized vocational guidance, and the multiattribute utility theory areas.

Computerized Testing. A number of the new computer-based predictor tests currently under development are expected to supplement ASVAB and to provide useful information for criterion prediction (Eaton & Goer, 1983; Kroeker et al., 1985). Further information concerning computerized tests and their potential can be found in Chapter 1.

Computerized Vocational Guidance. Kuder (1977) and others (Super, 1978) have long advocated the use of automated mechanisms to process information for career counseling purposes. Further discussion concerning current research in this area may be found in Chapter 3.

Multiattribute Models. Schmitz et al. (1984) have discussed the need to conceptualize the classification problem in terms of a number of salient decision attributes. The multidimensional nature of the classification criterion space calls for new approaches to the classical formulations of classification/assignment problems. For example, methodologies developed by Beach & Barnes (1983) and others, involving multiattribute utility models, might yield handsome dividends in the form of highly flexible yet powerful models.

SUMMARY

Today's military manpower and personnel managers require classification procedures that work effectively under a variety of conditions. Job options ranging from optimal to least acceptable must be identified rapidly for each potential recruit applicant. Specifically, this requirement demands a heavy emphasis on sequential assignment, goodness of fit, and person-job interaction.

The military services are attempting to meet the challenge of employing these concepts in part by developing new technological products and in part by adapting existing personnel accessioning procedures. To the extent that researchers succeed in these endeavors, managers will possess the tools they require for the optimal use of human resources.

REFERENCES

Alf, E. F., Jr., & Dorfman, D. D. (1967). The classification of individuals into two criterion groups on the basis of a discontinuous payoff function. *Psychometrika, 32*(2), 115–123.

Alf, E. F., Jr., & Wolfe, J. H. (1968). *Comparison of classification strategies by computer simulation methods* (STB 68–11). San Diego: Naval Personnel Research Activity.

Alley, W. E. (1978). *VOICE: Use and application in counseling and job placement* (AFHRL TR 78–62). Brooks Air Force Base, TX: Air Force Human Resources Laboratory.

Ash, P., & Kroeker, L. P. (1975). Personnel selection, classification, and placement. In M. Rosenzweig and L. Porter (Eds.), *Annual review of psychology*, Vol. 26 (pp 481–507). Palo Alto, CA: Annual Reviews.

Beach, L. R., & Barnes, V. (1983). Approximate measurement in a multi-attribute utility context. *Organizational Behavior & Human Performance, 32*(3), 417–424.

Beatty, T. M. (1977). *How to speed up your transportation model* (TR). Randolph Air Force Base, TX: Military Personnel Center.

Boldt, R. F. (1964). *Development of an optimum computerized allocation system* (TRR 1135). Washington, DC: Army Personnel Research Office.

Boldt, R. F., & Johnson, C. D. (1963). Computerized personnel assignment system. *Proceedings of the Second Army Operations Research Symposium*.

Boldt, R. F., Wiskoff, M. F., & Fitch, D. J. (1960). *An allocation technique applied to current aptitude input* (Research Memorandum 60–19). Washington, DC: Army Personnel Research Office.

Bolin, S. F., & King, S. H. (1958). *Improving assignment and allocation of personnel to combat units (research plans and beginnings)* (Research Study 58–1). Washington, DC: Army Personnel Research Office.

Borack, J., & Govindan, M. (1978). *Projections of the U.S. population of 18-year-old males in the post-1993 period* (NPRDC TR 78–16). San Diego: Navy Personnel Research and Development Center.

Brogden, H. E. (1946). An approach to the problem of differential prediction. *Psychometrika, 11*, 139–154.

————. (1954). A simple proof of a personnel classification theorem. *Psychometrika, 19*(3), 205–208.

Cardinet, J. (1959). The use of profiles for differential classification. *Educational and Psychological Measurement, 19,* 191–205.

Charnes, A., Cooper, W. W., Klingman, D., & Niehaus, R. J. (1973). *Static and Dynamic Biased Quadratic Multi-Attribute Assignment Models: Solutions and Equivalents.* Austin, TX: Center for Cybernetic Studies.

Charnes, A., Cooper, W. W., Lewis, K. A., & Niehaus, R. J. (1975). *A multi-objective model for planning equal employment opportunities.* Springfield, VA: NTIS, Department of Commerce.

Charnes, A., Cooper, W. W., Niehaus, R. J., & Stedry, A. (1969). Static and dynamic assignment models with multiple objectives and some remarks on organization design. *Management Science, 15*(8), B365–376.

Cleff, S. H. (1979). The Cleff job matching system: Introduction and review of developments. In G. Reber (Ed.), *Personalfuhring, Band VI: Personalinformations-systeme.* Wiesbaden: Gabler Verlag.

_____ . (1980. A strategy for hiring sales representatives. *Personnel, 57*(4), 58–68.

Cleff, S. H., & Hecht, R. M. (1971). Job/man matching in the 70's. *Datamation, 17*(3), 22–27.

Crawford, V. P., & Knoer, E. M. (1981). Job matching with heterogeneous firms and workers. *Econometrika, 49*(2), 437–450.

Creager, J. A. (1957). *Discriminant analysis and its role in the classification of airmen* (AFPTRC TN 57-127). Lackland Air Force Base, TX: Personnel and Training Research Center.

Cronbach, L. J., & Gleser, G. C. (1965). *Psychological tests and personnel decisions.* Urbana: University of Illinois Press.

Dantzig, G. B. (1951). Application of the simplex method to a transportation problem. Chapter 13. In T. C. Koopmans (Ed.), *Activity analysis of production and allocation,* Cowles Commission Monograph No. 13. New York: Wiley.

Dodd, B. T. (1980). *Proposals for fine-tuning personnel selection* (SP[N] TR 41). London: Naval Scientific Advisory Group.

Dow, A. N., Wolfe, J. H., Moonan, W. J., Swanson, L., & Taylor, C. W. (1964). *Feasibility study of the use of automation with enlisted classification procedures* (NPRA Memo Report 64-29). San Diego: Naval Personnel Research Activity.

Dubois, P. H. (1947). *The Classification Program* (Research Report No. 2), Army Air Forces Aviation Psychology Program: Washington, DC: U.S. Government Printing Office.

Dunnette, M. D. (1966). *Personnel selection and placement.* Monterey, CA: Brooks/Cole.

Dunnette, M. D., & Borman, W. C. (1979). Personnel selection and classification systems. In M. Rosenzweig and L. Porter (Eds.), *Annual review of psychology,* Vol. 30 (pp. 477–525). Palo Alto, CA: Annual Reviews.

Dwyer, P. S. (1953). *Selection and linear combination of tests in relation to multiple criteria and differential classification* (PRB Research Note No. 7). Washington, DC: Personnel Research Branch, The Adjutant General's Office, Department of the Army.

_____ . (1954). Solution of the personnel classification problem with the method of optimal regions. *Psychometrika, 19,* 11–25.

_____ . (1957). The detailed method of optimal regions. *Psychometrika, 22,* 43–52.

Eastman, R. F. (1978). *The assignment module: an element of an experimental computer-enhanced career counseling system for Army officers* (TP 294). Alexandria, VA: Army Research Institute.

Eaton, N. K., & Goer, M. H. (1983). *Improving the selection, classification, and utilization of Army enlisted personnel: Technical appendix to the annual report* (RN 83–37). Alexandria, VA: Army Research Institute.

Ewashko, R. C., Dudding, R. C., & Price, W. C. (1974). The integration of computer-based assignment models into the personnel management system of the Canadian Forces. In D. J. Glough, C. G. Lewis, & H. C. Oliver (Eds.), *Manpower planning models.* London: The English Universities Press.

Fine, S. A. (1958). Matching job requirements and worker qualifications. *Personnel, 34,* 52–58.

Flood, M. M. (1953). On the Hitchcock distribution problem. *Pacific Journal of Mathematics, 3*(2), 369–386.

Florian, M., & Klein, M. (1969). *An experimental evaluation of some methods of solving the assignment problem* (TR–41). New York: Operations Research Group, Columbia University.

Folchi, J., Foley, P., & Kroeker, L. P. (1984). *Development of Classification and Assignment within Pride (CLASP) school success parameters and equations.* Unpublished manuscript, Navy Personnel Research and Development Center, San Diego.

Ford, L. R., & Fulkerson, D. R. (1962). *Flows in networks.* Princeton, NJ: Princeton University Press.

Gale, D., & Shapley, L. S. (1962). College admissions and the stability of marriage. *The American Mathematical Monthly, 69*(1), 9–15.

Greenberg, H. M., & Greenberg, J. (1980). Job matching for better sales performance. *Harvard Business Review, 58*(5), 128–133.

Guilford, J. P., & Michael, W. B. (1949). *The prediction of categories from measurements.* Beverly Hills, CA: Sheridan Supply.

Hakel, M. D. (1986). Personnel selection and placement. In M. Rosenzweig and L. Porter (Eds.), *Annual review of psychology,* Vol. 37 (pp. 351–380). Palo Alto, CA: Annual Reviews.

Haltman, H. P. (1974). *Automated processing and classification of Air Force enlistees . . . whither and whence.* Unpublished manuscript, Human Resources Laboratory, Lackland Air Force Base, TX.

Harding, F. D., & Richards, J. A. (1971). *A descriptive analysis of the classification, assignment, and separation systems of the Armed Services* (AFHRL TR 71–15). Brooks Air Force Base, TX: Air Force Systems Command.

Hatch, R. S. (1971) Development of optimal allocation algorithms for personnel assignment. In A. R. Smith (Ed.), *Models of manpower systems.* New York: American Elsevier.

Hatch, R. S., Nauta, F., & Pierce, M. B. (1972). *Development of generalized network flow algorithms for solving the personnel assignment problem (Final Report.* Rockville, MD: Decision Systems.

Hatch, R. S., Pierce, M. B., & Fisher, A. H. Jr. (1968). *Development of a computer-assisted recruit assignment system (COMPASS II)*. Rockville, MD: Decision Systems.

Heflich, D. L. (1981). Matching people and jobs: value systems and employee selection. *Personnel Administrator, 26*(3), 77–85.

Hendrix, W. H. (1976). *Selection and classification using a forecast applicant pool* (AFHRL TR 76–13). Brooks Air Force Base, TX: Human Resources Laboratory.

Hendrix, W. H., Ward, J. H. Jr., Pina, M., & Haney, D. L. (1979). *Pre-enlistment person-job match system* (AFHRL TR 79–29). Brooks Air Force Base, TX: Human Resources Laboratory.

Hetter, R. D., & Abrahams, N. M. (1981). *Evaluation of aptitude and achievement composites for the initial classification of Marine Corps officers* (TR 81–21). San Diego: Navy Personnel Research and Development Center.

Horst, P. (1954). A technique for the development of a differential prediction battery. *Psychological Monographs, 68*(9), 1–31.

———. (1981). *Hierarchical clustering model for optimal differential assignment*. Unpublished manuscript.

Horst, P., & Sorenson, R. C. (1976). *Matrix transformation for optimal personnel assignments* (NPRDC TR 77–5). San Diego: Navy Personnel Research and Development Center.

Huber, G. (1966). *An approach for obtaining the cost matrix for the personnel assignment problem* (Firm and Market Workshop Paper 6609). Madison: University of Wisconsin Social Systems Research Institute.

Hunter, J. E., & Schmidt, F. L. (1982). Fitting people to jobs: the impact of personnel selection on national productivity. In M. D. Dunnette & E. A. Fleishman (Eds.), *Human performance and productivity: Human capability assessment*, Vol. 1. Hillsdale, NJ: L. Erlbaum.

King, W. R. (1965). A stochastic personnel-assignment model. *Operations Research, 13*(1), 67–81.

Klingman, D., & Phillips, N. V. (1982). *Topological and computational aspects of pre-emptive multicriteria military personnel assignment problems* (Research Report CCS 420). Austin: Center for Cybernetic Studies, University of Texas.

Kroeker, L. P. (1979). Policy specifying, judgment analysis, and Navy personnel assignment procedures. *Proceedings of the 21st Annual Conference of the Military Testing Association*, 592–598.

———. (1982). A procedure to revise estimates of psychological scale values. In B. Rimland (Ed.), *Independent research and independent exploratory development at the Navy Personnel Research and Development Center—FY81* (SR 82–27). San Diego: Navy Personnel Research and Development Center.

Kroeker, L. P., Bearden, R. M., & Laabs, G. J. (1985). Developing and evaluating a hands-on performance measure. *Proceedings of the 27th Annual Conference of the Military Testing Association*, 317–322.

Kroeker, L. P., & Folchi, J. (1984a). *Classification and assignment within PRIDE (CLASP) system: Development and evaluation of an attrition component* (NPRDC TR 84–40). San Diego: Navy Personnel Research and Development Center.

_____ . (1984b). *Minority fill-rate component for Marine Corps recruit classification: Development and test* (NPRDC TR 84–46). San Diego: Navy Personnel Research and Development Center.

_____ . (1985). *Marine Corps recruit classification: The program fill-rate component* (NPRDC TR 85–18). San Diego: Navy Personnel and Development Center.

Kroeker, L. P., & Rafacz, B. A. (1983). *CLASP: A recruit assignment model* (NPRDC TR 84–9). San Diego: Navy Personnel Research and Development Center.

Kuder, F. (1977). Career matching. *Personnel Psychology, 30*(1), 1–4.

Kuhn, H. W. (1955). The Hungarian method for the assignment problem. *Naval Research Logistics Quarterly, 2*, 83–97.

_____ . (1956). Variants of the Hungarian method for assignment problems. *Naval Research Logistics Quarterly, 3*, 253–258.

Lawler, E. E. (1974). More effective organization—match job to man. *Organizational Dynamics, 3*(1), 19–29.

Lee, S. M., & Schniederjans, M. J. (1983). A multicriteria assignment problem: a goal programming approach. *Interfaces, 13*, 75–81.

Liang, T. T. (1984). *Network formulation of multiple criterion problems for developing an integrated personnel distribution system in the Navy* (NPRDC TR 84–49). San Diego: Navy Personnel Research and Development Center.

Liang, T. T., & Thompson, T. J. (1986). *Optimizing personnel assignment in the Navy: The Seaman, Fireman, and Airman application* (NPRDC TR 86–10). San Diego: Navy Personnel Research and Development Center.

Lord, F. M. (1952). Notes on a problem of multiple classification. *Psychometrika, 17*, 297–304.

McWilliams, G. J. (1970). *A method for the approximate solution of transportation problems*. Unpublished Master's thesis, University of Texas, Austin.

Moore, B. E., & Sholtz, D. (1974). *Organizational tests of a static multi-attribute assignment model* (OCMM TR-20). Arlington, VA: Office of Civilian Manpower Management (Navy).

Moore, D. (1977). Capital job-matching people and jobs in London. *Data Processing, 19*(9), 24.

Morgan, F., & Roseen, D. (1974). *Recruiting, classification and assignment in the All Volunteer Force: Underlying influences and emerging issues* (R-1357-ARPA). Santa Monica, CA: Rand Corporation.

Munkres, J. (1957). Algorithms for the assignment and transportation problems. *Journal of the Society for Industrial and Applied Mathematics, 5*(1), 32–38.

O'Connell, D. P., & Shore, H. H. (1974). The Hungarian method in personnel work. *Personnel, 51*(4), 60–68.

Pierskalla, W. P. (1968). The multidimensional assignment problem. *Operations Research, 16*(2), 422–431.

Pina, M. (1974). *The assignment of airmen by solving the transportation problem* (TR 74–58). Lackland Air Force Base, TX: Human Resources Laboratory.

_____ . (1986, April). *The selection and classification of Air Force non-prior Service enlisted personnel*. Paper presented at the ORSA/TIMS Annual Meeting, Los Angeles.

Pollatschek, M. A. (1972). *Personnel-assignment by multi-objective programming* (TR 72–13). Stanford CA: Stanford University, Operations Research House.

Rafacz, B. A., & Halstead, D. (1977). *The sequential-assignment problem: Phase I—The development of a computer simulation program to evaluate a sequential assignment strategy* (NPRDC TN 77–13). San Diego: Navy Personnel Research and Development Center.

Roberts, D. K., & Ward, J. H., Jr. (1982). *General purpose person-job match system for Air Force enlisted accessions* (AFHRL SR 82–2). Brooks Air Force Base, TX: Human Resources Laboratory.

Ross, G. T., & Zoltners, A. A. (1979). Weighted assignment models and their application. *Management Science, 25*(7), 683–696.

Roth, A. E. (1982). The economics of matching: stability and incentives. *Mathematics of Operations Research, 7*(4), 617–628.

Schmitz, E. J., & McWhite, P. B. (1986). *Evaluating the benefits and costs of the Enlisted Personnel Allocation System (EPAS)* (MPPRG WP86–15). Alexandria, VA: U.S. Army Research Institute.

Schmitz, E. J., Nord, R. D., & McWhite, P. B. (1984). *Development of the Army's Enlisted Personnel Allocation System* (TR). Alexandria, VA: U.S. Army Research Institute.

Schoenfeldt, L. F. (1974). Utilization of manpower: development and evaluation of an assessment-classification model for matching individuals with jobs. *Journal of Applied Psychology, 59*, 583–595.

Schoenna, A. W. (1972). Matching man and job in a system perspective. *Personnel Journal, 51*(7), 484.

Sheibar, P. (1979). A simple selection system called "Jobmatch." *Personnel Journal, 58*(1), 26–29, 53.

Skinner, H. A., & Jackson, D. N. (1977). The missing person in personnel classification: a tale of two models. *Canadian Journal of Behavioral Science, 9*(2), 147–160.

Sorenson, R. C. (1965). *Optimal allocation of enlisted men—full regression equations vs. aptitude area scores* (TRN 163). Washington, DC: Army Personnel Research Office.

―――― . (1967). *Amount of assignment information and expected performance of military personnel* (TRR 1152). Washington, DC: Army Personnel Research Office.

―――― . (1968). Manpower system models in personnel allocation research. *Journal of the Human Factors Society, 10*(2), 99–105.

Srinivasan, V., & Thompson, G. L. (1973). Alternative formulations for static multi-attribute assignment models. *Management Science, 20*(2), 154–158.

Stillwell, W. G. (1983). *A review and comparison of personnel assignment systems with suggestions for a person-job matching model* (ARI Int. Report). Bethesda, MD: The Maxima Corp.

Super, D. E. (1978). From information retrieval through matching to counseling and to career development: Some lessons from the U.S.A. *Journal of Occupational Psychology, 51*, 19–28.

Swanson, L., & Dow, A. N. (1965). *Project COMPASS: A computer assisted classification system for Navy enlisted men* (NPRA SRR 66-6). San Diego: Naval Personnel Research Activity.

Thomas, G., Elster, R., Euske, K., & Griffin, P. (1984). *Development of an attrition severity index for selected Navy enlisted ratings* (NPRDC TR 85-1). San Diego: Navy Personnel Research and Development Center.

Thomason, J. S., & Rutledge, K. D. (1981). *A rating assignment procedure to increase first-term retention* (CRC 453). Alexandria, VA: Center for Naval Analyses.

Thorndike, R. L. (1950). The problem of classification of personnel. *Psychometrika, 15,* 215-235.

Thorpe, R. P., & Connor, R. D. (1966). *A computerized model of the Fleet Distribution system* (NPRDC SRR 66-13). San Diego: Naval Personnel Research Activity.

Votaw, D. F. Jr. (1952). Methods of solving some personnel-classification problems. *Psychometrika, 17*(3), 255-266.

———— . (1956). *Review and summary of research on personnel classification problems* (AFPTRC TN 56-106). Lackland Air Force Base, TX: Personnel and Training Research Center.

Votaw, D. F. Jr., & Dailey, J. T. (1952). *Assignment of personnel to jobs* (Research Bulletin 52-24). Lackland Air Force Base, TX: Human Resources Research Center.

Wagner, H. M. (1975). *Principles of Operations Research* (2nd ed.). Englewood Cliffs, NJ: Prentice-Hall.

Ward, J. H., Jr. (1958). The counselling assignment problem. *Psychometrika, 23*(1), 55-65.

———— . (1959). *Use of a decision index in assigning Air Force personnel* (WADC TN 59-38). Lackland Air Force Base, TX: Personnel Laboratory.

———— . (1977). *Creating mathematical models of judgment processes: From policy capturing to policy-specifying* (AFHRL TR 77-47). Brooks Air Force Base, TX: Human Resources Laboratory.

———— . (1979). Interaction among people characteristics and job properties in differential classification. *Proceedings of the 21st Annual Conference of the Military Testing Association*, 599-607.

———— . (1983). Strategies for capitalizing on individual differences in military personnel systems. In R. C. Sorenson (Ed.), *Human individual differences in military systems* (NPRDC SR 83-30). San Diego: Navy Personnel Research and Development Center.

Ward, J. H., Jr., Haney, D. L., Hendrix, W. H., & Pina, M. (1978). *Assignment procedures in the Air Force procurement management information system* (AFHRL TR 78-30). Brooks Air Force Base, TX: Human Resources Laboratory.

Ward, J. H., Jr. & Hook, M. E. (1961). *A hierarchical grouping procedure applied to a problem of grouping profiles* (ASD TN 61-55). Lackland Air Force Base, TX: Personnel Laboratory.

Ward, J. H., Jr., & Jennings, E. (1973). *Introduction to linear models*. Englewood Cliffs, NJ: Prentice-Hall.

Ward, J. H., Jr., & Sorenson, R. C. (1986). *Catalytic variables for improving personnel classification and assignment*. Unpublished manuscript, Navy Personnel Research and Development Center, San Diego.

Watt, R. (1973). *Enlisted personnel assignment system study* (OAD CR-62). McLean, VA: General Research Corporation.

Weil, R. L., Jr. (1967). Functional selection for the scholastic assignment model. *Operations Research, 15,* 1063–1067.

Whitehead, R. F., Suiter, R. N., & Thorpe, R. P. (1969). *The development of a computer assisted distribution and assignment (CADA) system for Navy enlisted personnel* (SRM 70-1). San Diego: Naval Personnel Research Activity.

Whitman, T. S., & Hyde, A. C. (1978). HRIS: Systematically matching the right person to the right position. *Defense Management Journal, 14*(2), 28–34.

3

Computerized Vocational Guidance Systems

HERBERT GEORGE BAKER and REGINALD T. ELLIS

INTRODUCTION

In the past two decades computerized occupational information and guidance systems have found wide applicability in the civilian community for vocational exploration and placement of young job seekers. During this same time frame, government research laboratories in the United States and Canada have been designing similar technologies that would be appropriate for the special environment of military service.

This chapter will review the development of military computerized vocational guidance systems, describing the organizational and individual requirements for these systems, the evolution of civilian systems, the evolution of civilian systems and their applicability to the military, and a future perspective on computerized guidance in the military.

REQUIREMENTS FOR VOCATIONAL INFORMATION AND GUIDANCE

Each year large numbers of individuals enter the armed services and receive training for a wide variety of military occupations. Enlistees are typically 18 to 20 years old, with little previous work experience, and with minimum knowledge of the military services and their occupational structures. Nevertheless, these young men and women must indicate their preference for military jobs at the point of entry into service, often under very stressful conditions of career choice.

The need for improved dissemination of military career information for purposes of occupational exploration and person-job matching has long been apparent to researchers and recruiting managers (Baker, 1983a).

Within the recruiting environment there are specific requirements for better informed job applicants, more comprehensive measurement of individual potential, and assistance to recruiters and military counselors.

With these needs, the computer appears as a bright spot on the horizon. Military researchers recognize that computerization offers hope for increasing the accessibility of accurate, timely, and personalized occupational information. Furthermore, computers can provide immediately scored self-assessment instruments, didactic counseling materials, and comprehensive, up-to-date, rapidly retrieved, personalized job information. Computers can deliver complete, standardized occupational information to the job applicant. With computers, individuals can benefit from impartial guidance without taxing the recruiter or relying on cumbersome printed materials.

The data generated in the course of applicant assessment can be used by both the organization and the job applicant. Data gathered for purposes of screening, selecting, and placing recruits will be used by the armed services to tailor the counseling and guidance process to the individual applicant. In turn, the job applicant can use the assessment data to increase self-knowledge and aid occupational exploration.

CIVILIAN APPROXIMATIONS OF CVG SYSTEMS

The development of automated occupational information and guidance systems can be seen as a progression from simple computerization to sophisticated, interactive programming. Rayman and Harris-Bowlsbey (1977) suggested a generational trichotomy—first, second, and third generations. Jacobson and Grabowski (1982) use a similar tripartite division—batch-processing systems, on-line career information systems, and on-line career guidance systems.

First Generation

The earliest efforts at guidance automation involved indirect inquiry, or batch-processing systems. In these systems, tests, questionnaires, requests, and so forth were forwarded to a computer center for batch processing with the results later returned to the counselor or counselee. The obvious disadvantage was turn-around time. An example of an indirect system is the Educational and Career Human Resources Information System (ECHRIS; Borow, 1973).

Second Generation

Computer-assisted guidance became practical and cost-effective in the 1960s (Ryan & Drummond, 1981). Counselees could be given direct access to individualized information (Borow, 1973). Automated data processing (ADP) capabilities were also used in connection with the testing features of counseling, thus avoiding delays in administration, scoring and actual interpretation of test results.

In *direct* inquiry systems, the person and the computer interact, on-line, in real time and at the same location. What is requested is immediately received. What is entered is acted upon without any appreciable delay. Users have much more control over the program and are aware of the effects of their choices (Oliver, 1977).

Even more significant was the genesis of monitoring—that is, the ability to track or keep track of. It is the process by which the computer analyzes and interprets user responses (Borow, 1973; Harris, 1974). As Harris (1972) noted, a direct inquiry system without system monitoring is simply a well-organized, fast, conversational, automated library. The Guidance Information System (GIS) is an example (Oliver, 1977).

There are two kinds of monitoring: system and personal. In *system monitoring*, the computer keeps a record of the user, the individual's data, use of the system, decisions, and so forth. This is convenient for personalizing visual displays and printouts. More importantly, it permits ongoing interaction from sign-on to sign-off and even into later return sessions. Of course, system monitoring was always possible and was sometimes used with indirect inquiry, but its effects are less significant when user and machine are separated spatially and temporally.

System monitoring makes interactive dialogue and a true conversational mode (or "counseling") possible. The Computerized Vocational Information System (CVIS) and the Educational and Career Exploration System (ECES) are examples of direct inquiry systems with system monitoring (Borow, 1973).

Computer-assisted guidance (CAG) systems have become increasingly prevalent (see Katz & Shatkin, 1980, for a conceptual analysis of CAG purposes and application). Some are remarkably broad in approach, firm in theoretical foundation, and thorough in occupational search and self-exploration. Many have undergone rigorous research and development, evaluation, and marketing. These second-generation systems include CVIS, ECES, GIS, the Career Information System (CIS), and the Coordinated Occupational Information Network (COIN; Rayman, Bryson, & Bowlsbey, 1978). Each of these has produced offshoots (see Minor, 1970, and Shatkin, 1980, for reviews of these systems).

Third Generation

Third-generation systems are those that approach personal monitoring and include significant teaching and guidance functions (e.g., they teach decision-making skills and help users to clarify values) in addition to providing self-assessment and occupational information. They are systems that can stand alone. They are very few in number, limited perhaps to DISCOVER (Rayman, Bryson, & Bowlsbey, 1978) and SIGI (Katz, 1974) and their descendants (Jacobson & Grabowski, 1982).

The necessary elements of a CVG system have been in various stages of preparation for many years. Initial efforts at combining sound theory and ADP equipment were undertaken nearly 20 years ago, as was simulation of a counselor's interview behavior. Computer-assisted guidance systems, meaning information retrieval systems used in conjunction with counseling, have been called CVG systems. However, strictly speaking, no true CVG systems exists; and true CVG has not been the subject of wide research. The reason is simple: the existing systems have been developed with the purpose of assisting counselors (Borow, 1973; Chapman & Katz, 1982; Harris, 1974; Jacobson & Grabowski, 1982; Katz & Shatkin, 1980; Rayman & Harris-Bowlsbey, 1977; Ryan & Drummond, 1981; Super, 1973). True CVG becomes possible with the advent of computer-assisted instruction (CAI) and personal monitoring (see Impellitteri, 1967, for a discussion of CAI; see Hickey & Newton, 1967, for a review of the CAI literature).

Now emergent, *personal monitoring* will allow the individual counselee to direct the guidance process to the greatest degree (Oliver, 1977; Rayman & Harris-Bowlsbey, 1977). Going beyond menu-driven, user-friendly software, personal monitoring (to the extent it becomes technologically possible and economically feasible) will enable genuinely interactive guidance, freeing the user to explore beyond programmed choices.

COMPONENTS OF A CVG SYSTEM

Essentially, a CVG system must include (1) personal assessment procedures to measure individual dimensions, or attributes, along a number of cognitive and noncognitive dimensions in order to provide selection and classification information to the organization and enhance the individual's self-awareness; (2) occupational information that is accurate, timely, sufficiently comprehensive, and personal to help an individual understand the requirements and conditions of occupations or careers; (3) a search strategy by which occupational information can be accessed using data generated by the individual assessment; and (4) a bridging mechanism that includes didactic or counseling materials useful in matching individual characteristics with organization and occupational requirements. Figure 3.1 illustrates some examples of the types of instruments and information that could be included.

Search strategies are a critical component of a CVG system and affect the system's time and cost requirements. Equally important is the impact of the

Figure 3.1
Computerized Vocational Guidance Elements

APPLICANT

ASSESSMENT

-Aptitude

-Interests

-Medical Evaluation

-Work Experience

-Career Maturity

OCCUPATIONAL

INFORMATION

-Job Requirements

-Training Provided

-Physical Demands

-Career Benefits

-Job Openings

SEARCH STRATEGIES/GUIDANCE MATERIALS

-Didactic Materials

-Accessing Occupational

Information

-Matching Personal

and Occupational

Characteristics

-Narrowing of Options

SYSTEM EVALUATION

-User On-Line Evaluation

-Interview

-Impact Evaluation

search strategy on the person-job match. Any effective procedure for matching persons with jobs must take into account both individual and institutional characteristics. Individual characteristics include abilities, preferences, interests, and goals. Institutional characteristics include priorities, objectives, training program vacancies, and personnel requirements. An effective search strategy, then, enables a narrowing-down of alternatives so that information is presented for those occupations that are best suited to the individual. Ultimately, the search strategy conduces to a choice of an occupation or an occupational field.

System evaluation is an additional component that can prove to be important. User evaluation (e.g., a series of multiple-choice questions administered on-line to assess general satisfaction with the guidance process and the interactively programmed computer system) may be combined with other, more formal evaluation and used as feedback to help improve the system.

MILITARY APPROXIMATIONS OF CVG SYSTEMS

Appropriateness of Civilian Systems to Military Environments

Civilian-developed systems generally have not been considered suitable for use in the military because of fiscal and temporal constraints as well as questions of their suitability for the military world of work.

When a qualified counselor is present and at work, second-generation systems are fully adequate. However, when professionals are not on hand to guide, vocational guidance is absent. Factors such a high turnover rate among counselors, geographic dispersion of counseling sites, and large numbers of individuals needing guidance (which are not limited to armed services recruiting; Arbeiter, 1981) call for the research and development of CVG systems within the military.

Baker (1984) reviewed and evaluated a number of previously developed CVG systems in the civilian community to determine their appropriateness for use in military recruiting and found no extant CVG system suitable, even with modifications. Of more significance, none of the systems has devoted effort to a military-based occupational classification system or focused on the uniqueness and the exigencies of military service. Finally, all of the operational systems would involve either licensing and royalty expenses, prohibitive length, or extensive programming for automation.

It was recommended that research and development be initiated on a CVG system for the military based on: a synthesis of vocational guidance theory, the unique aspects of military service, the characteristics of military applicants, the constraints of recruiting, and operational requirements.

Early U.S. Efforts

Navy Vocational Information System (NVIS). Nearly a decade of research by the U.S. Navy Personnel Research and Development Center (NPRDC) produced two important prototype systems: the Navy Vocational Guidance System and Automated Guidance for Enlisted Navy Applicants (AGENA). In fiscal year 1975, NPRDC began work on an advanced developmental effort called Project CONTRACT (Computerized Navy Techniques for Recruiting, Assignment, Counseling, and Testing). Two products of Project CONTRACT were (1) NVIS, an interactive CVG system; and (2) an optimal personnel assignment algorithm, Classification and Assignment Within PRIDE (CLASP), for use in the Navy's computerized job assignment system.

NVIS was programmed to run on IBM 360 mainframe and maintained an interactive dialogue with the user via a video display terminal (VDT). The system's data bases contained information on 279 civilian jobs, 114 worker trait groups, 79 entry-level Navy occupations, and more than 100 specialized Navy jobs. NVIS was designed to provide young men and women with personalized occupational guidance and a list of related civilian and Navy jobs that represented a good match between their own attributes and typical job requirements. It enjoyed excellent reception by the students.

One of the most interesting aspects of this effort was system mobility. In what may be considered a pioneering effort, computer terminals were installed in a mobile van that brought the system to the students (i.e., to a high school). There, through a modem link, the students interacted with the mainframe IBM 360. NVIS proved the feasibility of mobile systems during the 1970s.

Automated Guidance for Enlisted Navy Applicants (AGENA). NVIS was the precursor to a more advanced microcomputer-based system called AGENA. AGENA was designed as part of a more comprehensive prototypic personnel accessioning system, the Navy Personnel Accessioning System (NPAS), which was to integrate the many and wide-ranging tasks included in the military accessioning process (Baker, 1983a, 1983b; Baker 1985a; Baker, Rafacz, & Sands, 1983a, 1983b, 1983c).

AGENA used interactive programming to lead the person through a logical, thought-provoking dialogue that introduced the system and equipment, proceeded through preliminary aptitude screening, discussed how to plan for a career and discover personal interests and aptitudes, and ultimately allowed exploration of a number of Navy entry-level occupations that matched personal interests and aptitudes, with the opportunity to assess the availability of assignment options. All instructions were included in screen dialogue, and AGENA could be used by applicants without constant assistance by the Navy recruiter.

Within the broad function of person-job matching, three subfunctions were supported in the AGENA system: aptitude screening, vocational guidance, and assignment prediction. Because a minimum score on an Armed Services Vocational Aptitude Battery test composite must be attained to qualify for enlistment (and to enter certain occupational fields), AGENA included an aptitude screening instrument, known as the Computerized Adaptive Screening Test, which predicted the applicant's composite score. If a failing score was predicted, the recruiter could terminate the recruiting process.

Assignment prediction was another major component of AGENA, and research proved the potential feasibility of predicting school assignment. A mathematical model considered several individual and organizational factors, along with information on when the applicant was intending to go to the military entrance processing stations, take the ASVAB, and enter the Navy. This model determined which entry-level jobs were most appropriate for meeting the individual needs of the applicant and the institutional objectives of the Navy. In addition, the availability of these entry-level assignments was predicted for a three-month time frame. The substantial contributions Navy training can make to total career development were discussed in the AGENA dialogues, along with a brief discussion of the general value of Navy training and experience as well as additional benefits of Navy enlistment (e.g., medical benefits).

AGENA included two main data bases. The Navy ratings data base included information on the entry-level Navy jobs in two formats. An abbreviated version designed for VDT presentation included five sections: general description, related civilian jobs, qualifications, working conditions, and Navy opportunities. An extended description, available in hard copy as an option, included three additional sections that covered what the people in the rating do, sea and shore rotation, and the training provided by the Navy.

The civilian occupations data base gave descriptions on the VDT and hard copy of civilian occupations (or clusters of occupations) related to the Navy assignment opportunities. Besides a general description, the data base specified qualifications, training, pay, working conditions, employment outlook, and related Navy jobs.

The AGENA system was composed of nine separate modules: (1) system introduction, (2) aptitude screening tests, (3) interest inventory, (4) career planning, (5) ASVAB interpretation, (6) Navy jobs available, (7) related civilian occupations, (8) session/final summary, and (9) system evaluation. Figure 3.2 shows the AGENA processing sequence. Figure 3.3. shows a session in progress.

Figure 3.2
AGENA Guidance Process Flow

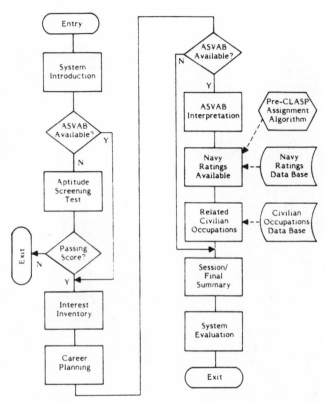

AGENA was developed only to the point of a very truncated demonstration system, which performed quite well in several demonstrations during the summer of 1981. AGENA exists only in a demonstration version, with programming limited to that purpose (except for CAST). No operational version was ever developed or field tested. Research and development ceased when funding was canceled in 1982.

CAST subsequently has been developed to operational capability, field tested, and incorporated in the Army JOIN system for use in all Army recruiting stations (Baker, Rafacz, & Sands, 1983b, 1983c, 1984).

Army Education Information System (AREIS). The U.S. Army Research Institute for the Behavioral and Social Sciences (ARI) sponsored the development of a prototypic, computer-based system that would provide information on military and civilian education programs as part of the Army

Figure 3.3
AGENA Guidance Session in Progress

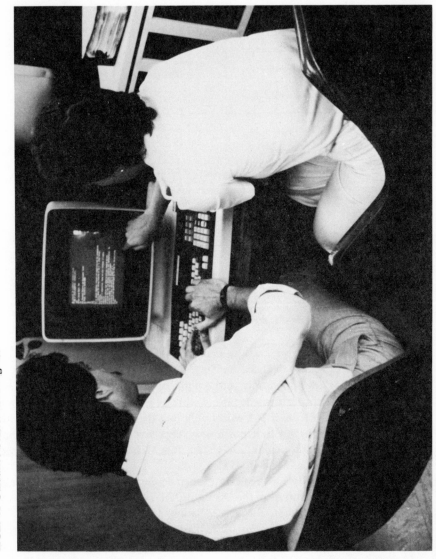

Continuing Education Service (ACES). The result was a computerized counseling system developed under contract by the DISCOVER Foundation during 1979–80 on the basis of a needs assessment conducted at Army Education Centers on bases throughout the world. Designed specifically for Education Center use, AREIS is an exception to recruiting-oriented developments in CVG.

Originally, AREIS was programmed on the Army's UNIVAC 1108 computer at Edgewood Arsenal, Maryland. Subsequent to a field trial, AREIS was changed to a microcomputer configuration. AREIS hardware now includes a microcomputer, color monitor, and printer.

AREIS includes four subsystems. All instructions for using the computer are presented on-line in simple language. Three of the subsystems are counselee-oriented and use interactive dialogues focused on subjects selected by the counselee. Conselees must enter through the Orientation subsystem. First-time users furnish demographic information to help construct a user record. Returning users bypass most of the entry procedure and go to the main directory or select which part of AREIS to use.

Orientation familiarizes the user with the equipment, provides information about the content of AREIS, explains the services of the Education Center, and gives an overview of ACES programs. After using the Orientation subsystem, a counselee may move from Self-Information to Goals and Planning or vice-versa (or between any of the subsections of these subsystems) at will.

Self-Information helps the counselee to assess work-related interests, aptitudes, skills, and values. Counselees may select from three assessment instruments. A list of a family of occupations is generated according to responses to the 90-item unisex edition of the American College Test (UNIACT; Lamb & Prediger, 1981). An aptitude assessment enables the counselees to compare their aptitudes with those of their peers. The values assessment assists in clarifying work-related values and produces a list of occupations keyed to these values. A summary consolidates all elements of counselee self-information.

Goals and Planning helps in establishing educational and vocational short- and long-range goals and provides information on ACES programs that may be useful in achieving these goals.

Counselor-Administrator, the fourth subsystem, stores counselee records and provides counselors with updated educational and vocational information for use in counseling. It is accessible only by Education Center staff and counselors, by means of a password. All data bases can be accessed through this subsystem.

AREIS data bases contain civilian occupations (information on more than 400 occupations), military occupational specialties (indicating correspondence of MOS to civilian occupations), and a master schedule of courses offered on or near the post.

A full evaluation of the complete microcomputer version of AREIS was conducted for nine months, beginning in the summer of 1982, at Education Centers at Fort Gordon, Georgia; Fort Meade, Maryland; and Mannheim, Germany. AREIS demonstrated counselor and counselee acceptance of computerized guidance functions in a military environment. It showed a microcomputer-based system capable of counselor-free operation, to the extent of its stated purposes. Assuming satisfactory results in the field trial, it will have demonstrated the utility of microcomputers in an environment logistically somewhat similar to recruiting (geographic dispersion, multiple users, frequent use, etc.). While the orientation is very broad, the counselee subsystems do reflect an excellent overall strategy of guidance flow: personal information, occupational and educational information, and planning.

However, AREIS was designed with a heavy emphasis on education and career orientation (for individuals already in service) and is, therefore, not suited to placement counseling without extensive modification. Furthermore, the occupational classifications fail to consider adequately military occupations that include huge segments of the Army (or other services). Specifically, no consideration is given to infantry, artillery, or combat arms in general.

The values clarification portion is inadequate in that it can result in profiles with all values equivalently rated. That is, weighting values in this system does not result in ipsative score reporting. Therefore, no relative importance of values is indicated. AREIS employs assessment instruments requiring licensing and royalty payment, which would make it very costly in military recruiting. Finally, AREIS presumes the presence of trained counselors and relies heavily on counselor intervention in the guidance process.

Officer Career Information and Planning System (OCIPS). OCIPS—a prototypic, interactive, computer-based system to provide career planning information to junior officers—was developed by ARI in 1971. OCIPS was programmed on a UNIVAC 1108 mainframe computer located at Edgewood, Maryland, with a terminal at Arlington, Virginia, connected by phone lines. The system used a printer for providing hard-copy summary data to users.

Conceptually based on Super's (1971) longitudinal study of career development, which emphasized the inevitability of choice and choice as an implementation of values that vary in different life stages, the system consisted of seven interactive dialogue subsystems and included exercises in skills and values clarification, career strategy formulation, choice-point identification, and personal career monitoring. Additionally, it provided information about the Army officer career structure and alternate specialty designations that junior officers are required to select.

The process of creating a career strategy was facilitated by use of a career planning game, SCOR, that included significant aspects of an officer's career. The game used an off-line playing board, SCOR-BOARD, for charting hypothetical career progression. Decision points required the player to deal with a number of career issues. The player started the game as a second lieutenant, selected menu-elicited goals, sought to move toward those goals in a series of computer-prompted decisions, and arrived at an end point that signified goal achievement.

Next, principles of creating career strategies were reviewed, and the user was presented with the Career Planning Wheel. This off-line chart was similar to the SCOR-BOARD but provided more detailed representation of an officer's career. The user could access career data related to the year of commissioned service in each topic on the wheel.

The user then evaluated the chosen career goals according to eight criteria for effective career planning. Revised goals were then translated into action plans for intermediate objectives, and the subsystems offered suggestions (e.g., choosing a specific standard for gauging success, identifying resources and barriers, setting checkpoints and deadlines).

The results of a field trial of parts of OCIPS (Cory, 1979; Phillips et al., 1980) showed that users found the content of the subsystems to be interesting, accurate, useful, and understandable and gave highly favorable ratings to the use of the computer as a method of transmitting career information. Users reported a decreased need for career information and an increased level of certainty and satisfaction with alternate specialty preference. Despite this positive reception, further development of the system was suspended.

Canadian Forces Career Information System (CFCIS)

Recruiting and selection in the unified Canadian Forces (CF) is carried out by nonspecialist military career counselors (MCCs), who are drawn from all branches of the service and assigned to CF recruiting centers for a two- or three-year tour. MCCs provide detailed vocational counseling to nonofficer applicants on over 60 entry-level trades across all three services. Recruitment, selection, trade assignment, and enrollment (accessioning) all occur at a common site as part of a single induction process. To cope with a high degree of variability in the level of counseling skills and vocational knowledge held by the MCCs, an integrated set of counseling tools was devised, employing up-to-date audiovisual and computer technology (Wilson, 1980). The CFCIS consists of an orientation file, an automated counseling system, and realistic job and life-style previews.

The 23-minute orientation video follows the careers of two young high school graduates from the point of their decision to visit a recruiting center, through enlistment, recruit training, military job training, and on to their duty stations. It provides a realistic organization preview by describing the roles and organization of the CF, its philosophy, and *raison d'être*. The film emphasizes the notions of commitment and teamwork and discusses what constitute good and poor reasons for entering the military. It is shown to all CF applicants as soon as possible after the first contact at the recruiting center.

The second component is the automated counseling system, an interactive computer system containing a large volume of vocational information on all entry-level CF trades. This is a stand-alone system (with periodic data upload to a mainframe) using a VDT interface with the user. Responding to inputs (test results, medical exam results, etc.) supplied by a clerk through a computer terminal early in the applicant processing stream, the computer generates a list of trades for which the applicant is eligible. The applicant then interacts with the computer and answers a series of questions on interests and goals.

Based on this, the computer compiles a list of trades for which the applicant is best suited and then provides extensive information on these trades. The applicant is encouraged to change answers and explore the effects on the suitability list. The system employs computer-assisted learning techniques to verify comprehension of the material presented. The applicant is given a hard copy of the conversation with the computer. In addition, a summary printout of the interaction is made available to the recruiter. These sources are used to structure the final trade assignment interview, during which a decision on trade selection is made.

The final component of CFCIS, the Trade and Lifestyle Videotapes (TLVs), is a library of five-minute realistic job previews on each of over 60 entry-level trades. The TLVs feature interviews with CF trades personnel drawn from the junior ranks. Each TLV has considerable footage on functions, equipment, and activities, which illustrate the verbal descriptions. Provision has been made for 25 percent of the library to be updated annually.

The two audiovisual components of CFCIS, both of which were implemented across the full recruiting system in April 1984, have been evaluated for user acceptance, effectiveness, and impact on the recruiting system. Evaluation of prototypic materials indicated their superiority to traditional print media in conveying information (Wilson & Flynn, 1982). They were judged to be accurate and realistic by a variety of subject matter experts; and they were seen as credible, realistic, and useful by applicants. A recent postimplementation study involving over 2,000 applications used pre- and postview ratings of interest in enrolling in specific trades to assess TLV impact (Miller & Ellis, 1986). Results indicated that the TLV library is functioning as intended, in that with few exceptions, exposure to TLVs resulted in a balance of increases and decreases in enrollment.

Funds were approved to construct two prototype Automated Counselling Systems (ACS; one in each of Canada's official languages, French and

English) at two large recruiting centers. Both of these were installed in late 1988. Evaluation of the effectiveness of the ACS, using a true experimental design, is planned for 1989 (Ellis, 1985). This study will assess increases in vocational knowledge, applicant and counselor reactions, and impact on commitment and the joining decision. Measures of job satisfaction, commitment, and trainees' perceptions of the adequacy of initial counseling will be gathered at the end of recruit training and at the end of trades training, along with data on differential turnover rates. Research has been conducted to determine the linkages between patterns of responses to CFCIS vocational interest questionnaire items and the probability of successful adjustment to conditions of service in each trade (Angus & Nethercott, 1987).

U.S. Army Joint Optical Information Network (JOIN) System

The U.S. Army is currently investigating the design of a recruiting-compatible CVG system to adequately tap the high-quality applicant market. JOIN, a stand-alone microcomputer-based system, is similar to the Navy Personnel Accessioning System. Technologically superior by virtue of advanced microcomputer capabilities, it has been implemented in Army recruiting offices nationwide. In the course of the recruiting process, Army-enlisted applicants directly interact with this state-of-the-art accessioning system.

When the Army became the first to apply the benefits of automation to the front-line recruiter, the opportunity for rapid interservice technology transfer became apparent. A very fruitful three-year interlaboratory program was initiated in 1982 between ARI and NPRDC (Sands, Gade, Bryan, 1982).

Several applicant assessment instruments were developed, tested, and refined. One is already in use in the recruiting milieu, the Computerized Adaptive Screening Test, and represents a milestone in computerized adaptive testing. Other instruments have undergone further validation and are being evaluated for possible implementation. Studies that are critical to the design of recruiting-compatible automated systems were completed and their results made available to the research and operational communities through a number of working papers, technical reports, professional papers, and journal articles (see, e.g., Baker 1985b; Baker, Sands and Rafacz, 1986; Diamond, 1986; Holland & Baker, 1986; Norris & Baker, 1986).

Recent studies have been conducted by the Army to evaluate JOIN's effectiveness. The first obtained information from Army enlistees concerning the realistic job previews provided by JOIN (Lockhart, Wagner, & Cheng, in press). It was concluded that: (1) providing new recruits with an accurate picture of the Army appears to be an effective means of improving job satisfaction, and (2) soldiers who saw JOIN videos believed that they received more complete information from their recruiter.

Another evaluation of JOIN tested the feasibility of deploying in post-secondary schools an Army automated computerized vocational guidance package, to enhance the recruiting of highly qualified young people, and to identify the best methods for providing Army career/vocational guidance in postsecondary schools (Faust, Warren, & Hertzbach, 1987). A field trial of the system was conducted in the career counseling centers of six community colleges in the Chicago, Baltimore, and Washington, DC, areas. The results demonstrated the appropriateness of the CVG components: (1) both students and counselors enjoyed the system; (2) the video portions were rated excellent; (3) an included interest measure was considered very beneficial by students in exploring occupations; and (4) the system functioned to increase the attractiveness of an Army career to the student users. With some modifications, the package could also be employed in high schools (Hertzbach, 1986; Faust, Warren, & Hertzbach, 1987).

The current Army career vocational guidance research project will assess vocational interests, provide realistic military occupational information, and provide incentive and program information. The strategy for implementing this program is to make it available to Army recruiters on JOIN and to provide it to institutions (e.g., two-year colleges and high schools) as a service. Students will receive information about themselves, as well as information about military occupations and the training required for these occupations.

CURRENT U.S. NAVY PROGRAMS

The most recent development in military CVG systems is the work under way at NPRDC. There, a comprehensive CVG system is being programmed to operate on an ultraportable microcomputer, or lap-top model.

Two studies essential to the development of a recruiting-compatible CVG system have outlined the organizational and operational considerations as well as theoretical and methodological issues (Baker, 1985b, in press). Many of the instruments developed in previous research have excellent potential for incorporation into a comprehensive computerized occupational information and guidance system on the ultraportable microcomputer. Automated career maturity, vocational interest, and work preference measures have been developed and field tested. Prototypes of life-style orientation and realistic job previews are also being developed.

The software package for this system will integrate applicant assessment, didactic counseling materials, occupational information, and choice elicitation. A small modem could permit tie-in with reservation systems, if desired.

When fully developed, the ultraportable CVG system will dramatically increase the range of possible uses for occupational information and vocational guidance materials by recruiting personnel. For example, a system like this could be taken to school job fairs, career days, and so on; it could even be brought to a prospect's home. A lap-top computer and small printer can easily be transported in a lightweight carrying case.

For less-mobile applications, the lap-top will interface with compatible peripherals, such as a software-controlled videodisc system. This will add the capability for showing military life-style orientation films and realistic job preview (RJP) vignettes to job applicants. The lap-top is programmed for IBM compatibility. A demonstration model of this system is currently being developed, with sample RJPs and occupational information dialogue complete. Current efforts focus on validation of an interest measure to be used in the system.

An interest measure, using Holland Codes, has been developed and pilot tested (Gottfredson, 1988). Further research is continuing with this instrument, prior to its conversion to automated form.

CONCLUSION

The various aspects of military service, coupled with the decline in available labor, impel increased attention to the individual assessment of enlistment applicants. With the goal of enhanced placement, tenure, and job satisfaction, efforts are moving ahead on the design and development of comprehensive systems to assist military job seekers in occupational exploration and help match personal characteristics and occupational choices. While many issues in the development of these systems remain (e.g., the level of occupational information specificity, and the degree of automation), these should be resolved once the objectives for the system are established.

The advances in the state of the art in computer hardware can be detected in the progression of system developments. As an example, the Navy's AGENA system, originally conceived as a mainframe-based system using time sharing, was subsequently reconceptualized to reside in a minicomputer. However, the rapid proliferation of extremely powerful stand-alone micro-computers obviated even those plans; and AGENA was programmed to run on an Applied Computer Systems table-top microcomputer consisting of a display terminal, a disk drive, and a printer. The logical successor is a system of interactive information and guidance that will run on lap-top portables for mobile application (with lightweight peripherals for semistationary uses) and on microcomputers for office use and networking to headquarters.

At present, there is an opportunity to escalate interservice cooperation and share the benefits of research and development. Hertzbach (1986) noted that efforts to develop an Army CVG system are at least in part dependent on the cooperation of the other services. The JOIN project is an exemplar of a trend within military personnel psychology research and development:

that is, maintenance of service-specific expertise bases, allied with decreasing research parochialism (Wiskoff, 1985). The time has come for a Department of Defense effort at CVG system development (Wiskoff, 1986). Given the close similarity in the recruiting efforts of the various services, the strong potential for interservice technology transfer, and the obvious leveraging of the government research dollar through cooperative endeavor, cooperative research and development is a rational approach to common problems. In that sense, the prospects for such a system appear good.

Military CVG systems have two clear objectives: to enhance awareness of military career options and to achieve optimal person-job matches that will enhance satisfaction and productivity while decreasing attrition and personnel turbulence. Through the enhanced career maturity engendered by personal assessment and the opportunity for occupational exploration, military job applicants will be in a better position to make sound, informed career decisions, which should enhance individual job satisfaction, commitment, and performance.

REFERENCES

Angus, E. J., & Nethercott, A. C. (1987). *Service member ratings of Vocational Preference Checklist items for entry-level CF occupations* (CFPARU TN 4/87). Willowdale, Ont.: Canadian Forces Personnel Applied Research Unit.

Arbeiter, S. (1981). Current and future delivery systems for adult career guidance. *New Directions for Continuing Education, 10,* 77–83.

Baker, H. G. (1983a). *Navy Personnel Accessioning System (NPAS): I. Background and overview of the person-job matching (PJM) and recruiting management support (RMS) subsystems* (NPRDC Spec. Rep. 83–34). San Diego: Navy Personnel Research and Development Center (AD-A129 325).

———. (1983b). *Navy Personnel Accessioning System (NPAS): II Summary of research and development efforts and products* (NPRDC Spec. Rep. 83–35). San Diego: Navy Personnel Research and Development Center (AD-A129 326).

———. (1984). *Computerized vocational guidance (CVG) systems: Evaluation for use in military recruiting* (NPRDC Tech. Rep. 84–21). San Diego: Navy Personnel Research and Development Center.

———. (1985a) A prototype computerized vocational guidance system for Navy recruiting. *Journal of Computer-Based Instruction, 12*(3), 76–79.

———. (1985b). *Designing a vocational guidance system for military recruiting: Problems and prospects I. Organizational and operational considerations* (MPL TN 85-5). San Diego: Navy Personnel Research and Development Center.

———. (in press). *Designing a vocational guidance system for military recruiting: Problems and prospects II. Theoretical and methodological considerations* (NPRDC TN 87). San Diego: Navy Personnel Research and Development Center.

Baker, H. G., Rafacz, B. A., & Sands, W. A. (1983a). *Navy Personnel Accessioning System (NPAS): III. Development of a microcomputer demonstration system* (NPRDC Spec. Rep. 83–36). San Diego: Navy Personnel Research and Development Center (AD-A129 319).

———— . (1983b, May). *Initial development of a computerized adaptive screening test (CAST) for use in a military recruiting station.* Paper presented at the 1983 Assessment Council Conference of the International Personnel Management Association. Washington, DC.

———— . (1983c, June). *Development and validation of a computerized adaptive screening test (CAST) for use in Army recruiting.* Paper presented at the 5th annual National Educational Computing Conference, Baltimore.

———— . (1984). *Computerized adaptive screening test (CAST): Development for use in military recruiting stations* (NPRDC Tech. Rep. 84–17). San Diego: Navy Personnel Research and Development Center.

Baker, H. G., Sands, W. A., & Rafacz, B. A. (1986). *Research and development in support of the Army Joint Optical Information Network (JOIN): Final report* (NPRDC Tech. Rep. 86–19). San Diego: Navy Personnel Research and Development Center.

Borow, H. (Ed.), (1973).*Career guidance for a new age.* Boston: Houghton Mifflin.

Chapman, W., & Katz, M. R. (1982). *Summary of a survey of career information systems in secondary schools and assessment of alternative types.* Princeton, NJ: Educational Testing Service.

Cory, C. H. (1979, October). Computer-aided career information systems. *Proceedings of the 21st annual conference of the Military Testing Association* (pp. 933–940). San Diego: Navy Personnel Research and Development Center.

Diamond, E. E. (1986, August). *An instrument to assess career maturity for use in military recruiting.* Paper presented at the annual convention of the American Psychological Association, Washington, DC.

Ellis, R. T. (1985). *Evaluation of the Automated Counselling Component of the Canadian Forces Career Information System: A Research Plan* (CFPARU TN 5/85). Willowdale, Ont.: Canadian Forces Personnel Applied Research Unit.

Faust, D. G., Warren, I. K., & Hertzbach, A. (1987, November). *Army vocational guidance in two-year colleges* (Res. Rpt. 1460). Alexandria, VA: Army Research Institute.

Gottfredson, G. D. (1988, February). *Development of the Civilian-Military Interest Survey (C-MIS)* (NPRDC TN 88–20). San Diego: Navy Personnel Research and Development Center.

Harris, J. E. (1972). *Analysis of the effects of a computer-based vocational information system on selected aspects of vocational planning.* Unpublished doctoral dissertation, Northern Illinois University, DeKalb.

———— . (1974). The computer: guidance tool of the future. *Journal of Counseling Psychology, 21*(4), 331–339.

Hertzbach, A. (1986, August). *Army career guidance for junior and community colleges.* Paper presented at the annual convention of the American Psychological Association, Washington, DC.

Hickey, A. E., & Newton, J. M. (1967). *Computer-assisted instruction: A survey of the literature.* Newburyport, MA: Entelek.

Holland, J. L., & Baker, H. G. (1986). *Preliminary classification of Army and Navy entry-level occupations by the Holland coding system* (NPRDC Tech. Rep. 87–5). San Diego: Navy Personnel Research and Development Center.

Impelliteri, J. T. (1967, November). The computer as an aid to instruction and guidance in the school. Paper prepared for the Regional Seminar and Research Conference in Agricultural Education, Cornell University.

Jacobson, M. D., & Grabowski, B. T. (1982). Computerized systems of career information and guidance: A state-of-the-art. *Journal of Educational Technology Systems, 10*(3), 235–255.

Katz, M. R. (1974). Career decision-making: A computer-based system of inter- active guidance and information (SIGI). *Measurement for self-understanding and personal development: Proceedings of the 1973 Invitational Conference* (pp. 43–69). Princeton, NJ: Educational Testing Service.

Katz, M. R., & Shatkin, L. (1980). *Computer-assisted guidance: Concepts and practices* (Res. Rep. RR 80–1). Princeton, NJ: Educational Testing Service.

Lamb, R. R., & Prediger, D. J. (1981). *Technical report for the unisex edition of the ACT interest inventory (UNIACT). Iowa City: American College Testing Program.*

Lockhart, D. C., Wagner, M., & Cheng, C. (in press). *The 1986 Early Career Satis- faction Survey: Analytic report.* Alexandria, VA: Army Research Institute.

Miller, D. A., & Ellis, R. T. (1986). The effect of trade and lifestyle videotapes on preference and interest in trade enrollment (CFPARU WP 86–6). Willow- dale, Ont.: Canadian Forces Personnel Applied Research Unit.

Minor, F. J. (1970). An experimental computer-based educational and career ex- ploration system. In D. E. Super (Ed.), *Computer-assisted counseling.* New York: Teachers College Press.

Norris, L., & Baker, H. G. (1986). *Development of an automated instrument to assess enlistment motivation* (MPL TN 86–9). San Diego: Navy Personnel Research and Development Center.

Oliver, L. W. (1977, January). *Computer-assisted career counseling.* Paper pre- sented at Army Education Counselor Career Counseling Workshop, Denver.

Phillips, S. D., Cairo, P. C., Myers, R. A., Ryan, T. G., Hoffer, G. L., & Croes- Silverman, M. (1980). *Career planning modules for the officer career informa- tion and planning system* (ARI Res. Rep. 1257). Alexandria, VA: U.S. Army Research Institute for the Behavioral and Social Sciences (AD–A100 959).

Rayman, J. R., Bryson, D. L., & Bowlsbey, J. H. (1978). The field trial of DIS- COVER: A new computerized interactive system. *The Vocational Guidance Quarterly, 26,* 349–360.

Rayman, J. R., & Harris-Bowlsbey, J. (1977). DISCOVER: A model for a systema- tic career guidance program. *The Vocational Guidance Quarterly,* September, 3–12.

Ryan, C. W., & Drummond, R. J. (1981). Differential impacts of a computer in- formation system on selected human services agencies. *Association for Educational Data Systems Journal,* Winter, 73–83.

Sands, W. A., Gade, P. A., & Bryan, J. D. (1982, November). *Research and development for the JOIN System*. Paper presented at the 24th annual conference of the Military Testing Association, San Antonio.

Shatkin, L. (1980). *Computer-assisted guidance: Descriptions of systems* (Res. Rep. RR 80–23). Princeton, NJ: Educational Testing Service.

Super, D. E. (1971). *Career decision tree*. New York: Teachers College, Columbia University.

_____ . (1973). Computers in support of vocational development and counseling. In H. H. Borow (Ed.), *Career Guidance for a new age*. Boston: Houghton Mifflin.

Wilson, F. P. (1980). Towards a more systematic counselling model for the Canadian Forces (CFPARU WP 80–3). Willowdale, Ont.: Canadian Forces Personnel Applied Research Unit.

Wilson, F. P. & Flynn, J. A. (1982). Introduction of trade and lifestyle videotapes (TLVs) into a Canadian Forces vocational counseling setting. Report 82–1. Willowdale, Ont.: Canadian Forces Personnel Applied Research Unit.

Wiskoff, M. F. (1985, August). Division 19 presidential address given at the annual convention of the American Psychological Association, Los Angeles.

_____ . (1986, August). Discussant remarks at a symposium on military occupational information and guidance. Annual convention of the American Psychological Association, Washington, DC.

4

Officer Aptitude Selection Measures

DIANNE C. BROWN

INTRODUCTION

Commissioned officers, the highest of military ranks, are charged with the leadership, command, and management of military personnel. They are drawn from the upper echelons of our nation's college-age population. Candidates who have leadership ability and who show strong academic potential and achievement are selected for officer training and education programs and, upon successful completion, are commissioned as second lieutenants in the Army, Marine Corps, or Air Force, or as ensigns in the Navy. Officer candidate programs such as the service academies, Reserve Officer Training Corps (ROTC), and Officer Candidate Schools (OCS) offer military science courses and military officer training, as well as specialized training in some cases, such as for flight officers.

To help ensure quality, a college education is a fundamental requirement for joining the officer corps. Officer candidate programs either incorporate a college education or overwhelmingly select college graduates. In addition to educational requirements, an assessment of aptitude is consistently a primary consideration in the selection of officer candidates. However, because of the numerous and decentralized officer commissioning programs, the specific aptitude selection measures can be best characterized as variable between and within services, as well as variable over time.

In contrast to enlisted accessions, the same aptitude test battery is not administered to all officer candidates. This variability is not only a function of policy that allows each officer candidate program to develop and practice its own selection methods, but is also a function of the candidates' education level upon entering the various officer candidate programs. That is, the appropriateness of an aptitude selection measure is largely determined by whether the officer candidate is a college graduate. Thus, with officer candidate programs for both college graduates (OCS and OTS [Officer Training School]), and undergraduates (the academies and ROTC), a variety of aptitude measures is deemed necessary. In attempting to procure the highest quality personnel for commissioning, the services have invested a great deal of time and effort in refining such officer selection measures.

This chapter first describes the various officer candidate programs. That is, it documents the officer training programs that ultimately lead to commissioned officer status. Current aptitude criteria used for officer candidate selection are then documented within this framework. A brief historical review of the development of officer aptitude selection tests is provided as well.

OFFICER CANDIDATE PROGRAMS

Officer candidate programs can be divided into two different categories: those that incorporate a college education, and those for college graduates. The programs that incorporate a college education include the service academies and ROTC. In return for a commitment to military duty, the services provide, either partially or totally, a college education. The academies and ROTC scholarship programs fully subsidize tuition. In the case of nonscholarship ROTC, a subsistence allowance is provided during the junior and senior years.

The academies offer a college education (bachelor of science degree) within a total military environment at one central location. Engineering and science curricula are the strong points of the academies; however, degrees in humanities and social sciences are offered. ROTCs, on the other hand, have several hundred locations at civilian and military colleges and universities, and reach a larger segment of the undergraduate population. Engineering and science majors are typically preferred, but not required. Additional programs (OCS and OTS) provide a means of drawing quality personnel from among the college-educated. As with ROTC, the technical majors are preferred, but not required.

Officer Candidate Programs for College Students

The service academies are essentially colleges that require military training and courses in addition to the regular curricula, which leads to the bachelor of science degree. The Army, Navy, and Air Force each have academies: the United States Military Academy (USMA), the United States Naval Academy (USNA), and the United States Air Force Academy (USAFA), respectively. The Marine Corps is permitted to commission up to

16 percent of the Naval Academy's graduates per year. These midshipmen are chosen from among those who apply and contract for service with the Marine Corps.

ROTC is another officer candidate program that includes a college education. In addition to the regular college curriculum, ROTC cadets take required military science courses and, typically, attend a summer training session either between the sophomore and junior years or between the junior and senior years. Upon graduation, ROTC cadets are commissioned as second lieutenants, or in the Navy as ensigns. ROTC has both scholarship and nonscholarship programs. Scholarships are primarily four-year, or are awarded to beginning college freshmen, but there are odd-year scholarships. The Army and Navy offer one-, two-, and three-year scholarships, and the Air Force additionally offers two-, two and one-half-, three-, and three and one-half-year scholarships. In the Navy, odd-year scholarships are awarded to students who have joined ROTC under the nonscholarship program and are subsequently recommended by commanding officers. Nonscholarship ROTC students can apply for either a four-year program or a two-year program. The two-year ROTC students must complete a six-week summer training session in order to apply to advanced ROTC, the final two years.

As with the Naval Academy, the Marine Corps is also permitted to draw 16 percent of Naval ROTC students per year. Again, these students are selected by the Marine Corps from among those applying to that service. Additionally, the Marine Corps, independently of the Navy's programs, operates two officer candidate programs that are intended for college undergraduates. Platoon Leaders Class (PLC) consists of two six-week summer training sessions and is for civilian college students. The Marine Corps Enlisted Commissioning Education Program (MECEP) is for enlisted personnel who are pursuing four-year college degrees. These students are assigned to NROTC units for the remainder of their college careers.

Officer Candidate Programs for College Graduates

Officer candidate or training schools are primarily for college graduates, and offer a variety of military and officer courses. The duration of these schools is typically three to four months. Most officer candidates who go through OCS or OTS are brought into the service as enlisted personnel, with the expressed intent of attending OCS upon completion of basic training. Other OCS officer candidates come from among eligible enlisted personnel. For example, the Air Force's Airmen Education and Commissioning Program is designed to prepare enlisted personnel for OTS. Through this program, enlisted personnel can complete the requirements for a bachelor of science degree (in engineering or science), and remain on active duty in the Air Force throughout college. Upon graduation, such individuals are eligible for OTS.

Army OCS is open to two types of applicants: college graduates who enlist in the Army, and enlisted personnel who have a minimum of two years of college. Those civilian college graduates enter the Army as enlisted personnel and upon successful completion of basic training go to OCS. The enlisted personnel can go through OCS and become commissioned, but they must complete college to be promoted above captain.

The Marine Corps offers two officer candidate programs for college graduates. The Officer Candidate Course (OCC) is for civilian college graduates, who enlist in the Marine Corps and then go through a ten-week training program. The Enlisted Commissioning Program (ECP) is for enlisted personnel and is similar to OCC. Marine Corps OCS is part of all of the officer candidate programs directly run by the Marine Corps (PLC, MECEP, OCC, and ECP). In other words, subsequent to completion of each of these programs, all Marine Corps officer candidates attend a six- or ten-week Marine Corps OCS to receive a commission.

Table 4.1 shows the number and percentage of active duty officers drawn from the various officer candidate programs by service for fiscal year (FY) 1986. These data show differences between the services in terms of the proportions of commissioned officers drawn by each source. The Army commissions the majority (72.5 percent) of its officers through ROTC, while the largest proportion of the Navy's officers (57.7 percent) go through OCS. Most of the Marine Corps' officers (61.6 percent) are drawn from PLC, and for the Air Force, AFROTC (40.0 percent) and OTS (44.3 percent) are the primary officer sources.

In essence, the first step in the selection of officer candidates is to target the defined population from which candidates are drawn; that is, college students and college graduates. Within this defined group, the services seek the individuals who are most likely to succeed in officer training and then serve effectively as officers. Aptitude measures are the primary selection tools used to identify those quality personnel. The following section describes the aptitude tests and other measures used by each of the services for the selection of officer candidates.

OFFICER APTITUDE SELECTION MEASURES

College admission examinations, either the Scholastic Aptitude Test (SAT) or the American College Test (ACT), are required of the majority of college students. These tests, likewise, have served as selection criteria for entrance into all three service academies. Officer candidate (or training)

Table 4.1
Number and Percent of FY 1986 Active Duty Officer Accessions by Service and Source of Commission

Service

Source of Commission	ARMY		NAVY		MARINE CORPS		AIR FORCE		Total DoD	
	N	%	N	%	N	%	N	%	N	%
ROTC[a] Scholarship	1,964	30.5	1,190	22.7	262	16.9	1,125	19.0	4,541	23.7
ROTC Non-Scholarship	2,705	42.0	174	3.3	40	2.6	1,244	21.0	4,163	21.7
Service Academy	1,023	15.9	849	16.2	173	11.2	938	15.8	2,983	15.6
OCS/OTS/AOC/NFOC[b]	750[c]	11.6	3,020	57.7	121	7.8	2,625[d]	44.3	6,516	34.0
PLC[e]	— f	—	— f	—	955	61.6	— f	—	955	5.0
Total Number	6,442	100.0	5,233	100.0	1,551	100.0	5,932	100.0	19,158	100.0

[a]Reserve Officer Training Corps.
[b]Officer Candidate School/Officer Training School/Aviation Officer Candidate/Naval Flight Officer Candidate.
[c]OCS only.
[d]OTS only.
[e]Platoon Leaders Class.
[f]Marine Corps only.
Source: Department of Defense (1986).

schools typically use tests developed within the specific services, which were developed to assess a variety of characteristics such as leadership ability, technical knowledge, or aviation aptitude as well as academic aptitude. The use of selection tests varies more across the services for the ROTC, with both civilian college entrance examinations and service-specific tests used.

This section documents the current aptitude criteria as well as other measures used for officer selection by service and source of commission. Although the emphasis of this section is on the various officer aptitude tests, the commissioning source context and other selection factors are provided to facilitate an understanding of how the tests are used.

Army

United States Military Academy (West Point). Selection into West Point is based on an applicant's "whole candidate score" (WCS), which is derived from weighting the following three factors:

- academic aptitude (60 percent);
- leadership potential, as assessed through evaluations of an applicant's participation in extracurricular and community activities (30 percent); and
- physical aptitude, as assessed by the Army's Physical Aptitude Examination (PAE) (10 percent).

There is no apparent documentation of the procedures used to determine the various weights assigned to these three components of the WCS. Use of the current version of the academic aptitude component began at the Academy in 1973, and the concept of a "whole man" evaluation dates back to 1958. The WCS in use today certainly evolved over time but specifically how and when is largely unknown because of either lack of documentation or lack of availability of such documentation.

Of primary importance is the academic aptitude portion, which is determined through either SAT scores statistically combined with high school rank (CEER score), or ACT scores statistically combined with high school rank (ACEER score).* Whether a candidate is given a CEER score or an ACEER score depends on which test was taken, and if both tests were taken, the test showing the higher score is used.

SAT, published by the Educational Testing Service, is the most widely used aptitude test for college admissions. SAT has Verbal and Mathematical subtests, and score scales for these have a mean of 500 with a standard deviation of 100. Validation studies correlating SAT scores with freshman

---

*CEER and ACEER are acronyms derived from *C*ollege *E*ntrance *E*xamination *S*cores and High School *R*ank or *A*merican *C*ollege *E*ntrance *E*xamination and High School *R*ank.

grade point average typically yield correlations of .35 for each subtest. Multiple regression coefficients around .54 are typical when combining both subtests with high school grades as predictors. ACT, published by the American College Testing Program, consists of four subtests: English, Mathematics, Social Studies, and Natural Sciences. Each subtest has a score range of 1-36, with means varying by subtest from 17.2 (Social Studies) to 20.8 (Natural Sciences), and all with a standard deviation of 5.5. Validity coefficients for ACT composite scores (the average of all subtests) correlated with college grade point average cluster around .40 and .50 (Anastasi, 1982).

There are no strict cut-off scores for SAT or ACT; rather, these are weighted and combined with high school rank to produce the CEER or ACEER score. These weights are empirically derived, using first-year grade point average as criterion (Davidson, 1977). There are general guidelines for SAT and ACT scores, and these fluctuate depending on the number and quality level of candidates.

Validation studies are conducted annually at the Academy, correlating all components of the WCS with performance criteria at West Point. A recent validation study correlating CEER scores with freshman academic quality point average produced a coefficient of .63 (Butler, 1985). Validities for CEER and ACEER are reportedly very consistent, usually between .60 and .65. One validation study, correlating CEER scores with first-year grade point average, reported coefficients for minorities of .41 and .52 (Davidson, 1977). However, "minority" was not defined in this report, and no documentation of validities by gender has been discovered.

Once an applicant meets the minimum qualifications, a nomination to the academy by a legal authority must be obtained. Although most nominations are obtained from a member of Congress, some are from the vice president or the delegate from the District of Columbia. Completed files for each candidate who is qualified and nominated then go to the admissions committee for final selection. The admissions committee consists of a group of junior and senior officers drawn from the staff at the Academy. Selection at this point, although guided by the number of openings at the Academy, is largely subjective. Members of the admissions committee review applicant files and choose those they deem best qualified.

Army Reserve Officer Training Corps. Nonscholarship ROTC uses a new selection system, referred to as the Precommissioning Assessment System (PAS). PAS was instituted for use in school year 1986/87, based on recommendations of the Review of Education and Training for Officers study group, which was formed through the Military Personnel Center. Precommissioning selection typically takes place at the beginning of the junior year in college, when students contract with the Army, agreeing to serve on either active or reserve duty upon commissioning.

Factors that are considered in precommissioning selection include:

- the Army's physical readiness test (which all ROTC students must pass twice a year);
- a structured interview by a professor of military science to assess student motivation;
- grade point average;
- participation in extracurricular activities;
- ROTC writing requirements, which are part of military qualification skills, taught and assessed through military science courses;
- Officer Selection Battery Forms 3 & 4 (OSB 3&4) scores.

In selection, these elements are obtained for each applicant and are reviewed in terms of the "whole person package," rather than being quantified, weighted, and combined to form a single qualifying score. There are minimum standards, or cut-off scores for those factors that are quantified, such as grade point average and OSB 3&4 scores. If an applicant is lacking in one area, such as participation in extracurricular activities, the entire record is reviewed to identify strengths in other areas, or perhaps a justification for the apparent shortcoming, such as part-time work.

The OSB 3&4 was developed by the Army Research Institute for the Behavioral and Social Sciences. The test content is based on a job analysis of Army lieutenants conducted to identify performance dimensions. The resulting performance dimensions that are assessed with the OSB 3&4 are as follows: initiative, decision making, administration, communication, interpersonal manner, technical knowledge, and combat performance.

The OSB 3&4 is scaled on an Army standard score with a mean of 100 and a standard deviation of 20. Validation of the OSB 3&4 against faculty ratings of officer potential for a sample of 2,805 college juniors enrolled in ROTC produced coefficients of .26 for Form 3 and .28 for Form 4. Form 3 was additionally validated against final grade in Officer Basic Course, required of all Army officers upon commissioning, which resulted in a correlation of .52. Validities for subgroups (shown in Table 4.2) were found to be comparable (Fischl et al., 1986).

The four-year scholarship program uses a whole person score (WPS) for selection. The weighted factors that make up the WPS are as follows: SAT or ACT score (25 percent), high school class standing (25 percent), participation in extracurricular activities and other factors that demonstrate leadership ability (40 percent), and PAE (10 percent). The WPS is on a scale of 1 to 999. Cut-off scores change from year to year, depending on the applicant population and the Army's needs. Although the WPS is used to determine entry into the four-year scholarship program, there are specific

Table 4.2
Officer Selection Battery Forms 3 and 4 Validities for Subgroups

	Validity Coefficient[a]	
Group	Form 3	Form 4
Black	.27	.34
White	.24	.23
Hispanic	.33	.31
Male	.26	.25
Female	.30	.33
Total	.26	.28

[a]Criterion was faculty rating of officer potential.
Source: Fischl et al. (1986).

cut-off scores for SAT and ACT, and if these minimums are not met, the applicant is not accepted.

For the three-year scholarship ROTC program, which covers the last three years of college, SAT or ACT scores are used in screening applicants. A candidate must meet the minimum SAT and ACT scores to be competitive. If the minimum SAT or ACT score is met, then the whole person package is reviewed.

SAT and ACT scores are not used in the selection process for the two-year ROTC scholarship program. Instead, a minimum 2.0 college grade point average (GPA) is required on a 4.0 scale, 4.0 being the highest. GPA is used in the two-year program the same way SAT scores are used for the three-year scholarship program; the minimum must be met to be competitive. If the candidate has a GPA of 2.0 or above, then the whole person package is reviewed.

Army Officer Candidate School. Factors considered in the selection of candidates to OCS include the Army's PAE, college grade point average, letters of recommendation from former employers or professors, college major (engineering and science are preferred), and an interview by the battalion board. Aptitude measures used for selection into Army OCS are the Officer Selection Battery Forms 1 & 2 (OSB 1&2) and the General-Technical (GT) composite of the Armed Services Vocational Aptitude Battery. As with ROTC, these factors are not weighted, but are all reviewed in a whole person evaluation.

The OSB 1&2 is a completely separate test from the OSB 3&4, although it too was developed by ARI. It consists of the seven subtests presented in Table 4.3. Although the entire battery is administered to all OCS applicants, only

Table 4.3
Officer Selection Battery Forms 1 and 2 Subtests and Content Description

SUBTEST	DESCRIPTION OF CONTENT
Combat Leadership (Cognitive)	Military tactics; practical skills in a variety of areas ranging from outdoor activities to mechanical and electronic applications
Technical-Managerial Leadership (Cognitive)	History, politics; culture; mathematics; physical sciences
Career Potential (Cognitive)	Technological knowledge relevant to military requirements
Combat Leadership (Non-Cognitive)	Combat leader qualities, occupational interests, sports interest, outdoor interests related to combat leadership
Technical-Managerial Leadership (Non-Cognitive)	Mathematics and physical sciences skills and interest; urban or rural background; scientific interest and ability; decisive leader qualities; and verbal-social leadership
Career Potential (Non-Cognitive)	Clerical-administrative interest versus white collar interest, combat interest
Career Intent	Intention of making the Army a career choice

Source: Gilbert (1978).

one subtest enters into the formal selection decision. The Army OCS uses the Technical-Managerial Leadership (Cognitive) subtest scores as a criterion for entry.* This subtest is scaled to an Army standard score scale ($\bar{x}$ = 100, SD = 20). In a study that validated the OSB 1&2 Technical-Managerial subtest with Officer Basic Course (OBC) final grades for a sample of 4,622 officers who attended OBC in FY 1974, a significant correlation, uncorrected for range restriction, was found (r = .29, p < .01). Significant correlations were found for subgroups, as well. Validities for males and females were .29 and .33, respectively. The coefficient for the

---

*Other OSB 1&2 subtests have been used in ROTC as career guidance tools to aid students in assessing aptitudes or interests in the various areas.

black sample was .29, as compared with that of the white sample, which was .22 (Gilbert, 1978).

The ASVAB, used for the selection and classification of enlisted personnel in all four services, consists of ten subtests (shown in Table 4.4). For selection and job classification purposes, these ten subtests are combined to form various composites. The General-Technical (GT) composite of the ASVAB, used by the Army for OCS selection, comprises the Word Knowledge, Paragraph Comprehension, and Arithmetic Reasoning subtests. The GT composite, like the OSB 1&2, is scaled on a standard score scale with a mean of 100 and a standard deviation of 20. ARI conducted a study validating ASVAB composites with performance of second- and third-tour enlisted personnel. Skill Qualification Test (SQT) scores in 195 different military occupational specialties (MOS) were used as the criterion measure. SQTs are administered every year and are specific to MOS and skill level within MOS. In correlations between the ASVAB GT and SQT scores, 84 percent were significant positive coefficients (Grafton & Horne, 1985). No information was available on validities for subgroups and no validity studies have been conducted on the specific use of the ASVAB GT composite in OCS.

To be eligible to apply to Army OCS, an applicant must attain the minimum score on the Technical-Managerial Leadership (Cognitive) subtest of the OSB, and a minimum score of 110 on the GT composite of the ASVAB. If these minimums are met, a candidate's application will go to a selection board. The selection board then rates each applicant, assigning a numerical value and, based on the number of available positions in OCS, the highest rated individuals are selected.

Navy

United States Naval Academy. The Naval Academy uses a whole person evaluation system for admission. Several variables are combined and

Table 4.4
Armed Services Vocational Aptitude Battery Subtests

1	Word Knowledge (WK)	6	General Sciences (GS)
2	Paragraph Comprehension (PC)	7	Mathematics Knowledge (MK)
3	Arithmetic Reasoning (AR)	8	Electronics Information (EI)
4	Numerical Operations (NO)	9	Mechanical Comprehension (MC)
5	Coding Speed (CS)	10	Automotive-Shop Information (AS)

weighted to produce a numerical score, the "candidate multiple" (CM). The factors included in the CM are as follows:

- SAT or ACT Verbal and Mathematical scores;
- high school class rank;
- evaluations by high school teachers on communication skills, interpersonal relations, personal conduct, and leadership potential;
- participation in extracurricular activities;
- specially adapted scales from the Strong-Campbell Interest Inventory designed to assess interests and to predict career retention.

Optimal weightings of variables are derived empirically, using multiple regression analyses (Neumann, in press). Weights are validated and adjusted annually. Based on 1986 standards, SAT/ACT scores comprise approximately 60 percent of the CM. To be competitive, normal qualifying scores are required for SAT or ACT.

The Naval Academy annually conducts studies validating all of the CM predictor variables against several performance variables, which include GPA, military performance, and attrition from the academy. In a recent validation study correlating predictor variables with second-year academic quality point average, coefficients (corrected for range restriction in predictor variables) of .45, .62, and .58 were found for verbal subtest score, mathematical subtest score, and high school rank, respectively. The corrected validity coefficient for the combined CM was .62 (Neumann, in press). Another study that compares validities for males and females shows comparable validities for the three aptitude predictors, but markedly different validities for the total CM; .51 for males compared to .43 for females (Neumann & Abrahams, 1982).

Similar to West Point, all minimally qualified and nominated applicant files are reviewed by an admissions board of 17 members that comprise senior officers and faculty from the academy. During the selection process, the admissions board reviews an applicant's CM, its separate components, and additional information such as the applicant's written statement, and reference letters from high school teachers. The admissions board may adjust an applicant's CM by up to 20 percent during this review process. The rationale behind this method is that reviewers can subjectively detect relevant information on a candidate that can be overlooked in the empirical derivation of the CM. Candidates are then rank-ordered based on the adjusted CM and the highest ranked are offered appointments based upon the number of openings.

Navy Reserve Officer Training Corps. Selection for the NROTC four-year scholarship program consists of two processes: the initial screening process and the final selection process. For the initial screening process, SAT or ACT scores serve as the criterion and for those who qualify, a subsequent selection board review occurs. If an applicant meets the minimum required SAT or ACT scores, a selection board further reviews the candidate's qualifications. A composite score is derived for each candidate based on several factors and using optimal weights for each variable. The factors and their effective weights are as follows:

• SAT (or ACT) Verbal and Mathematical scores combined (19 percent);
• high school rank (56 percent);
• results of a structured interview by a Navy officer to assess candidate's potential (10 percent);
• results of a scale developed from the Strong-Campbell Interest Inventory to predict career tenure (9 percent);
• score derived from a biographical questionnaire designed to predict retention (5 percent).

Optimal weights for the variables were derived empirically using multiple regression analyses. Correlating the composite with sophomore GPA produced a validity coefficient, uncorrected for range restriction, of .28 (Mattson, Neumann, & Abrahams, 1986). Apparently, there is no published documentation of validation for subgroups.

The nonscholarship portion of NROTC is called the college program. College program students are selected by individual units, and standards vary by unit; there are no set admission criteria. Selection of college program students for one-, two-, and three-year scholarships also takes place within the various units, with no uniform criteria.

Officer Candidate School and Aviation Officer Candidate School. The Navy OCS and AOCS programs, for college graduates, review an applicant's GPA, extracurricular activities, employment record, and a physical examination. The Aviation Selection Test Battery was developed by the Naval Medical Command (MEDCOM), formerly the Bureau of Medicine and Surgery (BUMED), and is used as the primary aptitude screening instrument for these programs. Applicants must first meet the minimum requirements on the Aviation Selection Test Battery, and then the whole person package is reviewed. The Aviation Selection Test Battery consists of four subtests, with different subtests used depending on whether the examinee is an aviation training (AOCS) or nonaviation training (OCS) applicant.

The four subtests of the Aviation Selection Test Battery, described in Table 4.5, are the Aviation Qualification Test (AQT), the Mechanical Comprehension Test (MCT), the Spatial Apperception Test (SAT—not to be

Table 4.5
U.S. Navy and Marine Corps Aviation Selection Test Battery

TITLE	LENGTH	ITEM CONTENT
Part I: Academic Qualification Test (AQT)	105 items, 60 mins.	Quantitative Ability Verbal Ability Practical Judgment Clerical Speed and Accuracy Following Directions
Part II: Flight Aptitude Rating (FAR)		
1. Mechanical Comprehension Test (MCT)	75 items, 40 mins.	Mechanical Aptitude
2. Spatial Apperception Test (SAT)	34 items, 10 mins.	Spatial Orientation
3. Biographical Inventory (BI)	160 items Unlimited	Evidence of early maturity, early risk taking behavior, informal acquisition of aerospace knowledge, selected personal history items related to aviation success, selected attitudes and interest items related to aviation success.

Source: Petho (1980).

confused with the Scholastic Aptitude Test mentioned previously), and the Biographical Inventory (BI). These subtests are divided and grouped to comprise two parts of the Aviation Selection Test Battery. The first part is the AQT—consisting only of that subtest—which is a test of general intelligence and includes items that assess quantitative and verbal ability. This score is intended to predict performance in nonaviation school. The second part is the Flight Aptitude Rating (FAR) composite, which consists of the other three subtests (MCT, SAT, and BI). This composite is intended to predict performance in pilot training. One other score derived from the Aviation Selection Test Battery is the Officer Aptitude Rating (OAR). The OAR, used in the selection of nonaviation applicants, is obtained by combining the AQT and MCT scores.

The AQT-FAR scores are scaled in stanines, (i.e., scores range from 1 through 9 with a mean of 5). The OAR is scaled in T scores, with a range of 0 through 100 and a mean of 50. MEDCOM establishes minimum acceptable scores for these tests though the Naval Military Personnel Command may set higher standards. The current MEDCOM cut-off scores are 3 on both the AQT and the FAR for Naval Flight Officers, and 3 on the AQT and 5 on the FAR for Aviation Officer Candidates (AOCs). Validation of the AQT-FAR shows a corrected correlation of .30 between AQT score and a pass/fail criterion at the undergraduate level of training, and .52 between FAR and pass/fail criterion (Doll, 1977). Validity information for subgroups and for OAR specifically is apparently not available.

Navy OCS uses OAR as a preliminary screening device and requires an applicant to obtain a minimum score to be competitive. If this minimum is met, the applicant's whole person package, mentioned previously, is reviewed to determine qualification. In an effort to make Naval OCS equally accessible to racial and ethnic minorities, members of such groups who score slightly lower than the minimum on OAR can be accepted and then go to Officer Candidate Preparatory School (OCPS) before OCS. AOCS uses the AQT-FAR for preliminary screening. As with OCS, if minimum scores are met, the whole person package is then reviewed.

Marine Corps

Marine Corps Officers Accessed from Navy Officer Programs. The Marine Corps may commission up to 16 percent of the Naval Academy graduates per year. These midshipmen go through the Naval Academy's selection procedures as previously described. Similarly, 16 percent of NROTC students are permitted to enter the Marine Corps. The only difference between the Navy and the Marine Corps in aptitude selection criteria for NROTC may be evidenced in different minimum score requirements.

Marine Corps Officer Programs. The Marine Corps uses the whole person concept for selection, reviewing all relevant qualifications of an applicant. For most of the Marine Corps officer programs, the following factors are among those considered: recommendations from professors or employers, college or high school transcripts, physical examination, and employment/ military record. The Marine Corps OCS, as described previously, serves as an additional screening process as well as a training program for Marine Corps officer candidates. While the whole person package is considered for selection into programs, factors are not weighted into a formula that produces a numerical score. The various programs do, however, have minimum acceptable scores for aptitude measures.

For selection into Platoon Leaders Class, Officer Candidate Course, Marine Corps Enlisted Commissioning Education Program, and Enlisted

Commissioning Program, the Marine Corps uses SAT or ACT, and scores of the ASVAB Electrical (EL) composite. The EL composite is made up of the following ASVAB subtests: General Science, Arithmetic Reasoning, Mathematics Knowledge, and Electronics Information. The EL composite is scaled on a standard score scale with a mean of 100 and a standard deviation of 20.

In a validation study, performed through the Center for Naval Analyses, ASVAB EL and SAT scores were correlated with performance in The Basic School, (TBS), which is a comprehensive five-month program that is required of every Marine Corps commissioned officer. TBS academic grade was used as the performance criterion for this validation. Validities, corrected for range restriction, were .73 for the ASVAB EL composite and .72 for the SAT. Estimated reliability for the ASVAB EL was .94 (Stoloff, 1983). There is apparently no published data on subgroup validities for these measures.

Air Force

Air Force Academy. The Air Force Academy uses a whole person package, referred to as the Selection Composite, as the criterion for admission. The Selection Composite is made up of an academic component (70 percent), a leadership component (15 percent), an interview, and a physical fitness test (15 percent). The academic component comprises SAT or ACT scores statistically combined with high school rank. If an applicant meets the minimum requirements, his or her application package goes to a selection board where the whole person package is reviewed. However, if a candidate is lacking in one area but exceptional in most other areas, the application can be accepted.

The Air Force Academy performs validation studies annually, correlating all of the variables in the Selection Composite, as well as the academic component and its separate components, with freshman GPA. Validities for the academic variables typically range from a low of .48 to a high of .62. More specific information on validity, validity for subgroups, and weighting procedures is internal to the Air Force and not available for public release.

Air Force Reserve Officer Training Corps. For admission into AFROTC's four-year scholarship program, SAT or ACT scores, high school rank, participation in extracurricular activities, and work experience are among the factors considered. An applicant's intended major is also important, since four-year scholarships are primarily for students pursuing engineering degrees. However, to be competitive, minimums must be met for high school GPA, high school rank, and SAT or ACT scores. If minimum requirements are met, all factors, though not actually weighted and combined, are reviewed by a selection board.

For the other scholarship programs and the nonscholarship program, the Air Force uses the Air Force Officer Qualifying Test (AFOQT) for selection. The AFOQT consists of 16 subtests that are grouped to form five composites, which are shown in Table 4.6. The Pilot composite is designed to assess characteristics essential to successful completion of pilot training, and the Navigator-Technical (Nav-Tech) composite predicts success in navigator training. These composites are used primarily for classification. Verbal and mathematical abilities are measured by the Verbal and Quantitative composites, and the Academic Aptitude composite comprises these two composites.

The 16 AFOQT subtests consist of varying numbers of items. The number of correct responses for each subtest is summed to comprise a raw score. Raw scores for composites are then obtained by summing the raw scores on the subtests that make up that composite. Composite raw scores are then converted to percentiles, which are based on a large sample of Air Force applicants tested in the late 1970s.

In a recent validation study of the AFOQT for nonrated officers, each of the five composites was correlated with final school grade in one of 37 nonrated technical training courses. Statistically significant positive correlations were obtained for the majority of variables. Most correlations ranged from .20 to .40 (Arth, 1986). In another study, a meta-analysis was conducted on 47 validities of the AFOQT for nonrated specialties producing a mean weighted coefficient of .39 (Hartke & Short, 1986). A study of subgroup validities for the AFOQT is being conducted currently at the Air Force Human Resources Laboratory.

For the two-, two and one-half-, three-, and three and one-half-year AFROTC scholarships, the same basic procedures for selection are followed as with the four-year scholarship program—that is, certain minimums must be met and then the whole person package is reviewed. The major differences are that college GPA is used instead of high school GPA, and AFOQT scores (Verbal and Quantitative) are required.

For selection into nonscholarship AFROTC, applicants are given a Quality Index score. This score comprises four factors that are assigned approximately equal weights: Detachment Commander's rating, cumulative GPA, SAT or ACT score, and AFOQT scores (Academic Aptitude composite score, Quantitative score, and Verbal score). Weights were derived using multiple regression analyses. There are no minimum requirements for GPA, SAT score, or ACT score. These variables are simply weighted into the Quality Index score. The Air Force-required minimum AFOQT scores are applied so that an applicant must meet the cut-off scores to be eligible to apply.

It should be noted that all AFROTC participants eventually must have a Quality Index score. The Quality Index score is used for admission into the

Table 4.6
Construction of AFOQT Form O Composites

AFOQT SUBTESTS	PILOT	NAVIGATOR-TECHNICAL	AFOQT COMPOSITES ACADEMIC APTITUDE	VERBAL	QUANTITATIVE
Verbal Analogies	X		X	X	
Arithmetic Reasoning		X	X		X
Reading Comprehension			X	X	
Data Interpretation		X	X		X
Word Knowledge			X	X	
Math Knowledge		X	X		X
Mechanical Comprehension	X	X			
Electrical Maze	X	X			
Scale Reading	X	X			
Instrument Comprehension	X				
Block Counting	X	X			
Table Reading	X	X			
Aviation Information	X				
Rotated Blocks		X			
General Science		X			
Hidden Figures		X			

Source: Arth (1986).

last two years of AFROTC, the Professional Officer Course (POC), when students actually contract with the Air Force, agreeing to serve upon commissioning. Ultimately, even the four-year scholarship students will take the AFOQT to compete for entry into POC and keep their scholarships.

Air Force Officer Training School. Entry into Air Force OTS also requires meeting the Air Force minimum AFOQT scores. Applications of candidates who meet minimum scores go to a central selection board where they are rated. The selection board considers such factors as education level, GPA, AFOQT scores, college major, work/military experience, and leadership potential, though there is no weighting formula that produces a numerical value.

As is evident in this documentation of officer selection tests, obtaining quality personnel is of primary importance to all of the services. For this reason much time and effort has been expended to develop valid selection methods. Aptitude tests are heavily relied upon to identify those who are likely to succeed as military officers. An historical review of the development of the services' officer aptitude selection tests, provided in the following section, gives some insight as to why such measures are important.

BRIEF HISTORICAL REVIEW OF OFFICER SELECTION TESTS

Officer aptitude selection tests were developed to meet the specific needs of each service. Much of the initial impetus for developing such tests arose from the tremendous demands for officer personnel that came with World War II. High attrition rates and less-than-adequate performance pointed to the need for a relatively quick, cost-effective, and accurate means of selecting quality officer personnel. Over the years, the services have invested great efforts toward developing their selection instruments and these efforts resulted in the officer selection practices of today. This historical overview is intended to outline the major developments of the various officer selection tests and to show how the current tests evolved.

The Officer Selection Battery

In 1955 the U.S. Army Research Institute for the Behavioral and Social Sciences, then called the Personnel Research Office (USAPRO), initiated a large-scale research effort called the Officer Prediction Task (Willemin, 1962). The purpose of this effort was to provide the Army "improved techniques and prerequisites for selecting officers who have aptitudes and other characteristics to meet the differing demands of successful performance in different kinds of asssignment" (Willemin, 1964). The emphasis of the research was on the development of a test battery that would be differentially predictive—that is, would predict performance in specific assignment areas. Prior to this time, selection and classification of Army officers was based on the theory that broadly trained officers could generalize their knowledge and skills to any assignment (Willemin, 1962). The U.S. Army Behavioral Science Research Laboratory (BESRL), also ARI under a different name, undertook this longitudinal study which would span a decade.

The Officer Prediction Task began with the development of the Differential Officer Leadership Experimental Test Battery (DOL), a test that took three days to administer. The DOL was administered to over 6,000 lieutenants in 1958 and 1959, and validated against their performance ratings after 18 months of service. Results of these administrations led to the development of the Differential Officer Battery (DOB), which was a shortened version of the DOL and took two days to administer. The DOB was administered to 4,000 lietutenants in 1962 and, as with the DOL sample, performance ratings were obtained after 18 months. In addition, 900 of the lieutenants who took the DOB reported to the Officer Evaluation Center (OEC) at Fort McClellan, Alabama, after approximately 18 months of service. This provided more extensive performance measures to be used in validation efforts.

The Differential Officer Performance Battery (DOPB) was used as the performance measure at the OEC. The DOPB consisted of 15 situational performance tests that were administered under conditions of total simulation. The officers were called into simulated emergency situations and required to perform under stressful conditions (e.g., little sleep, abrasive superiors, and commanding troops in simulated combat situations) while, unknown to them, they were being evaluated on three major factors. These factors were derived from BESRL's job analysis of 400 Army officer military occupational specialties. Three broad areas were identified as the most differential: combat, administrative, and technical. The 15 situational tests of the DOPB were divided equally among these three areas (Willemin, 1967). The data obtained from the Officer Prediction Task were then analyzed to identify factors that were most differentially predictive.

The Cadet Evaluation Battery (CEB) was developed by ARI as a result of the Officer Prediction study. Essentially, the CEB was a refined and shortened version of the DOB, measuring cognitive abilities and interest in three areas: combat leadership, technical-managerial leadership, and career potential (Rumsey & Mohr, 1978). The Technical-Managerial Leadership (cognitive) subtest of the CEB was used for selection into advanced ROTC from 1972 through 1983. The CEB was then renamed the Officer Selection Battery Forms 1 and 2 which is currently used for selection into Army OCS.

In a validation study conducted through ARI for the OSB 1&2, the multiple correlation coefficient for the entire test battery and grades in Officer

Basic Course was .42. The coefficient for the specific subtest used in the selection of officer candidates (the Technical-Managerial Leadership cognitive subtest) was .29. Both coefficients are significant at the $\alpha = .01$ level (Gilbert, 1978).

As noted previously (in subsection "Army Reserve Officer Training Corps" of the main section "Officer Aptitude Selection Measures"), the Officer Selection Battery Forms 3 and 4 is a brand new test, separate from the OSB 1&2. ARI began developing the OSB 3&4 in the early 1980s with a job analysis to develop criterion constructs. This job analysis consisted of interviews with Army lieutenants to determine what activities were required of their positions, and interviews with supervising captains to develop a list of critical incidents of both successful and unsuccessful performance. The performance dimensions developed through these two methods were then evaluated on relevance and importance by another 89 captains. The resulting performance dimensions were combined to form a list of criterion constructs that was then compared to recent literature on the job dimensions of Army lieutenants. The final set of dimensions is as listed in the "Army ROTC" subsection.

A pool of 1,400 test items was developed based on test content derived from the performance dimensions. Item difficulty was established according to the test target population—college sophomores. A total of 8,778 ROTC students, primarily juniors, was tested at 233 schools. This sample was stratified for race and gender composition. Faculty ratings of overall officer potential, assessed through a standardized Cadet Rating Form covering the identified performance dimensions, were obtained for the sample and served as the criterion. Final items were chosen to comprise two parallel forms of the test, 110 items per form, based on item external validity, item content, and difficulty.

These forms were then administered to a standardization sample of 2,836 ROTC sophomores. Measures of internal consistency, assessed using coefficient alpha, were .92 for Form 3 and .94 for Form 4. A portion of the schools in the standardization sample completed the Cadet Rating Form, providing a criterion measure for estimating validity. The coefficient for Form 3 was .26, and for Form 4, .28. Form 3 was additionally administered to 577 Army lieutenants enrolled in Officer Basic Course and the resulting validity coefficient with OBC final grades was .52 (Fischl et al., 1986).

The Navy and Marine Corps Aviation Selection Test Battery

A comprehensive treatment of test instruments used in aviator selection is presented in Chapter 5. This section contains an historical overview of one service research program to evaluate aviator candidates.

Research on the selection of Navy aviator candidates began in the 1920s. At this time, selection of flight candidates was primarily based on physical standards as assessed by medical examiners. It became apparent that simply using physiological standards for selection was inadequate since those passing the physical were not in all cases successful in flight school. So a psychological interview of sorts was incorporated into the medical examination. Based on several studies conducted at the time, medical examiners attempted to assess such attributes as an individual's character, motivation, and intelligence. In light of high attrition rates of flight candidates and data on World War I pilot casualties, which indicated that human error was more often the cause than mechanical failure, it was obvious that a standardized method of psychological assessment was necessary.

In 1939 the Civilian Pilot Training (CPT) program was developed by the Committee on Selection and Training of Aircraft Pilots. The committee was initiated by the National Research Council and funded through the Civil Aeronautics Administration. This program was intended to develop a civilian pilot combat force that would be suitable for Army and Navy flight programs. Selection variables examined in the course of developing the CPT program included biographical inventories, psychomotor tests, and paper-and-pencil cognitive tests. Predictive validities were difficult to obtain because of a lack of good criterion measures, a problem that plagued the Navy's earlier attempts to develop valid selection measures (North & Griffin, 1977).

With World War II came increasing demands for Naval aviators, and because of the high cost involved in training aviators, the Navy had to develop selection procedures that would minimize failure in training. That selection procedure came to be developed as a result of the Pensacola 1000 Aviator Study. This study evaluated the predictive validities of roughly 60 psychological, psychomotor, and physical tests using more than 900 Naval flight candidates. As was suspected during earlier Naval research, physical tests showed very little predictive utility. Based on the findings of the study, three tests were chosen to be incorporated into a Naval selection battery: the Wonderlic Personnel Test (PT), the Bennett Mechanical Comprehension Test (MCT), and the Purdue Biographical Inventory (BI). These paper-and-pencil tests were initially used in the CPT program. Although results from the study indicated that psychomotor tests were useful in predicting flight performance, they were never used as selection devices by the Navy because they were expensive, not easily administered, and tended to be unreliable measures.

In 1942 the first Naval aviation selection test battery was implemented. The BI and the MCT were combined to make up the Flight Aptitude Rating. The following year, the PT was replaced with the Aviation Classification

Test (ACT), a test of general intelligence that included judgment, arithmetic, vocabulary, meter-reading and checking. The Aviation Classification Test and the Flight Aptitude Rating were refined and the new forms were implemented in 1944.

In 1945 the Chief of Naval Air Training (CNATRA) requested the BUMED to conduct more research on the Navy's aviation selection instruments because of refined training techniques. Additionally, CNATRA wanted measures that would serve to select candidates with officer potential. In response, the Pilot Candidate Selection Research Program (PCSRP) was initiated and became operational in 1947. This research led to the revised Aviation Selection Test Battery (ASTB), which was implemented in 1953. Since results showed that spatial orientation was a significant differentiating trait for aviation training, the Spatial Apperception Test was included in the ASTB. New forms of the Aviation Classification Test that contained more items and had higher reliability coefficients were incorporated and renamed the Aviation Qualification Test. Although no significant changes are noted in the MCT or the BI, previous forms were replaced with new ones. So the 1953 version consisted of the AQT, MCT, BI, and Spatial Apperception Test.

In 1971 a revised ASTB was implemented. Educational Testing Service had revised SAT and the BI and BUMED revised the AQT and MCT. In 1972 the Officer Aptitude Rating was introduced for use in the selection of nonaviation officer candidates. The OAR consists of combined AQT and MCT scores (personal communication, September 1986).

The Air Force Officer Qualifying Test

The Air Force Officer Qualifying Test has a long history of extensive research and development, which began with the establishment of the Aviation Psychology Program in the early 1940s. Prior to U.S. involvement in World War II the Army Air Corps (the Air Force's predecessor) began to expand, and with World War II came an increasing demand for aircrew personnel (pilots, navigators, and bombardiers), and thus the need for selection and classification methods that would bring in the necessary manpower but assure the quality of personnel as well. The mission of the Aviation Psychology Program was to develop these selection methods.

Before the tremendous demand for aircrew personnel became apparent, candidates for aircrew training were required to have completed two years of college. In 1941 this requirement was dropped because of the limitations it imposed on the applicant population. The Aviation Psychology Program then developed the Aviation Cadet Qualifying Examination (ACQE) for screening aircrew officers to replace the two-year college requirement

(Flanagan, 1948), and it was used until 1947. The ACQE was useful in prediction training but selection and classification methods for identifying quality aircrew members was still needed.

Also developed by the Aviation Psychology Program was the Aircrew Classification Battery (ACB) in 1942. The ACB was not only used for classification but for selection of aircrew members as well. It consisted of both paper-and-pencil tests and psychomotor tests. In 1943 the Officer Quality score was included, a composite that is currently the Academic Aptitude composite of the AFOQT. The 1944 version of the ACB included revisions of the composites to include a total of seven, which included two separate Pilot composites and three separate Gunner composites. The final version of the ACB, developed in 1945, combined the three Gunner composites into one (DuBois, 1947). Since the applicant flow had decreased significantly after the war, in 1947 the ACB was discontinued and those applicants having the required two years of college and a passing score on the ACQE were accepted.

The following year, an experimental test called the Aviation Cadet-Officer Candidate-Qualifying Test (AC-OC-QT) was designed to screen OCS applicants, screen for aviation training aptitude, and nonaviation aptitude (Tupes, 1953). This test was revised in 1950, retitled the Aviation Cadet Qualifying Test (ACQT), and replaced the ACQE operationally (Zachert & Hill, 1952). In 1951 the ACB was again implemented for the selection of aircrew personnel. Because the Air Force was growing rapidly at that time, the two-year college requirement was again dropped in order to facilitate recruitment. At this time, Verbal and Quantitative composites were included in the ACB to predict success in nonaviation officer duties. The ACB was used until 1955 when psychomotor testing was discontinued because of administrative and reliability problems.

The AFOQT was developed in 1951 and the preliminary form incorporated the AC-OC-QT. It was designed to predict success in OCS and to screen for aircrew training. There have been many revisions of the AFOQT since that time, but for the sake of parsimony, only the forms with the most prominent changes will be discussed here.

Forms B through G were developed between 1955 and 1963. These early forms of the AFOQT were normed using applicants to the Air Force Academy (AFA). In 1960, use of the AFOQT for selection at the AFA was discontinued because it was too time-consuming to administer both the AFOQT and the College Entrance Examination Board tests. Form G was the last form that was used for selection of AFA applicants, and the CEEB tests were retained because of their use in civilian colleges and universities. In 1963 the AFOQT-64 was implemented. In addition to some format changes in AFOQT-64, this form had a new normative base using the sample tested with the Project TALENT battery which was developed by the American Institutes for Research (AIR). The Project TALENT battery, consisting primarily of aptitude and achievement tests, was used to survey a sample of approximately 400,000 secondary school students. Additionally, it was administered to 3,300 basic airmen. Through regression analysis and equipercentile equating procedures, TALENT composites and Air Force variables (to include the AFOQT) were related to a subsample of 12th grade males. Thus, a normative base of a nationally representative sample of 12th grade males was derived for the AFOQT (Daily, Shaycroft, & Orr, 1962). The AFOQT-68 included another set of norms from junior officers that facilitated two separate conversion tables based on education level: one for ROTC and one for OTS (Miller, 1968).

Form N, implemented in 1978, had a new normative base that consisted of subjects from three precommissioning sources, as well as active-duty second lieutenants and airmen in Basic Military Training. This sample was drawn to be representative of the full range of ability expected in the officer applicant population, and it is the normative base for the current forms of the AFOQT. Form O, implemented in 1981, is equated to Form N, the anchor test, through common items (Rogers, Roach & Short, 1986). It was decided that because education level does not vary significantly among applicants for a particular program, the education conversion tables were unnecessary and a potential source of error. Thus, education conversion tables were not developed for Form O. Forms P1 and P2 of the AFOQT comprise the first version of the test to have parallel forms to be randomly distributed to applicants.

In a validity study conducted through the Air Force Human Resources Laboratory (AFHRL), the AFOQT Form O was validated against final school grade in 37 different nonrated (nonaviation) technical training courses. Correlations were mostly in the range of .20 to .40 (Arth, 1986). Also through AFHRL, a meta-analysis of AFOQT validities was conducted on 47 different validity coefficients of nonrated positions. The resulting weighted mean correlation was .39 (Hartke & Short, 1986).

As discussed in the previous section, a variety of measures are used to screen officer candidates. College grades, college entrance examination scores, work experience, and the like were incorporated into the selection process as their predictive value became apparent. The use of aptitude measures and other tests designed specifically for officer selection has evolved over the years as well. Although some documentation of the development of officer selection tests exists, there is little (and incomplete) historical information on other selection measures and the development of the selection process as a whole.

SUMMARY AND CONCLUSIONS

The variety of officer candidate programs facilitates the procurement of quality personnel for commissioning. The many dispersed locations, the accommodation of differing education levels, and the opportunity for both civilians and enlisted personnel are all factors that aid the services in procuring "the best and the brightest." Although the academies provide a good method of selecting and educating college-bound youth, ROTC's many dispersed civilian university locations enable the services to procure the needed quantity of this scarce resource. To broaden the applicant pool even more, OCS and OTS draw candidates primarily from among college graduates. The common thread among the various programs is a college education—again, to ensure officers of high caliber. To further screen for quality, aptitude measures are used to identify those with the highest potential of becoming successful officers.

The aptitude tests currently used to select officer candidates are summarized by service and source of commission in Table 4.7. In general, the service academies use Scholastic Aptitude Test or American College Test scores and high school class rank. With the exception of the Marine Corps, OCSs employ aptitude tests specifically developed for officer selection. These tests typically assess not only academic apititude, but such attributes as leadership potential and aptitude for more specific technical areas (e.g., mechanical, aviation). Like the academies, ROTC programs also use SAT/ACT scores, and some use additional measures of aptitude as well. For example, the AFROTC additionally uses AFOQT scores for selection into the Professional Officers Course, and the Army ROTC uses the OSB Forms 3 and 4 for its nonscholarship program. Although the Marine Corps uses the same aptitude measures for each of its officer training programs, one must keep in mind that the Marine Corps does not run its own academy or ROTC. Except for Marine Corps officers who go through the Naval Academy and NROTC, all Marine Corps officer program candidates must have SAT/ACT scores and ASVAB Electrical composite scores.

One might wonder why the services do not use the same aptitude measures for each source of commission. The use of different aptitude measures seems to be primarily a function of the point at which a person is entering the officer training/education program. In viewing aptitude test use across the services, the two officer commissioning sources that are most consistent in terms of applicant education level are also the most consistent in the types of aptitude tests used for selection. Specifically, the service academies all have entering college freshmen and all use the same aptitude measures— SAT/ACT scores and high school class rank. These are traditional measures of academic ability used for incoming freshmen in the academies,

Table 4.7

Aptitude Measures Used in the Selection of Officer Candidates by Service and Source of Commission, 1987

1987

Source of Commission	Service			
	ARMY	NAVY	MARINE CORPS	AIR FORCE
Academy -	SAT/ACT, H.S. Rank	SAT/ACT, H.S. Rank	From Naval Academy; Same Measures	SAT/ACT, H.S. Rank
Scholarship Reserve Officer Training Corps	SAT/ACT, H.S. Rank, College GPA[a]	SAT/ACT, H.S. Rank, H.S. GPA[a]	From NROTC; Same Measures	SAT/ACT, H.S. Rank, H.S. GPA, College GPA, AFOQT[a]
Non-Scholarship Reserve Officer Training Corps	OSB 3&4	Criteria Vary by Individual Unit	From NROTC; Same Measures	AFOQT, SAT/ACT, College GPA
Officer Candidate or Training School (OCS/OTS)	OSB 1&2, GT of ASVAB, College GPA	OAR	--	AFOQT, College GPA
Aviation OCS	--	AQT-FAR	--	--
Marine Corps Programs	--	--	SAT/ACT, EL of ASVAB	--

SAT= Scholastic Aptitude Test   ASVAB= Armed Services Vocational Aptitude Bat
ACT= American College Test   GT= General Technical Composite
H.S.= High School   OAR= Officer Aptitude Rating
GPA= Grade Point Average   AQT-FAR= Aviation Qualification Test- Flight
AFOQT= Air Force Officer Qualifying Test   Aptitude Rating
OSB= Officer Selection Battery   EL= Electrical Composite

[a] These measures used separately or in various combinations depending upon scholarship program-- two, three, or four-year.

scholarship ROTC programs, and general civilian college programs alike. Total, or even partial, provision of a postsecondary education is a large investment for the services, so a primary concern is prediction of success in college. Developing and implementing a selection test is also costly, and SAT and ACT are valid and reliable measures of general academic aptitude available to the academies at virtually no institutional cost.

OCS and OTS have primarily college graduates entering the programs, and all of these use the service-specific tests. In these cases, the services are tasked with selecting the best from among a group of applicants with proven academic success. Therefore, the services can concentrate on assessing more specific aptitudes or characteristics that predict officer performance.

ROTC programs, with the most variation in education levels of applicants, are the most varied in the use of aptitude tests for selection. Similar to the academies, scholarship ROTC programs, with most candidates entering as college freshmen, all use SAT or ACT scores. The non-scholarship ROTC programs, with selection and contracting taking place primarily for college juniors, show more varied aptitude tests. The Army uses its OSB Forms 3 and 4; the Navy's tests vary with individual NROTC units; and the Air Force uses the AFOQT in addition to SAT or ACT scores. Again, as applicants demonstrate a proven academic record, selection testing is more geared toward predicting additional attributes that are related to success as a military officer.

Substantial efforts have been put forth to devise the most appropriate selection methods. There have been many changes in officer selection methods since World War I when screening was based primarily on physical standards. High attrition rates in officer training schools drew attention to the fact that physical requirements alone were insufficient for selecting officer candidates who were likely to succeed in training and as military officers. For example, casualties of flight personnel served as a more drastic indicator of the need for more stringent selection systems. Educational requirements, either a high school diploma or two years of college, were the first evidence of set standards of mental ability. Prior to, and during, World War II, awareness of the need for psychological screening devices that would predict successful performance grew. This period marked the beginning of the extensive research and development of officer aptitude tests. Early efforts included studies of aptitude tests, psychomotor tests, personality inventories, and biographical inventories, to mention a few.

Over the many years, each of the services conducted its research systematically, and with the same basic goal of developing valid predictors of military officer performance. Many avenues were explored and as one approach proved inadequate in the prediction of officer performance, efforts were concentrated all the more toward other predictors. Research continues in the same vein, with efforts toward improving, updating, and revalidating the tests currently used as well as exploring the comparative utility of new selection tests. Perhaps because of the decentralized nature of officer commissioning programs, such research is conducted rather independently, with seemingly little shared among either the officer programs or the services. Although the services and officer programs have varying needs and objectives, more open communication on test development and validation research may be beneficial in light of the continuous efforts to improve officer selection.

The military's system for the procurement and training of commissioned officers is specially designed to obtain officers of high quality. The emphasis on a college education defines a select population from which officer candidates are drawn. The variety and dispersed locations of officer training programs enable the services to target, commission, and train sufficient numbers of the most select of this population. Aptitude measures serve to identify those with the greatest potential to become successful officers. These selection methods are designed to facilitate the commissioning and retention of individuals with high aptitude, high leadership ability, and a high overall performance level.

REFERENCES

Anastasi, A. (1982). *Psychological testing*. New York: Macmillan.

Arth, T. O. (1986). *Validation of the AFOQT for non-rated officers* (AFHRL-TR-85-50). Brooks Air Force Base, TX: Air Force Human Resources Laboratory.

Baisden, A. (1986, September). Personal communication.

Butler, R. P. (1985). "Display of admission variables" (Memorandum for record). West Point, NY: Office of Institutional Research.

Daily, J. T., Shaycroft, M. F., & Orr, D. B. (1962). *Calibration of Air Force selection tests to Project Talent norms* (PRL-TDR-62-6). Lackland Air Force Base, TX: Personnel Research Laboratory.

Davidson, T. G. (1977). *CEER/ACEER as a predictor of academic grade point average* (77-014). West Point, NY: Office of the Director of Institutional Research.

Department of Defense. (1986). *Active force officer accessions by Service* [Table provided by the Directorate for Accession Policy, Office of the Assistant Secretary of Defense (Force Management and Personnel)].

Doll, R. E. (1977). *Estimating the "true validity" of the Naval Aviation Selection Tests*. Paper presented at the 1977 Annual Convention, Aerospace Medical Association, Las Vegas.

DuBois, P. H. (1947). *The classification program* (AAF Aviation Psychology Program Research Report No. 2). Washington, DC: U.S. Government Printing Office.

Educational Testing Service (1987, May). Personal Communication, Division of Educational Research and Evaluation.

Fischl, M. A., Edwards, D. S., Claudy, J. G., & Rumsey, M. G. (1986). *Development of Officer Selection Battery Forms 3 and 4* (Technical Report 603). Alexandria, VA: U.S. Army Research Institute for the Behavioral and Social Sciences.

Flanagan, J. C. (1948). *The aviation psychology program in the Army Air Forces* (AAF Aviation Psychology Program Research Report No. 1). Washington, DC: U.S. Government Printing Office.

Gilbert, A.C.F. (1978). *Predictive utility of the Officer Evaluation Battery (OEB)*. Paper presented at the 20th Annual Conference of the Military Testing Association (MTA), Oklahoma City.

Grafton, F. C., & Horne, D. K. (1985). *An investigation of alternatives for setting second-to-third tour reenlistment standards* (Technical Report 690). Alexandria, VA: U.S. Army Research Institute for the Behavioral and Social Sciences.

Hartke, D. O., & Short, L. O. (1986, August). *A meta-analysis of Air Force Officer Qualifying Test validities*. Paper presented at the 1986 Annual Convention of the American Psychological Association, Washington, DC.

Mattson, J. D. Neumann, I., & Abrahams, N. M. (1986). *Development of a revised composite for NROTC selection* (MPL Technical Note 87-7). San Diego: Navy Personnel Research and Development Center.

Miller, R. E. (1968). *Predicting first year achievement of Air Force Academy cadets, class of 1968*. (AFHRL-TR-68-103). Lackland Air Force Base, TX: Personnel Research Division, Air Force Human Resources Laboratory.

Neumann, I. (in press). *Revision of the United States Naval Academy selection composite*. San Diego: Navy Personnel Research and Development Center.

Neumann, I., & Abrahams, N. M. (1982). *Validation of Naval Academy selection procedures for female midshipmen* (NPRDC TR 82-54). San Diego: Navy Personnel Research and Development Center.

North, R. A. & Griffin, G. R. (1977). *Aviator selection 1919-1977* (Special Report 77-2). Pensacola, FL: Naval Aerospace Medical Research Laboratory.

Petho, F. C. (1980). *A brief description of the United States Navy and Marine Corps aviation selection tests* (Technical Memorandum 80-1). Pansacola, FL. Aerospace Psychology Department.

Rogers, D. L., Roach, B. W., & Short, L. O. (1986). *Mental ability testing in the selection of Air Force officers: A brief historical overview* (AFHRL-TR-86-23). Brooks Air Force Base, TX: Air Force Human Resources Laboratory.

Rumsey, M. (1986, September). Personal communication.

Rumsey, M. G., & Mohr, E. S. (1978). *Male and female factors on the Cadet Evaluation Battery* (Technical Paper 331). Alexandria, VA: U.S. Army Research Institute for the Behavioral and Social Sciences.

Stoloff, P. (1983). *Officer selection study* (CNR 53). Alexandria, VA: Center for Naval Analyses.

Tupes, E. C. (1953). *The validity of the Aviation Cadet-Officer Candidate-Qualifying Test AXA and AXB for prediction of success in USAF Officer Candidate School* (Technical Report 53-35). Lackland Air Force Base, TX: Personnel Research Laboratory, Human Resources Research Center, Air Research and Development Command.

United States Air Force Academy (1986, February). Personal communication, Research Department.

United States Military Academy (1986, February). Personal communication, Office of Institute of Research.

Willemin, L. P. (1962). *Prediction of effective officer performance* (Research Study 62-3). Washington, DC: U.S. Army Personnel Research Office.

_____ . (1964). *Prediction of officer performance* (Technical Research Report 1134). Washington, DC: U.S. Army Personnel Research Office.

_____ . (1967). *Officer prediction research of the U.S. Army Behavioral Science Research Laboratory*. Paper presented at Conference of DA Military Personnel Management Team Chiefs, Washington, DC.

Zachert, V., & Hill, F. L. (1952). *The Aviation Cadet Qualifying Test, PRT 3 and 3A, compared with the April 1951 Aircrew Classification Battery* (Research Note PERS 52-34). Lackland Air Force Base, TX: Human Resources Center, Air Training Command.

5

Aviator Selection

DAVID R. HUNTER

INTRODUCTION

The selection of aircrew personnel, in particular pilots, has come a long way
since Orville and Wilbur flipped a coin in 1903. In the ensuing 80 years,
almost every test in the psychological arsenal has been evaluated at one time
or another to determine its applicability for aircrew selection. This chapter
reviews that research, with particular emphasis on the contributions made
by personnel associated with the member organizations of the Military
Testing Association.

A review of English-language journals and military technical reports
revealed over 200 articles dealing with aviator selection. Depending upon
the principal selection instruments described, these were divided into four
general categories: paper-and-pencil cognitive ability tests; personality, interest, and background information tests; psychomotor and information
processing tests; and light-plane and job-sample tests. This chapter is
organized in accordance with these categories.

The question of why the selection of a comparatively few individuals for
aircrew training has received so much attention has often been posed. Some
argue that this is because of the essential nature of the pilot's job, the level
of pilot responsibility for an increasingly expensive machine, and the pilot's
relative independence of action. In the final analysis, however the answer
centers on money. Pilot training is, almost without exception, the most expensive of the many training programs conducted by the military services.
Two factors contribute to this expense. First, it takes a long time to train a
pilot. Initial training in most services takes from nine months to a year or
more. After that, the pilot goes on to additional training in an operational
aircraft. Although services differ in their opinions regarding precisely when

an individual can truly be called a fully operational pilot, the period varies from a few months after initial training for helicopter pilots to two or three years for a Royal Air Force (RAF) Harrier pilot.

The second factor is the cost of operating the aircraft used both in initial and in subsequent operational transition training. The operating costs of light planes such those used by civilian recreational flyers may be only $20–$50 per hour. However, operating a modern jet trainer or fighter may cost thousands of dollars per hour.

An example may make this clearer. During this period 1981–82 the average cost of a person failing in pilot training in the United States Air Force (USAF) was approximately $50,000. With an average flow of 2,000 trainees per year and an attrition rate of approximately 20 percent, this resulted in a net loss to the Air Force of $20 million annually. A quick inspection of these figures shows that every 1 percent reduction in the attrition rate results in a cost saving of approximately $1 million. Similar losses are experienced by the other air forces, with somewhat lower figures for the Armed Forces because of the lower cost of helicopter training.

These figures show why the services have a keen interest in research aimed at improving pilot selection procedures. Even a test with minimal predictive validity, especially if inexpensive to administer, can result in a significant saving in training funds.

Because of high training costs, each service has developed extensive procedures for screening pilot trainee applicants. All services administer paper-and-pencil cognitive ability tests to prospective pilots. Some services, notably the United States, have developed extensive paper-and-pencil test batteries taking many hours to administer. (See Chapter 4 for a description of these procedures.) However, other services, such as the British, use only a single paper-and-pencil test, and place more emphasis on psychomotor coordination testing. With the exception of the United States, which abandoned psychomotor testing in the early 1950s, all services have psychomotor tests. The use of personality and biographical measures is also widespread, with some services, such as the United States, using a short biographical inventory. Others, particularly the Scandinavian countries, have an extensive battery of personality tests. The utility of light-plane screening prior to pilot training is also generally recognized. Belgium is the only country that does not use this procedure. A wide range of programs exists, with some prospective pilots receiving as few as 10–15 hours of light-plane training, while other receive 40–50 hours. The efforts that have gone into developing these selection procedures and the continuing efforts to find improved means for selection will be addressed in the following sections.

PAPER-AND-PENCIL COGNITIVE ABILITY TESTS

The use of paper-and-pencil tests of general cognitive abilities for the selection of pilots is universal. While some of these tests may have little face validity and only marginal predictive validity, their low cost and ease of administration have led to their adoption, at least as an initial screening device, by all services.

World War I and World War II

The use of such tests dates back to the beginning of aviation, and to the start of the mass-testing movement—at around the time of World War I. Dockeray and Isaacs (1921) reported that the first extensive research program directed toward pilot selection was conducted in Italy. Among the several measures examined by Italian psychologists before and during the war were measures of reaction time, emotional reaction, equilibrium, perception of muscular effort, and attention. While most of these tests were apparatus-based, the attention test used a paper-and-pencil format.

Flanagan (1942), in his review of the selection and classification of aircrews between 1924 and 1942, noted that in the selection battery of 1942 a general mental examination entitled the Aviation Cadet Qualifying Examination was used to measure "the types of proficiency in comprehension and in problem solving which are typical of those required in the training schools of the Army Air Forces." The development of this examination, and that of the other tests that made up the selection battery, was an outcome of the work started by the Civil Aeronautics Authority in 1939 and initially aimed at the training of civilian pilots. A description of this program and its contribution to the development of the military pilot selection program was given by Viteles (1945), who noted the development and evaluation of a wide range of tests, including general intelligence, aviation classification and mechanical comprehension.

World War II stimulated a great deal of effort in the development of more effective pilot selection measures. In a series of U.S. Army Air Force reports, A. W. Melton (1947) provided a comprehensive description of the paper-and-pencil tests used for aircrew selection and classification. Correlations with a criterion of pass/fail in training typically ranged from .40 to .51 for tests of general information, instrument comprehension, mechanical principles, dial and table reading, and spatial orientation.

Fiske (1947) reported on U.S. Navy research conducted during 1941–42 that evaluated the Wonderlic Personnel Test and Bennett's Mechanical Comprehension Test for three samples of approximately 2,000 aircrew each. Correlations with pass/fail in training were almost all significant and ranged from .08 to .35. Fiske also reported a correlation of .43 between pass/fail and a Flight Aptitude Rating consisting of a combination of the Biographical Inventory and the Mechanical Comprehension Test. In addition, he noted a positive relationship ($r = .24$) between training success/failure and previous flight training, and an inverse relationship ($r = -.19$) between training outcome and age.

In his description of research conducted by the RAF during World War II, Parry (1947) cited the contributions of F. C. Bartlett in the development of a General Intelligence Test, an Elementary Mathematical Test, and a Pilot Coordination Test. Selection boards were free to use or ignore the test results as they felt appropriate, but the introduction of the tests did advance the selection process, if only on a modest scale. Because of the increasing demand for pilots, in 1944 a two-day testing program was instituted with 18 paper-and-pencil and 5 apparatus tests. While he did not provide individual validity coefficients for these tests, Parry did provide some validity figures for the combined category index. Correlations were .26 (.47 corrected) and .29 (.47 corrected) between the index and initial pilot training performance and initial ground training, respectively.

In another description of World War II aircrew selection procedures, Signori (1949) reported on the Royal Canadian Air Force (RCAF) program at Arnprior, Ontario. Two paper-and-pencil tests, Mental Ability and Mechanical Reasoning, were found to correlate .06 and .21, respectively, with pass/fail for a sample of 366 trainees.

The Allies were not alone in their efforts to improve aircrew selection prior to and during the war. Hopkins (1944) commented on observations made before the war in Tokyo, Budapest, and Berlin, while Geldard and Harris (1946) described the aircrew selection and classification systems in use by the Japanese army and navy during the war. At the end of the war with Japan, Geldard and Harris interviewed many of the officials who had been actively engaged in the administration of psychological tests and interviewing. They noted that, because of an order issued just prior to the final surrender, most of the records of the Japanese selection and classification programs were destroyed. However, some copies of the various tests used by both services were recovered. These instruments included an intelligence test (based on the U.S. Army Alpha) and a mental addition test. Former Japanese officials estimated the validities of both of these tests to be approximately .50.

Post-World War II

Levine and Tupes (1952) noted that postwar military research continued at a greatly reduced rate and that the main focus of research turned to monitoring the validity of the existing tests, which according to Levine and

Tupes, was around .57–.60 for the Air Force stanine. Slightly lower validities for the USAF stanine were reported by Fleishman (1954), who also reported the validities of a number of other paper-and-pencil tests.

Want (1962) described a study that assessed the validity of tests used in the selection of Royal Australian Air Force (RAAF) pilots. This battery was based largely upon the results of U.S. and British research during World War II and was implemented by the RAAF in 1955. Want reported multiple correlations of .63 with pass/fail, .68 with pass/elimination-for-flying-deficiency. All of the eight tests reported by Want were significantly correlated with the criterion (.23 to .46), except for a measure of verbal intelligence.

In addition to training U.S. service personnel, the USAF also trains many foreign students. Mullins, Keeth, and Riederich (1968) reported a study in which a battery of 24 paper-and-pencil tests and two psychomotor tests were evaluated using 120 foreign students entering USAF pilot training. Except for the instructions, which were translated into 10 languages, all the tests were "language free." Of the 39 predictors, three paper-and-pencil tests (Division, Wheels, and Table Reading) and one psychomotor test yielded a multiple correlation of .53 (p < .01) with the pass/fail criterion.

McMullin and Eastman (1973) reported the validities of a battery of tests used for the selection of warrant and commissioned officer aviators. The Flight Aptitude Selection Test (FAST) has been operational since 1966 and encompassed four content areas: personality and leadership, spatial aptitude, mechanical aptitude and knowledge, and aviation information. McMullen and Eastman reported that this battery yields correlations of .38 and .44 between training outcome (pass/fail) and the warrant officer and commissioned officer FAST composite scores, respectively.

Efforts to refine and improve the Army aviator selection process continued. In a report on the development of a Revised Flight Aptitude Selection Test (RFAST), Brown, Dohme, and Sanders (1981) noted that the development of a revised battery was brought about because of changes in the mission of the Army aviator and because of difficulties (primarily administrative) in the FAST itself. Whereas the FAST had 12 tests and two versions, one for warrant officers and one for commissioned officers, the RFAST had a single version, and was reduced to seven tests: biographical information, mechanical principles, helicopter information, instrument comprehension, complex movements, and stick and rudder orientation.

Brown et al. reported a corrected validity coefficient of .33 for the RFAST, based upon a sample of 178 warrant officer candidates. This is comparable to the correlations reported by McMullen and Eastman (1973), but is somewhat less than the correlation Hertli (1982) reports for the original FAST battery. In a concurrent validity study of 1,618 warrant officer graduates, Hertli found an uncorrected correlation of .29 between FAST scores and an Overall-Grade criterion. This yielded a correlation of .48 after correction for restriction of range. Along with those for the FAST, age, and education, Hertli also reported the concurrent validities of several of the Army composites from the Armed Services Vocational Aptitude Battery, which is used as a preliminary selector for Army aviators. These correlations ranged from .13 to .24, with the best predictor being the ASVAB skilled technician composite.

Hunter and Thompson (1978), in a study of selection for USAF pilot training, described the subscales that comprised the pilot composite of the Air Force Officer Qualifying Test, Forms M and N. The subscales comprising AFOQT Form N were: verbal analogies, table reading, electrical maze, block counting, scale reading, tools, mechanical comprehension, instrument comprehension, and a biographical and attitude scale. The composition of the AFOQT Form N was attributed by Hunter and Thompson to the results of an unpublished study by Robert Miller (1976).

Seven subscales from the battery developed by Miller and included in the AFOQT Form N correlated .25 (p < .05) with a pass/fail criterion in the Miller study, and .17 (nonsignificant) for an additional sample (N = 131) collected by Hunter and Thompson. The multiple correlations with a pass/flying-deficiency-elimination criterion for the two samples were .26 (p < .05) and .35 (p < .05), respectively. Hunter and Thompson reported an estimated validity for the AFOQT pilot composite of .30 to .40 within the restricted sample, and indicated that the unrestricted correlation would be on the order of .40 or greater.

Summary and Current Research Status

Two general results are consistent across the many studies using paper-and-pencil cognitive tests. First, there seems to be little relationship between general intelligence and pilot performance. Several studies have used the Otis Quick Scoring Test, measures of verbal intelligence, and academic ability tests (which typically correlate highly with traditional measures of IQ), with equivocal results. Correlations with these sorts of measures and pilot training success range from negative, nonsignificant, to as high as .34. In general, flying does not seem to require a high degree of intellectual capacity.

Second, there are two measures, instrument comprehension and mechanical comprehension, that have demonstrated consistent relationships with pilot training. Both of these tests have been used since before World War II and have demonstrated validities of .20 to .40. Whether these measures tap some latent ability or whether, as is quite likely given the nature of the tests, they are measuring the interests of the examinees, is open to question.

Table 5.1 summarizes some of the results noted earlier in this section, along with the results from studies not described in detail owing to space limitations. The table provides a ready means of comparison of the

Table 5.1
Summary of Paper-and-Pencil Cognitive Ability Tests

TEST	N	VALIDITY	CITATION REFERENCE
General Information	1000	.51	Melton, 1947
Instrument Comprehension	1000	.48	Melton, 1947
Mechanical Principles	1000	.43	Melton, 1947
Dial & Table Reading	1000	.40	Melton, 1947
Mechanical Comprehension	2356/1818/2073	.35/.32/.27	Fiske, 1947
Mechanical Reasoning	366	.21	Signori, 1949
Math & Physics Proficiency	366	.14	Signori, 1949
Practical Mechanical Ability	366	.17	Signori, 1949
Otis Quick Scoring Test	37	-.14	Lane, 1947
Aviation Information	37	.35	Lane, 1947
Mechanical Comprehension	37	.31	Lane, 1947
Otis Quick Scoring Test	88	-.16	Greene, 1947
Mechanical Comprehension	88	.28	Greene, 1947
Aviation Information	88	.19	Greene, 1947
Arithmetic Reasoning	3308	.10	Fleishman, 1954
Dial & Table Reading	3308	.24	Fleishman, 1954
General Information	3308	.32	Fleishman, 1954
Instrument Comprehension	3308	.17	Fleishman, 1954
Mechanical Information	3308	.26	Fleishman, 1954
Mechanical Principles	3308	.21	Fleishman, 1954
Mechanical Comprehension	108	.22	Bair et al., 1956
General Intelligence	108	-.09 to .15	Bair et al., 1956
Mathematics	108	.15 to .23	Bair et al., 1956
Minnesota Peg Board	108	.24	Bair et al., 1956
DAT Space Relations	108	.10 to .17	Bair et al., 1956
Dial Reading	117	.27	Want, 1962
Instrument Comprehension	117	.46	Want, 1962
General Information	117	.25	Want, 1962

Table 5.1 (continued)

TEST	N	VALIDITY	CITATION REFERENCE
Verbal Intelligence	117	-.11	Want, 1962
General Mathematics	117	.23	Want, 1962
General Science	117	.27	Want, 1962
Mechanical Comprehension	958	.35	Peterson et al., 1967
Academic Ability	958	.34	Peterson et al., 1967
Instrument Comprehension	400-500	.14	Berkshire, 1967
Mechanical Comprehension	1150	.14	Booth & Peterson, 1968
Mechanical Principles	245	.10	Hunter & Thompson, 1978

NOTE: In those cases where more than one sample and correlation is shown on a single line, the author reported the use of the same test with more than one sample in the same study.

validities of various tests. This list is certainly not exhaustive, but it attempts to show the validities typical of the various types of tests, particularly those that have been investigated widely.

At present, there seems to be little interest in the development of new paper-and-pencil measures of cognitive ability. Although some work is under way to update existing tests, in general current efforts are directed at the maintenance of existing measures and the simplification of testing processes. For example, the current version of the USAF Officer Qualifying test has been considerably simplified in terms of number of answer sheets, use of fewer conversion scales, and use of automated optical scanning and scoring. Instead, research emphasis has shifted to the areas considered in the following sections of this chapter.

PERSONALITY, INTEREST, AND BACKGROUND
INFORMATION TESTS

The notion that correlates of pilot training and operational performance may be obtained from measures of personality and other noncognitive tests has been a persistent, if unrewarded, concern of aviation psychologists. The image of a pilot, created usually by nonpilots, of a dashing individual with nerves of steel and a sports car (or motorcycle) parked on the ramp, suggests that these are qualities one could successfully measure.

The 1940s and 1950s

Except for generalizations based upon limited, almost anecdotal studies, little in the way of scientific investigation of the relationships between personal characteristics and background and flying performance was conducted until World War II, although Hopkins (1944) did report that some measures of what were termed *Lebenslauf-Analyse* were in use by the Germans during his visit to Berlin in 1936. The first extensive examination of personality measures was reported at the end of World War II, when Viteles (1945) described the studies conducted in conjunction with the Civilian Pilot Training Program. He cited several studies using a Biographical Inventory for pilot selection, along with a Personal-History Inventory, Desire-to-Fly Inventory, "Ability-to-Take-It" Test, "Self-Description" Test, Strong Vocational Interest Blank, Humm-Wadsworth Temperament Scale, Guilford STDCR Test, Maslow Dominance Test, Projection Tests (Rorschach), and other interest and attitude scales.

Probably the most successful of these measures is the Biographical Inventory, which has been used in many subsequent studies. Fisk (1947), in describing the selection procedures used by the U.S. Navy during World War II, reported biserial correlations between a shortened version of the Biographical Inventory and flight training pass/fail for three samples of approximately 2,000 trainees each. These correlations ranged from .30 to .35. A considerably lower correlation of .06 (N = 366) was noted by Signori (1949) for an Aircrew Information Sheet that assessed biographical data used by the RCAF. For the same sample, an Aircrew Interview Report Form that was purported to assess motivation and attitude correlated .14 with the pass/fail criterion.

Levine and Tupes (1952) reported that the attitude survey was "the best single predictor of motivational elimination yet investigated" (p. 160); with a biserial correlation of .45 for that category of elimination. The attitude survey, along with a biographical inventory, general information test, practical judgment test, and biographical data blank yielded a multiple correlation of 0.62 with a graduation versus flying-deficiency-elimination criterion (N = 430–583).

In two studies of the Minnesota Multiphasic Personality Inventory (MMPI) (Gordon, 1949; R. S. Melton, 1954), no significant correlations were noted between flying criteria and individual scales. Melton (1954), however, noted that one clustering of flight failures was found for those individuals with low scores (T < 40) on the hysteria (Hy), masculinity-femininity (Mf), and hypomania (Ma) scales. A discriminant function computed on the failure and the opposition clusters (high Hy, Mf, Ma) generated a variate that correlated .26 with the pass/fail criterion (N = 935).

In a study of 50 successful pilot trainees and 50 trainees eliminated from training because of overt personality disturbances, Holtzman and Sells (1954) found "there is little doubt that the clinical assessments of beginning aviation cadets have no relationship to a criterion of adjustment in the basic flight-training program" (p. 488). The six tests used in this study were: Background Information, Ink-Blot Test, Feeling and Doing (a psychosomatic inventory), What Is He Saying (a sentence completion test), L-D Test (a group test version of the Szondi Test), and Drawing Test (a group test version of the Draw-a-Person Test).

In an extensive study of personality variables and their relationship to pilot performance, Sells and his associates (Sells, 1955, 1956; Sells & Trites, 1957; Sells et al., 1958) investigated a large number of personality measures. A critical point of difference between this and preceding research was the explicit recognition of the impact of aptitude on initial training success, and the direction of the research toward the prediction of posttraining adaptability criteria. Regarding this orientation, Sells (1956) noted:

Earlier we made mention of the fact that ability factors have been found to be of overwhelming importance in relation to success in flight training. It follows that personality factors are subordinate to ability in this phase. It has also been our thesis that the relative importance of ability and personality factors shifts after completion of training, the personality factors increasing in influence (p. 446).

Hence, the criterion reported in this series of reports was seldom simple pass/fail in pilot training, but rather a global success measure gathered from personnel records (Form 66) to include such items as rate and extent of promotion, types of assignment, extent of command responsibility, types of aircraft qualifications held, flying duties, and effectiveness reports. Another criterion, termed "purified pass-fail," was also used in which "the high group represented both graduation from training and evidence of good adjustment whereas the low group included men who failed for reasons of poor motivation, excessive emotional reaction or overt symptoms attributable to stress in the program" (Sells, 1956, p. 441). These criteria were used in the evaluation of 26 tests, which included both standard clinical instruments and specially developed tests. In discussing the studies conducted to assess the validities of these tests, Sells indicated correlations of .37 to .41 with a purified pass/fail criterion for the Personal History and the Background Information Inventory. Using the published scales of the MMPI, correlations ranging from .10 to .40 were obtained with a purified pass/fail criterion. A special scale formed by item analyses of seven MMPI scales was developed and cross-validated using 200 B-29 (Bomber) aircraft commanders. The cross-validity of the special scale with that sample was .20. In another study of the MMPI, in which a predictor score consisting of the unweighted sum of the psychopathic deviate, hypochondriasis, and question raw scores was formed, a significant correlation of 0.22 was obtained with the purified pass/fail criterion in a cross-validation sample, and a correlation of 0.16 was obtained with an unpurified (traditional) pass/fail criterion for a sample of 442 aviation cadets.

To evaluate the contribution of ability and personality factors to early and late criteria, Sells (1956) correlated the Pilot Stanine and three personality tests with both pass/fail and Form 66 criteria. The results showed that the efficiency of the aptitude predictor (Pilot Stanine) declined while the effectiveness of the personality predictors was unchanged. Sells also reported separately a correlation of 0.23 (p. < .001) between Form 66 criterion and scores from a Self-Enhancement Scale derived from the Sentence Completion Test.

Flying is often described as "hours of boredom separated by moments of sheer terror." Hence, the capacity to deal effectively with those moments, and perhaps with the anticipation of those moments built up during the long hours of boredom, might well differentiate successful from unsuccessful pilots. Voas, Blair, and Ambler (1956) pointed out that flying is generally considered to require an above average tolerance for stress. To assess the capacity of aviation cadets to deal with stress under realistic conditions, Voas et al. evaluated the performance of cadets during altitude chamber training. During this training, the cadets were required to remove their masks to experience the effects of high altitude, but could, if they wished, replace their masks before the end of the exercise. Voas et al. took the incidence of mask replacement, along with the cadets' reports of "ear-blockage" during the descent phase of the exercise, as indicators of low stress tolerance. On a sample of 1,540 cadets, Voas et al. found that "significantly more of those who withdrew [from flying training] because of anxiety toward flying had anxiety reactions in the decompression chamber than those who completed [training]" (p. 397). In a further study of student naval aviators, Bucky and Spielberger (1973) also found that, in a sample of 316 pilot candidates, those who were more anxious, as measured by the

State-Trait Anxiety Inventory, were more likely to drop out of training, and that the more anxious the student, the earlier the student dropped out.

In a study of the use of the Kuder Preference Record (KPR) as an indicator of the vocational interests of naval aviation cadets, Rosenberg and Izard (1954) found significant differences on several scales of the KPR between cadets still in training after nine months and those who had left training. In addition, Rosenberg and Izard (1954) developed a Voluntary Withdrawal Scale (VWS) based upon an item analysis of the KPR. For the 137 cadets in their study, the VWS produced a biserial correlation of .56 with the success/withdrawal criterion. Voas (1959), however, in a study of 605 naval aviation cadets, found a significant but considerably lower biserial correlation of .17 between the VWS and a success/withdrawal criterion. While the VWS also showed significant differences between the successful group and a total elimination group, when differences in mechanical ability were held constant the differences became nonsignificant. Voas (1959, p. 73) concluded that the validity of the KPR was largely due to its relationship to measures of mechanical ability, and that "the vocational interest measured by this inventory does not have an important relationship to success in flight training."

Research after 1960

In an extensive study of biographical items and personality measures, Taylor et al. (1971) developed two biographical inventories and an activities index. These instruments were administered to 645 students scheduled for pilot training at the USAF Officer Training School. A priori key scores from the biographical inventories were found to correlate significantly with a pass/fail in pilot training criterion for only the creativity key, which correlated .10 (p < .05) with pass/fail. None of the keys correlated significantly with a criterion of success versus self-initiated elimination (SIE). Of 30 activities index need scores, only five correlated significantly with the pass/fail criterion, and five correlated significantly with the Pass/SIE criterion. Those scales that predicted both criteria were energy, harm avoidance, and sensuality. These correlations ranged from .09 to .18. An audacity measure was the only one of 12 activities index factor scores to correlate significantly with either of the two criteria. In addition to using the a priori keys, Taylor et al. also divided their sample into development and hold-out groups and developed empirical keys for a number of other criteria. Application of the keys obtained from analyses of the development group to the hold-out group yielded a correlation of .26 (p < .01) between a pass/fail criterion and a key developed to predict the pass/SIE criterion. The pass/SIE key score correlated .32 (p < .01) with the pass/SIE criterion in the holdout group. Taylor et al. also developed keys using items contained in the existing Air Force Pilot Biographical Inventory and Officer Biographical Inventory. The Total Attrition Key score was found to correlate .22 (p < .01) with pass/fail in the hold-out group.

The use of biographical data for the selection of USAF pilot trainees has also been investigated by Guinn, Vitola, and Leisey (1976), and in a follow-up study by Hunter and Thompson (1978). Guinn et al. gave a 116-item inventory containing background and attitudinal items (Officer Background and Attitude Survey-OBAS) to 593 officer trainees slated to attend pilot training. This sample was split in half and four keys were developed from item analyses. The validities of those four key scores ranged from .32 to .40 and .06 to .14 for the development and cross-validation samples, respectively. Hunter and Thompson (1978) applied the Total Elimination and the Flying Deficiency Elimination Keys to the item responses of an independent sample of 257 pilot trainees who took the OBAS while in officer training. They found that these two scores correlated .15 and .13 (both p < .05) with a pass/fail criterion—values that are quite close to those obtained by Guinn et al. for their cross-validation sample.

In addition to the OBAS, Guinn et al. also administered the Strong Vocational Interest Blank (SVIB). Several of the standard scales of the SVIB were found to correlate significantly with a pass/fail criterion, the four highest being librarian (r = .22), army officer (r = .15), air force officer (r = .15), and computer programmer (r = .15).

Hunter and Thompson (1978) also reported validities for the SVIB, but did not give the correlations for the standard SVIB scales. Instead they reported correlations of .13, .16, (both p < .05) and − .06 (not significant), between a pass/fail criterion and three SVIB scales attributed to but not reported by Guinn et al. (1976).

The use of the SVIB has also been investigated by Robertson (1975) who found that naval aviator SVIB scales that he constructed could be used effectively in career guidance and to increase career retention. Use of the SVIB has also been investigated by DeVries et al. (1975), who administered the SVIB, along with the Cattell 16PF, State-Trait Anxiety Inventory, and Motivational Analysis Test, to both cross-sectional and longitudinal samples of USAF navigator trainees. None of the traditional personality measures showed any strong relationships to training outcomes, the best predictor being obtained from an "Attitude Toward Navigation" scale that assessed the magnitude and direction of attitudes toward navigation as a career field.

Fleischman et al. (1966) evaluated five personality scales as predictors of success in U.S. naval aviation training. The scales used were Cattell 16PF, Taylor Manifest Anxiety, Alternate Manifest Anxiety Scale, Pensacola Z

Scale (measure of authoritarianism), and Adjective Check-List. The majority of these personality measures were essentially unrelated to the training criteria. Only the Taylor Manifest Anxiety Scale and Factor C from the 16PF showed significant but small ($r = .10$) relationships with a pass/fail criterion.

Similar results were found by Bale and Waldeisen (1969) in a study of the Objectively Scorable Apperception Test (OAT), a forced-choice version of the Thematic Apperception Test developed by Stricker (1962). The OAT added to existing selection measures in an initial validation sample, but the results did not replicate in the cross-validation sample.

In a study of causes of attrition in U.S. Army Initial Entry Rotary Wing (Helicopter) training, Roth (1980) administered a battery of tests prepared by Elliott, Joyce, and McMullen (1979) to matched samples of attritional and nonattritional subjects. Significant differences were found on three of the 16 scales of the Cattell 16PF (assertiveness, suspiciousness, and practical/imaginative). Roth also reported having given the Strong-Campbell Interest Inventory to the same samples, but did not give the results.

Jessup and Jessup (1971) (also reported in Jessup, 1969), administered the Eysenck Personality Inventory (EPI) to 167 RAF pilot trainees and found significant differences in failure rates among individuals in all four quadrants of the EPI (introvert, extrovert, neurotic, stable). Failure rates were highest (60 percent) among those individuals in the neurotic-introvert quadrant and lowest (14 percent) among those in the stable-introvert quadrant.

Based upon an extensive review of personality measures as predictors of pilot training outcomes conducted by Rossander (1980), Joaquin (1980) administered the Personality Research Form (PRF) to 102 Anglophone pilot trainees in the Canadian Forces. A factor analysis of the results yielded seven factors, none of which correlated significantly with a pass/fail criterion. The only significant outcome was a correlation of .22 ($p < .05$) of a Vocational Preference Scale (aggressive leadership) from the PRF with pass/fail.

Recently, a great deal of interest has been expressed, principally by European air forces, in the use of the Defense Mechanism Test (DMT). Development of the DMT is attributed to Professor Ulf Krach of the University of Lund, Sweden, around 1962. (However, the present author has been unable to locate any English-language journals that describe the development of the DMT.) The DMT is a projective test, in which pictures depicting ambiguous situations that might be construed as vaguely threatening are displayed tachistoscopically many times, with the length of exposure of each stimulus picture gradually becoming longer. After each exposure, the subject must make a sketch of what he or she has seen and give a brief description of the scene. Two pictures are commonly used, both of which feature a young man seated in the foreground and an older threatening man in the background. The descriptions produced by the subjects are analyzed for a number of signs of defense mechanisms. Signs are given weights according to previous empirical relationships to prediction of inadequate adaptive behavior (including failure in flying training) and the weighted scores are then summed to produce an overall Perceptual Defense Organization (PDO) score, which is transformed into a DMT score with a range of 1 to 5.

Stoker (1982) reported two validation studies conducted using RAF pilot trainees. In the first study, which used an individual testing procedure, a nonsignificant biserial correlation of $-.25$ between the DMT score and a criterion of pass/fail in basic flying training was found. In the second study, which used a group-testing mode, a nonsignificant biserial correlation of .12 was found. Stoker noted that the change of testing mode (individual to group administration) may have acted to disrupt the personality aspects assessed by the DMT. He also cited one Danish and two Swedish studies that indicated favorable results for this test. Nevertheless, he also pointed out that individual administration of such lengthy tests (approximately three hours for administration and scoring) is probably not feasible when processing large numbers of applicants for pilot training. Further study of this test procedure is warranted only if a group or computer-based administration protocol can be devised that can retain the validity purported to be commanded by the individually administered version.

Summary and Current Research Status

The results of several representative studies using personality, interest, and background information tests are summarized in Table 5.2. Measures of background information have shown the most consistent relationships to success in training. All three U.S. services include some measure of background information in their operational selection tests, as do many of the European services.

The utility of other measures for the prediction of success in training as opposed to later operational performance (as used by Sells and his associates) is more equivocal. Projective techniques have generally failed to show a consistent reliable relationship to training success, as have other more objective measures, such as the MMPI. Recent studies conducted by the European services have indicated some promise for the EPI and the DMT. However, it remains to be seen whether these results can be replicated.

In particular, the RAF recently conducted an extensive study of the DMT (Burke, 1988). The test protocol was administered by a team of psychologists

Table 5.2
Summary of Personality, Interest, and Background Information Tests

TEST	N	VALIDITY	CITATION REFERENCE
Biographical Inventory	2000	.30 - .35	Fiske, 1947
Aircrew Information (Biographical Inventory)	366	.14	Signori, 1949
Aircrew Interview (Motivation)	366	.06	Signori, 1949
Biographical Inventory	37	.30	Lane, 1947
Attitude Survey	500	.45	Levine & Tupes, 1952
MMPI	935	.26	Melton, 1954
Biographical Inventory	1003/ 3308	.25/.28	Fleishman, 1954
Aviation Interest	2070/ 4509	.23/.34	Sells et al., 1958
Biographical Inventory	958	.15	Peterson et al., 1967
Biographical Inventory	1150	.02	Booth & Peterson, 1968

trained by the test developer to a sample of over 200 individuals selected for pilot training. The results of the test administrations, without identifying information, were forwarded to the developer for scoring. The DMT scores were then sealed pending the completion of training of all the individuals in the study. This study showed little contribution of the DMT to the existing RAF selection measures. Based upon these results, the RAF has no plans at present to implement the DMT.

The USAF, while expressing some interest in the results of the DMT studies, is also pursuing the development of an Aviation Information questionnaire to assess level of interest in an aviation career as a function of level of prior study of the area.

PSYCHOMOTOR AND INFORMATION-PROCESSING TESTS

Psychomotor Tests

Research on how to select pilots began almost as soon as the Wright brothers made their first sortie, and was further stimulated by the need for pilots during World War I. Henmon (1919) and Stratton et al. (1920) reported a variety of measures, including such tests as Perception of Tilt, Complex Reaction Time, and Equilibrium, as predictors of pilot performance. In addition, Dockeray and Isaacs (1921) noted that similar tests were under evaluation by the Italians, French, and British.

Between World Wars I and II, attention was given mainly to measures of psychomotor coordination. Mashburn (1934a, 1934b) reported the development of a "Complex Coordinator" that measured the speed of movement of aircraft-like controls while aligning rows of lights. At about the same time Bartlett and Craik (1939) were working on a device known as the "Reid Machine" (similar to the "Complex Coordinator") for the RAF.

Both of these devices later found service as operational pilot selection devices. The "Complex Coordinator" became the Complex Coordination Test used by the USAF, while the "Reid Machine" became the Sensory Motor Apparatus (SMA) used by the RAF. Data from Williams (1940) support the validity of the SMA as a pilot selection measure, and a large body of data has been reported (e.g., A. W. Melton, 1947) to show the validity of the Complex Coordination Test. Viteles (1945) also indicated that the Complex Coordination Test was valid for the selection of U.S. Navy pilots but did not report specific validities. In addition, Viteles mentioned a number of other tests that were developed as part of the Civil Aviation Administration program, including such tests as the Seashore Serial Reaction Time Test, Ranseen Coordinator, and Snoddy Star Test. Validities for these tests were not provided.

Hopkins (1944), reporting the results of a visit to Berlin in 1936, and Fitts (1946), reporting on German World War II selection procedures, both mentioned the use of complex coordination tests and reaction time tests by the German air force. In addition, Geldard and Harris (1946) noted that the Japanese air force used two tracking tests and a digit recognition test as part of their aircraft classification procedures, while the Japanese navy used two pursuit tracking tasks, a selective reaction task, memory of speed task, and figure regeneration task in their aircrew selection.

In a study of 366 RCAF pilot trainees, Signori (1949) found that a Visual Link Test of Flying Aptitude, which he described as a ground psychomotor ability test, correlated .41 ($p < .01$) with a pass/fail criterion. An updated version of this test, the Visual General Aviation Tester, is used by the Canadian Forces to the present day.

In the early 1950s psychomotor testing was abandoned by the USAF, largely due to the unreliability of the electromechanical apparatus, which at the time was being shipped around the country to various testing sites. Research into the use of such measures continued, however. Fleischman (1954) reported the development of a Direction Control Test (DCT), similar in some respects to the Discrimination Reaction Time Test used by the U.S. Air Force during World War II, and Compensatory Balance Test (CBT), which involved rolling a ball through a tilting maze. Based upon samples of approximately 1,000 pilot trainees each, correlations with a flying training pass/fail criterion of .33 and .21 to .27 were obtained for the DCT and CBT, respectively. All correlations were significant and were supported by similar correlations obtained from studies of the two tests using U.S. Navy pilot trainees.

Fleishman (1956), in a review of post-World War II pilot selection research, also provided a summary of the validities of several operational tests used during the war by the USAF. The best predictor of pass/fail was the Complex Coordination Test (r = .45), followed by the Rudder Control Test (r = .40), Two-Hand Coordination Test (r = .30 to .35), Direction Control Test (r = .34), Rotary Pursuit Test (r = .30), and Pursuit Confusion Test (r = .30).

Trankell (1959) described the use of a measure of simultaneous capacity to select pilots for the Scandinavian Airlines System. Trankell's procedure required the subjects to hold a pencil in each hand and to place one dot in each of a series of circles connected by straight lines. One series of circles was used for the left hand and one series for the right hand. The subject alternately moved left and right hands from circle to circle following the lines. The biserial correlation between performance on this test and success in the copilot training course was .42 (p < .001, N = 363). A somewhat higher correlation of .55 was obtained from a psychologist's assessment of the subjects' simultaneous capacity (based upon viewing the subjects' performance during the objective testing) and the training criterion. Of the 14 tests reported by Trankell, including measures of verbal intelligence, maturity, and tact, the measure of simultaneous capacity had the highest correlation with the training criterion.

The RAF has continued to use perceptual/motor testing for pilot selection since World War II. This has been made possible, in part, by the use of a centralized pilot selection center (Officer and Aircrew Selection Center) at RAF Biggin Hill. The two principal selection tests in the RAF have been the Sensory Motor Apparatus (SMA, a compensatory tracking task similar to the Complex Coordination Test) and the Control of Velocity Test (CVT), a pursuit tracking task with a velocity input control. Knight (1978) reported the biserial correlations (corrected for range restriction) between a pass/fail criterion and the SMA and CVT to be .21 and .18, respectively (N = 183, p < .05 for both correlations). Another test that has been used for the past several years for pilot selection is the Aircrew Film Test. This test purports to measure scheduling ability—the capacity to plan ahead and optimally allocate cognitive resources. In the study by Knight (1978), however, this test was not found to correlate significantly with pilot training pass/fail (r = .12).

More recently, Burke (1980) reported the development and validation of an additional tracking test for use with RAF pilots. However, this test, which used two-axis tracking in both pursuit and compensatory tracking modes, failed to correlate significantly with pilot training pass/fail for a sample of 40 trainees (r = .06). Burke also reported considerably reduced correlations of − .02 and .13 for the SMA and CVT, respectively.

Computer-Based Psychomotor Tests

Following Fleishman's work in the 1950s, there followed a fairly quiet period of USAF research using psychomotor/perceptual tests. This period lasted until the mid 1960s when, under the sponsorship of the Air Force Human Resources Laboratory, Passey and McLaurin (1966) conducted an extensive review of perceptual/motor ability testing and produced a suggested test battery (McLaurin & Passey, 1967) for the selection of aerospace ground personnel. While oriented toward the selection of enlisted technical personnel, the battery contained many tests that were potentially useful in aircrew selection. Shortly thereafter, the USAF instituted a program of computer-based selection test development that has continued and gradually increased in scope.

Sanders, Valentine, and McGrevy (1971) described the first system used for the development of two psychomotor coordination tests in a computer-based format. These tests were the Complex Coordination Test and the Two-Hand Coordination Test, modeled after their World War II namesakes. The Complex Coordination Test was a compensatory tracking task using both foot pedals and a large, floor-mounted joystick. The Two-Hand Coordination Test was a pursuit tracking task in which the subject used two desk-mounted joysticks to control the left-right and up-down movements of a cursor while tracking a target that moved about the screen in a circle.

Valentine and McGrevy (1971), and McGrevy and Valentine (1974) reported the results of two validation studies of these tests. On a sample of 121 pilot trainees tested before entering training, a consistent pattern of negative correlations (error scores were used) was obtained between test performance and success in flying training. These correlations ranged from − .04 to − .24 for the 15 scores obtained from the Two-Hand Coordination

Test, and from − .09 to − .42 for the 20 scores obtained from the Complex Coordination Test. Because of a programming error, no valid scores were obtained for the rudder-bar portion of the Complex Coordination Test in the first study. Therefore, after correcting the fault, Valentine and McGrevy administered that test to an additional sample of 92 individuals slated to attend pilot training. A similar set of correlations was obtained, ranging from .06 to − .33, with 17 of the 25 correlations being significant (p < .05).

Hunter and Thompson (1978) cited an additional, unpublished study of the Two-Hand Coordination Test and Complex Coordination Test conducted by McGrevy in which performance on the fourth and fifth minutes of the two tests was compared to training performance for a sample of 150 pilot trainees. In that study, the correlation between the pass/fail criterion and the four scores obtained from the Two-Hand Coordination Test ranged from − .14 to − .20, while the correlations for the six scores obtained from the Complex Coordination Test ranged from − .15 to − .24. In addition, Hunter and Thompson also performed their own investigation of these two tests as part of a larger study of several potential selection instruments. They administered the tests to a sample of 137 individuals prior to pilot training and obtained correlations with a pass/fail criterion ranging from − .13 to − .21 for the Two-Hand Coordination Test and from − .16 to − .22 for the Complex Coordination Test (Hunter & Thompson, 1978, Table 2, p. 8). In addition, they reported a correlation of − .29 (p < .01) between the pass/fail criterion and a single Psychomotor Composite Score, formed by taking the simple arithmetic sum of the six scores obtained from minutes four and five of the Complex Coordination Test.

Studies that demonstrated the consistent validity of the laboratory-based tests led to the development of a portable apparatus suitable for the administration of the Two-Hand Coordination Test and Complex Coordination Test at field sites. Hunter (1982) provided a brief description of that device, and the results of some initial validation studies. On a sample of 475 Reserve Officer Training Corps cadets tested while still attending university, correlations with a pass/fail criterion of − .14 and − .16 (both p < .05) were obtained with the X-axis and Y-axis control scores, respectively, from the Two-Hand Coordination Test. Correlations of − .14, and − .12, and − .12 (all significant) were obtained with the X-axis, and Y-axis, and Z-axis (Rudder-bar) control scores, respectively, from the Complex Coordination Test. Composite Scores, formed by summing the transformed (Z-score) value for each control score, were generated for both the Two-Hand Coordination Test and the Complex Coordination Test, and were found to correlate − .16 and − .17, respectively, with the pass/fail criterion. In a second sample, consisting of 209 individuals attending the Officer Training School prior to entry into flying training, correlations of − .125 and − .156 were found between the pass/fail criterion and composite scores from the Two-Hand Coordination Test and Complex Coordination Test, respectively. Correlations between the simple control scores and the criterion were similar to those found in the larger sample of ROTC cadets.

Information-Processing Tests

In recognition of the increasing automation of aircraft attitude controls (autopilots, direct-link navigation systems, etc.) and the growing view of humans as information-processing systems, there has been a movement away from the view of piloting as principally a psychomotor coordination task toward a recognition of the importance of other cognitive factors. In this view, the pilot does not simply move the controls in a complex compensatory tracking task, but acts as an information processor and systems manager (compare Hulin & Alvares, 1971; Eddowes, 1974; Leshowitz, Parkinson, & Waag, 1974; Imhoff & Levine, 1981).

This view was reflected in the studies of several researchers concerned with pilot selection beginning with Gopher and Kahneman (1971). Basing their work on studies on experimental psychology dealing with focused or divided attention, Gopher and Kahneman developed a dichotic listening test in which the subject was required to attend selectively to one of two messages simultaneously presented to the two ears. In a study of 100 cadets attending flight training in the Israeli Air Force, a correlation of .26 (p < .01) was found between a three-point flying performance criterion (failure in light aircraft, early failure in jet aircraft, graduation to advanced jet training) and omissions in Part I of the Dichotic Listening Test. A correlation of .36 (p < .01) was found between the same criterion and performance during Part II of the test. In a concurrent validity study conducted at the same time, Gopher and Kahneman found that pilots of faster aircraft performed significantly better on the test than pilots of slower (transport) aircraft.

Recently, Gopher (1982) published a follow-up study in which a group of 2,000 Israeli flight cadets took the Dichotic Listening Test. In this study significant differences were noted between successful and unsuccessful flight training groups on omission, intrusions, and switching error scores. Correlations between the three test scores and a graded flight criterion (scaled 1 to 7) were − .15, − .13, and − .18, for the omissions, intrusions, and switching error scores, respectively. All correlations were significant (p < .01). While these correlations were somewhat lower than expected based upon the previous study, Gopher pointed out that they nevertheless can make a substantial contribution to the selection algorithm as they are essentially orthogonal to the other selection measures.

Another aspect of human performance that has generated a great deal of interest has been the capacity to perform two (or more) tasks simultaneously. Gopher and North (1974) and North and Gopher (1976) have described a procedure to assess an individual's capacity through the manipulation of the demands of two concurrent tasks. Their procedures required the subject to perform a one-dimensional tracking task and/or a digit processing task. Subjects performed each task singly to obtain a base-line performance level, and then both tasks together. During the dual-task phase, the single-task performance levels were used as performance objectives, and both tasks were given equal priority. During a third phase of dual-task performance, the relative priorities of the two tasks were varied, and the desired performance level was based upon performance during phase two.

Several measures taken from the dual-task portion of this test procedure were subsequently found to correlate reliably with instructor's ratings of flying potential made after 10 hours of dual instruction in a civilian light plane training program. The single-task measures, however, did not discriminate between the high- and low-potential groups.

Damos (1978) used a similar technique in which the tracking task was considered to be primary and the digit processing task secondary. Performance on the tracking task was kept constant through manipulation of the task difficulty so as to maintain a consistent allocation of attention to the task. The measure of interest, median response time to the secondary task, was found to correlate significantly ($r = .68$, $p < .05$) with performance on a flight check ride given after 30 hours of training, but not with performance at the 10- or 20-hour levels. Damos attributed this relationship, and the increasing correlations as the training progresses, to an increase in the importance of residual attention and decrease in the importance of psychomotor factors, as the student progresses through flight training. However, the sample used in the study was small ($N = 16$), making interpretation difficult.

In a second study, Damos and Lintern (1979) addressed more specifically the existence of a unique time-sharing ability and its possible relationship to flying training performance. The procedure in this instance used two identical one-dimensional tracking tasks—one task, controlled by the right hand, was displayed. Under the dual-task condition both tasks were displayed. The subjects completed four single-task trials, followed by 25 dual-task trials, and finally, one single-task trial with each hand. All trials were one minute long. Having the subjects perform the single task both before and after the introduction of the second task allowed Damos and Lintern to verify the stability of performance on a single task. Hence, any improvement in dual-task performance could be attributed to the development of time-sharing skills. A sample of 57 flight-naive civilian volunteers were tested using this procedure and then given a course of instruction on a light-plane simulator followed by a simulator performance test. When the simulator performance was correlated with the scores from the single-and dual-task trials a pattern similar to that reported earlier by North and Gopher (1974) was obtained. The correlations between the simulator score and the dual-task performance increased, and the correlations between the simulator score and the single-task performance decreased, except for the last two trials.

Damos and Lintern interpreted these results as indicating the development of a time-sharing skill that, as it becomes more developed, increases in its relationship to the flying training criterion. They further attributed the anomalous increase in validity of the single-task performance for trials 30 and 31 to a change in the response strategy being used by the subjects as a result of having learned a superior control technique (small control movements) while performing the dual task. As they noted, that interpretation is open to question and the phenomenon is deserving of additional research.

In a study utilizing Canadian Forces personnel, Fowler (1981) described an information-processing approach to pilot selection that resulted in the development of an Aircraft Landing Test. This was a simulation, presented on a cathode ray tube display, of the approach and landing of a light aircraft onto a runway. Movement of the aircraft was controlled by a stick and throttle, and the display consisted of a simple representation of an aircraft centered in the display, the horizon line and the runway outline, and power, altitude, heading, and airspeed indicators. Subjects practiced landing the aircraft on the runway for up to three 30-minute sessions, with standardized instruction being provided during the first 15 minutes of the first session. Several scores were produced, including number of approaches to first safe landing and number of approaches to three safe landings in a row. Flying performance criteria were obtained from two standardized flight grading tests administered at 7 and 12 flying hours in a light aircraft as part of the Canadian Forces flying training system. Correlations between the flight performance criteria and test performance for a group (N = 104) with no previous flying experience ranged from .30 to .41 (both significant, $p <$ .01).

Summary and Current Research Status

Psychomotor tests, especially those that require more than simple pursuit tracking, have historically proven valid for the selection of aircrew. A summary of the various tests and their validities is given in Table 5.3. The table shows that some tests, notably the tracking measures subsumed under the

Table 5.3
Summary of Psychomotor and Information Processing Tests

TEST	N	VALIDITY	CITATION REFERENCE
Visual Link Test	366	.41	Signori, 1949
Direction Control Test	1000	.33	Fleishman, 1954
Compensatory Balance Test	1000	.21 - .27	Fleishman, 1954
Complex Coordination Test	1000	.45	Fleishman, 1956
Rudder Control Test	1000	.40	Fleishman, 1956
Rotary Pursuit Test	1000	.30	Fleishman, 1956
Two-Hand Coordination	1000	.30 - .35	Fleishman, 1956
Direction Control	1000	.34	Fleishman, 1956
Rudder Control	120	.35 - .49	Mullins et al., 1968
Complex Coordination Test	120	.21 - .25	Mullins et al., 1968
Simultaneous Capacity	363	.42	Trankell, 1959
Complex Coordination	117	.31	Want, 1962
Sensory Motor Apparatus	118	.21	Knight, 1978
Control of Velocity Test	118	.18	Knight, 1978
Sensory Motor Apparatus	40	-.02	Burke, 1980
Control of Velocity Test	40	.13	Burke, 1980

Table 5.3 (continued)

TEST	$\underline{N}$	VALIDITY	CITATION REFERENCE
Two-Hand Coordination Test	121	.04 - .24	McGrevy & Valentine, 1974
Complex Coordination Test	121	.09 - .42	McGrevy & Valentine, 1974
Two-Hand Coordination Test	150	.14 - .20	Hunter & Thompson, 1978
Complex Coordination Test	150	.15 - .24	Hunter & Thompson, 1978
Portable Two-Hand Coordination	209/475	.13/.16	Hunter, 1982
Portable Complex Coordination	209/475	.16/.17	Hunter, 1982
Dichotic Listening Test	100	.26 - .36	Gopher & Kahneman, 1971
Dichotic Listening Test	2000	.13 - .18	Gopher, 1982
Dual-Task Performance	16	.68	Damos, 1978
Dual-Task Performance	57	.14 - .29	Damos & Lintern, 1979
Aircraft Landing Test	130	.27 - .46	Fowler, 1981

title Complex Coordination, have demonstrated consistent, reliable correlations with pilot training, although there does seem to be a tendency for the correlations to decrease. Whether that trend is attributable to defects in the design of the tests or, as many would argue, to a decrease in the importance of psychomotor coordination in flying training, is yet to be determined. Nevertheless, it does tend to reinforce the present emphasis on other cognitive information-processing skills.

More recent research, drawing upon the interpretations of human performance provided by the information-processing paradigm, has also identified measure of relevance to flight training success/failure. Whether these newer measures will supplement or replace psychomotor measures remains to be seen. In any event several services are engaged in extensive research projects aimed at the identification of relevant cognitive abilities and the validation of such measures against pilot training outcomes. The USAF has produced a battery of tests called the Basic Abilities Test (BAT), which implements the recommendations made by Imhoff and Levine (1981). Several of the European services (including the USSR) have purchased an instrument called the Precise Instrument Coordination Analyzer (PICAR), which assesses psychomotor coordination and some other cognitive factors. The RAAF along with the RAF are looking forward to the replacement of their aging psychomotor test units (Sensory Motor Apparatus and Control Velocity Test) with modern computer-based equipment. For example, the RAF is evaluating computer-based versions of the CVT and SMA. Also, under the sponsorship of the British army, a research group at the University of Hull has developed a computer-based selection battery (MICROPAT) for possible use in the selection of helicopter pilots (Bartram, Dale, & Smith, 1982, 1983).

LIGHT-PLANE AND JOB-SAMPLE TESTS

It is commonly agreed that the more closely a selection procedure resembles the job for which it is being applied, the greater will be its validity. Obviously, one way to select personnel would be simply to take everyone into training, and then retain only those personnel who survive the training process. The relationship between test and criterion here is apparent—they are one and the same. Since that approach obviously cannot be used when there are more applicants than training positions, and especially when the cost of training is very high, one must retreat somewhat from the perfect concordance of test and criterion and select a subset of the tasks performed during actual training. This sample of the available job tasks is called a job sample (or sometimes a miniature job). (For more general treatments of the job-sample testing approach, see Mount, Muchinsky, & Hanser, 1977; and Siegel, 1978.)

Light-Plane Tests

Not suprisingly, this approach to selection has been tried for pilots. The RAF used such a process during World War II, where applicants for pilot training were given a short course of training in a small single-engine aircraft, during which their performance was carefully graded. Their performance during this "grading" procedure determined whether they were passed on to the basic flying training course. Signori (1949) reported correlations of .44 and .39 between assessments made after 7 and 11 hours, respectively, and success in pilot training for 366 RCAF pilots.

In the USAF, Boyle and Hagin (1953) and Flyer and Bigbee (1954) described the results of a long-term study in which 120 students were given 25 hours of light-plane training prior to entering pilot training and were matched against a sample of 120 control students who received no such training. Boyle and Hagin reported that 87 percent of the 120 students who received the training graduated, and that there were only four accidents. This was compared to the control group, of whom 62 percent graduated and which experienced 11 accidents. In the continuation of this study, Flyer and Bigbee (1954) reported correlations ranging from .18 to .51 between success in pilot training and a variety of measures taken from the light-plane training. They found that "flight instructor evaluations made during the light plane phase emerged as the most promising single variable" (p. 9).

In another pair of studies using a single data base, Cox and Mullins (1959) and Mullins and Cox (1960) evaluated an experimental flying program for ROTC university students. While these two studies were not concerned with using the flying program as a selection device, they demonstrated, as did the previous studies, that those students who received the flying program before entry into training had a significantly lower failure rate (14 percent as compared to 21 percent for those students who did not receive the training).

Similar results were noted by Berkshire and Ambler (1963) in a study of 196 students given a one-week Flight Indoctrination Program (FIP) consisting of four flights with a total of 5.9 flying hours. Here, too, the students receiving the training had significantly lower attrition rates than matched controls (overall 26.5 percent for experimental group compared to 32.1 percent for controls). In addition, they found that measures taken during the indoctrination program correlated significantly with later performance during flying training. A further study (Ambler & Waters, 1967) of the flight indoctrination program among U.S. Navy ROTC students produced similar evidence that such a program reduces attrition in training (15 percent attrition for the FIP group, 30 percent attrition for the non-FIP group), as did a study of Canadian Forces personnel by Ingram (1968). In addition, the study by Ingram showed that assessments made during the light-plane training could significantly improve the accuracy of pilot training pass/fail predictions.

Simulator-Based Testing

To move another step away from perfect concordance between the task and the test, one may ask whether the abilities assessed during light-plane training that seem to reliably predict later success in the actual flying training could also be assessed through simulated flight. While simulations do not possess all the attributes associated with real flight—in particular the motion and outside-the-cockpit visual stimuli—what one loses in fidelity may be made up for in increased control of the situation (i.e., replicability of the training and testing situations) and increased reliability of the measurement systems. In light-plane screening, one is dependent upon an instructor and, possibly, a flight examiner to generate the assessment scores. In a simulator, the unreliability of human assessors may be overcome by direct recording of flight parameters and student responses.

Hill and Goebel (1971) described the development of such a simulator-based job sample, based upon a GAT-1 light-plane simulator connected to a small minicomputer. Using that system, Goebel, Baum and Hagin (1971) administered a six-hour syllabus of flight instruction to a sample of approximately 100 students prior to their entry into the T-41 light-plane screening program used by the USAF to determine admission to Undergraduate Pilot Training (UPT). The subjects learned tracking tasks that involved tracing outlines of contours on the wall outside the GAT-1 with a dot of light projected from the nose of the GAT-1, as well as aircraft maneuvers such as straight-and-level instrument flight, turns, and descents. While Goebel et al. collected objective performance data using the computer system, their report addresses only the subjective predictors provided by the flight instructors who administered the syllabus. The correlation between the GAT-1 Instructor Evaluations and the Final T-41 Grade (adjusted to provide a 12-category scale similar to that used in the GAT-1 instructor's grades) was found to be .50. Correlations between the GAT-1 Instructor Evaluations and performance in basic (T-37 aircraft) flying training were .23, .29, .16, and .30, for the Midphase, T-37 Trainer (Final), T-37 Instrument (Final), and T-37 Contact (Final), grades, respectively. Of these correlations, only that between the GAT-1 and T-37 Instrument grades was nonsignificant. Correlations between the T-41 and T-37 grades, as listed before, were .12, .38, .16, and .19, respectively. Of these, only the correlation between the T-41 and T-37 Trainer (Final) grades was significant. As Goebel et al. note, however, some attenuation of the correlations between the T-41 and T-37 grades must be expected, as performance in the T-41 was used to eliminate individuals from training.

Continuing this avenue of research, Long and Varney (1975) developed an Automated Pilot Aptitude Measurement System (APAMS), which consisted of two GAT-1 simulators connected to a single minicomputer. In this system, however, an automated instructional sequence was employed, with no human instructor required. A five-hour syllabus of instruction, administered over a ten-day period, was delivered using computer-controlled film/sound strips in a projector mounted inside the cockpit of the GAT-1. This syllabus covered the function and movements of all the instruments and controls, and worked the students through a progressively more involved series of flight maneuvers, beginning with straight-and-level flight, through climbs and descents, turns, and, eventually, take-off and landing. Feedback on performance on individual maneuvers was provided via a computer display mounted on the nose of the simulator, and all maneuvers were performed without outside visual references. Automatic recording of relevant flight parameters (i.e., heading, bank angle, altitude, etc.) was performed by the minicomputer.

Because of the mass of data this approach generated, Long and Varney elected to use a factor-analytic approach to coalesce the data into a more manageable format. They found correlations ranging from 0.25 to 0.50 between various UPT criteria and the factor scores obtained from the APAMS. While many of these correlations were statistically significant, interpretation was made difficult by the fact that the factor analysis was performed on 190 variables using a sample of only 112 subjects. The stability of the factor structure obtained from such an analysis (the rule-of-thumb is to have 10 times as many subjcts as variables) is questionable.

This aspect was noted by Hunter and Thompson (1978) who conducted a follow-on study using the APAMS. They collected APAMS performance data on two samples of 140 and 116 subjects, respectively. In addition to factor scores, they also generated simple parameter scores (i.e., average pitch angle deviation, average bank angle deviation, etc.), and composite performance scores produced by simple summations of Z-Scores for the parameter scores. Factor scores for the second sample were generated using factor weights derived from the first sample to demonstrate the shrinkage attributable to unreliability of the factor weights when produced from such a disproportionate rate of subjects to variables. Correlations of the simple parameter scores with pass/fail ranged from .19 to .28 for the first sample and from .09 to .28 for the second sample. Correlations of the composite scores generated from the simple parameter scores (in standard score form) with UPT pass/fail were .30 and .25, for samples one and two, respectively. Both correlations are significant at $p < .01$.

Based upon the results of this series of studies, several other investigators have initiated studies of the feasibility of using simulators for selection purposes. Rauch (1980) has described ongoing research projects in the West German armed forces that use an APAMS-like system, while Kells and Joaquin (1980) and James (1985) described similar activities in the Canadian Forces. Researchers at the U.S. Army Research Institute, Fort Rucker, Alabama, adapted the APAMS concept for implementation on an operational flight simulator (UH-1 Helicopter Simulator) with encouraging results (Marco et al., 1979).

Summary and Current Research Status

The studies reviewed here have shown a consistent reliable relationship between performance in flying training and performance in either a light-plane screening program or a job-sample test given in a flight simulator—a relationship that is reflected in the almost universal use of light-plane screening for pilot selection. While some may question the cost benefit of using an increasingly expensive light-plane screening program, there can be little doubt as to the validity of the process.

A recent, unpublished study by the author (Hunter, 1985) showed that of 26 individuals admitted to flying training despite having failed in the USAF flying screening program, 18 (69 percent) failed in training, compared to a failure rate of 26 percent for those who passed flying screening. These results, and those like them in the other studies summarized in Table 5.4, have encouraged the services to keep their flying screening programs, while searching for less expensive but equally valid means of assessing the attributes measured during flying screening. As noted earlier, the approach taken has been to use flight simulator programs. All of the U.S. services, along with the Canadian Forces and German air force, have conducted, or are now conducting, studies in this area.

DISCUSSION AND CONCLUSIONS

As we have seen in this chapter, aircrew selection research has been a topic of continuing, intense interest over the last 80 years. Historically, we find that the operational measures used by the various services are those that have demonstrated consistent validity in the research program. Specifically, these include some measure of general intellectual capacity, usually some measure of instrument and mechanical comprehension, an instrument to assess relevant biographical factors, often a test of psychomotor coordination, and almost always a short screening program in an inexpensive light plane.

Table 5.4
Summary of Light-Plane and Job-Sample Tests

PREDICTOR	N	VALIDITY	CITATION REFERENCE
Light-Plane 7/14 hrs	366	.44/.39	Signori, 1949
Light-Plane	120	.18-.51	Flyer & Bigbee, 1954
Light-Plane	196	.34-.36	Berkshire & Ambler, 1963
Light-Plane 30 hrs	448	.38	Baxter, 1978
Light-Plane	100	.12-.38	Goebel, Baum, & Hagin, 1971
Simulator	100	.16-.30	Goebel, Baum, & Hagin, 1971
Simulator	128	.00-.24	LeMaster & Gray, 1974
Simulator	112	.25-.50	Long & Varney, 1975
Simulator	140/116	.30/.25	Hunter & Thompson, 1978

In addition to these generally recognized areas of measurement, researchers have also tried other approaches, including physical fitness (no relationship), stress reactivity (equivocal), physiology (evoked cortical potentials, again equivocal), age (consistent negative correlation), and education (equivocal). Despite, or perhaps thanks to, these efforts, the attrition rates of the principal services linger around 20 percent. This has led to suggestions that the utility of existing selection measures, particularly of the paper-and-pencil tests used by the U.S. forces, has peaked, and that there is little likelihood of achieving further reduction in attrition through improvement in these tests. This has resulted in the services investigating the use of computer-based tests to assess aspects of human performance that the information-processing paradigm of cognitive psychology has indicated are critical (e.g., Sternberg Test, measures of iconic decay rate and iconic masking, etc.).

An equally cogent argument might be made that the existing selection procedures are delivering to the training programs individuals who are fully capable of succeeding, and that the observed failure rates are due to the unreliability of the extensive training. Precisely what the reliability of a one-year course of highly technical training is, to the best of my knowledge, has never been addressed. Since the observable validity coefficients are a joint function of the reliability of the tests and the reliability of the training, such an analysis would be of considerable interest.

Nevertheless, selection researchers continue to struggle to develop new, hopefully more valid selection procedures, trusting their colleagues in training systems to provide reliable criteria. Certainly, the faith of these researchers seems undiminished, as there are more projects aimed at the improvement of pilot selection under way now, than has been the case since World War II. The U.S. services, principally the Air Force, are investigating computer-based cognitive testing along with more background and interest measures, while the European forces are pursuing the development of the Defense Mechanism Test. Additionally, the RAF is actively engaged in the computerization of its aircrew selection center, and will be evaluating many unique selection instruments over the coming few years.

Intranational cooperative efforts, so long lacking, are now the order of the day. Within the United States efforts are under way to coordinate aviator selection research among the Army, Navy, and Air Force through a joint working group. A similar group is in place in the United Kingdom, and doubtless such groups exist within other member nations of the Military Testing Association. Beyond intranational efforts, however, there is a growing movement toward true international cooperation and collaborative efforts. In addition to the exchanges of ideas and results of studies at the meetings of the Military Testing Association, the Technical Cooperation Program, North Atlantic Treaty Organization working parties, and the various professional organizations, there are also exchanges of personnel for periods of a year or more among the various services. The RAF (Science-3) and the USAF (Human Resources Laboratory) have conducted an exchange program for several years. The German air force and the RAAF also have placed personnel within the USAF for extended periods. Having participated in these programs via a two-year assignment from the AFHRL to Science-3, I can testify to their value in identifying new techniques and ideas and in forming the personal contacts essential to a viable international collaborative effort.

These international collaborations are now taking place, to the benefit of all concerned. Recently, data have been collected in Australia on portable testing devices on loan from the USAF and similar efforts have taken place in Europe under the sponsorship of the Euro-NATO Aircrew Selection Working Group. Beyond the practical implications of these efforts, which may identify improved selection methods and shorten the time required to collect samples adequate for test validation, there is also great value in the opportunity these activities provide for cross-cultural research.

This international and local research must continue if the services are to adapt their aviator selection procedures to keep pace with the changing requirements of military aviation. Gone for the most part is lone-wolf, seat-of-the-pants flying with its emphasis on motor coordination. In its place is externally controlled, systems-management flying aided by computer systems that a few years ago would have filled a building. The air forces are planning for transorbital and space vehicle operations, while the predominantly helicopter-oriented army forces are developing new vehicles to fly and fight at nap-of-the-earth altitudes at night and under adverse weather conditions. The systems that allow these operations are amazing in their sophistication, sometimes overpowering in the requirements they place on the operators, and may well require us to reconsider, or at least reorder, the abilities and skills we attempt to assess in aviator selection. In 80 years of aviation many changes have taken place, both in the technology of aircraft and in the technology of aviator selection. One can only wonder what the next 80 years will bring.

REFERENCES

Ambler, R. K., & Waters, L. K. (1967). *The value of an NROTC flight indoctrination program to Naval aviation training.* Pensacola, FL: Naval Aerospace Medical Center.

Bair, J. T., Lockman, R. F., & Martoccia, C. T. (1956). Validity and factor analysis of naval air training predictor and criterion measures. *Journal of Applied Psychology, 40,* 213–219.

Bale, R. M., & Waldeisen, L. E. (1969). *The relationship of the objectively scoreable apperception test (OAT) to success in naval aviation training.* Pensacola, FL: Naval Aerospace Medical Center.

Bartlett, F. C., & Craik, K. J. (1939). *Report on the Reid Machine* (Report No. 59). London: Flying Personnel Research Committee, Royal Air Force, Ministry of Defence.

Bartram, D., Dale, H. C. A., & Smith, P. (1982). *Leconfield trials of the micropat system* (Report ERG/Y6536/82/5). Hull: Ergonomics Research Group, University of Hull.

Bartram, D., & Dale, H. C. A. (1983). *A description of the fully automated personnel selection testing system being developed for the Army Air Corps* (Unnumbered Report). Hull: Ergonomics Research Group, University of Hull.

Baxter, T. D. (1978). *Predicting undergraduate pilot training (UPT) performance for Air Force Academy graduates* (SRL-TR-78-0004). Colorado Springs: U.S. Air Force Academy, Frank J. Seiler Research Laboratory.

Berkshire, J. R. (1967). *Evaluation of several experimental aviation selection tests.* Pensacola, FL: Naval Aerospace Medical Center.

Berkshire, J. R., & Ambler, R. K. (1963). The value of indoctrination flights in the screening and training of Naval aviators. *Aerospace Medicine, 34,* 420–423.

Booth, R. F., & Peterson, F. E. (1968). *Expansion of the Navel flight officer student prediction system* (NAMI-1038). Pensacola FL: Naval Aerospace Medical Center.

Boyle, D. J., & Hagin, W. V. (1953). *The light plane as a pre-primary selection and training device: I. Analysis of operational data.* (Technical Report 53-33). Goodfellow Air Force Base, TX: Human Resources Research Center.

Brown, W. R., Dohme, J. A., & Sanders, M. G. (1981). Changes in the U.S. Army aviator selection and training program. In R. W. S. Jensen (Ed.), *Proceedings of the First Symposium on Aviation Psychology* (Technical Report APL-1-81). Columbus: Aviation Psychology Laboratory of the Ohio State University.

Bucky, S. F., & Spielberger, C. D. (1973). State and trait anxiety in voluntary withdrawal of student naval aviators from flight training. *Psychological Reports, 33,* 351-354.

Burke, E. F. (1980). *Results of a preliminary study on a new tracking test for pilot selection* (Note No. 9/80). London: Science 3 (Royal Air Force), Ministry of Defence.

_____ . 1988. Personal communication.

Cox, J. A., & Mullins, C. J. (1959). *Evaluation of light plane training among AFROTC student officers* (WADD-TN-59-43). Lackland Air Force Base, TX: Personnel Laboratory, Wright Air Development Center.

Damos, D. L. (1978). Residual attention as a predictor of pilot performance. *Human Factors, 20,* 435-440.

Damos, D. L., & Lintern, G. (1979). *A comparison of single- and dual-task measures to predict pilot performance* (Technical Report Eng Psy-79/2). Urbana-Champaign: University of Illinois at Urbana-Champaign.

DeVries, P. B., Yakimo, R., Curtin, J. G., & McKenzie, J. F. (1975). *Undergraduate navigator training attrition study* (AFHRL-TR-75-62). Williams Air Force Base, AZ: Flying Training Division, Air Force Human Resources Laboratory.

Dockeray, F. C., & Isaacs, S. (1921). Psychological research in aviation in Italy, France, England, and the American Expeditionary Forces. *Journal of Comparative Psychology, 1,* 115-148.

Eddowes, E. E. (1974). *A cognitive model of what is learned during flying training* (AFHRL-TR-74-63). Williams Air Force Base, AZ: Flying Training Division, Air Force Human Resources Laboratory.

Elliott, T. K., Joyce, R. P., & McMullen, R. L. (1979). *The causes of attrition in initial entry rotary wing training* (Report TF-79-B1). Alexandria, VA: U.S. Army Research Institute.

Fiske, D. W. (1947). Validation of naval aviation cadet selection tests against training criteria. *Journal of Applied Psychology, 31,* 601-614.

Fitts, P. M. (1946). German applied psychology during World War II. *American Psychologist, 1,* 151-161.

Flanagan, J. C. (1942). The selection and classification program for aviation cadets (aircrew-bombardiers, pilots, and navigators). *Journal of Consulting Psychology, 5,* 229-238.

Fleischman, H. L., Ambler, R. K., Peterson, F. E., & Lane, N. E. (1966). *The relationship of five personality scales to success in naval aviation training* (NAMI-968). Pensacola, FL: Naval Aerospace Medical Institute.

Fleishman, E. A. (1954). *Evaluations of psychomotor tests for pilot selection: The Direction control and compensatory balance tests* (AFPTRC-TR-54-131). Lackland Air Force Base, TX: Air Force Personnel & Training Research Center.

————. (1956). Psychomotor selection tests: research and application in the United States Air Force. *Personnel Psychology, 9,* 449–467.

Flyer, E. S., & Bigbee, L. R. (1954). *The light plane as a pre-primary selection and training device: III. Analysis of selection data* (AFPTRC-TR-54-125). Lackland Air Force Base, TX: Air Force Personnel & Training Research Center.

Fowler, B. (1981). The aircraft landing test: an information processing approach to pilot selection. *Human Factors, 23,* 129–137.

Geldard, F. A., & Harris, C. W. (1946). Selection and classification of aircrew by the Japanese. *American Psychologist, 1,* 205–217.

Goebel, R. A., Baum, D. R., & Hagin, W. V. (1971). *Using a ground trainer in a job sample approach to predicting pilot performance* (AFHRL-TR-71-50). Williams Air Force Base, AZ: Flying Training Division, Air Force Human Resources Laboratory.

Gopher, D. A. (1982). Selective attention test as a predictor of success in flight training. *Human Factors, 24,* 173–183.

Gopher, D., & Kahneman, D. (1971). Individual differences in attention and the prediction of flight criteria. *Perceptual and Motor Skills, 33,* 1335–1342.

Gopher, D., & North, R. A. (1974). *The measurement of operator capacity by manipulation of dual-task demands* (Technical Report ARL-72-21). Urbana-Champaign: Aviation Research Laboratory, University of Illionois at Urbana-Champaign.

Gordon, T. (1949). The airline pilot's jobs. *Journal of Applied Psychology, 33,* 122–131.

Greene, R. R. (1947) Studies in pilot selection. II. The ability to perceive and react differentially to configuration changes as related to the piloting of light aircraft. *Psychological Monographs, 61,* 18–28.

Guinn, N., Vitola, B. M., & Leisey, S. A. (1976). *Background and interest measures as predictors of success in undergraduate pilot training* (AFHRL-TR-76-9). Lackland Air Force Base, TX: Personnel Research Division, Air Force Human Resources Laboratory.

Henmon, V. A. C. (1919). Air Service tests of aptitude for flying. *Journal of Applied Psychology, 3,* 103–109.

Hertli, P. (1982). *The prediction of success in Army aviator training: A study of the warrant officer candidate selection process* (Unpublished Report). Fort Rucker, AL: U.S. Army Research Institute Field Unit.

Hill, J. W., & Goebel, R. A. (1971). *Development of automated GAT-1 performance measures* (AFHRL-TR-71-18). Williams Air Force Base, AZ: Flying Training Division, Air Force Human Resources Laboratory.

Holtzman, W. H., & Sells, S. B. (1954). Prediction of flying success by clinical analysis of test protocols. *Journal of Abnormal and Social Psychology, 49,* 485–490.

Hopkins, P. (1944). Observations on army and air force selection and classification procedures in Tokyo, Budapest, and Berlin. *The Journal of Psychology, 17,* 31–37.

Hulin, C. L., & Alvares, K. M. (1971). *An evaluation of three possible explanations of the temporal decay in prediction pilot performance* (AFHRL-71-5). Williams Air Force Base, AZ: Flying Training Division, Air Force Human Resources Laboratory.

Hunter, D. R. (1977). Pilot selection research in the Air Force. *Proceedings of the 19th Annual Meeting of the Military Testing Association.*

_____ . (1982). Air Force pilot selection research. Washington, DC: 90th Annual Meeting of the American Psychological Association.

_____ . (1985). *Analysis of the predictive validity of the flying screening program.* San Antonio: Air Force Human Resources Laboratory.

Hunter, D. R., & Thompson, N. A. (1978). *Pilot selection system development* (AFHRL-TR-78-33). Brooks Air Force Base, TX: Personnel Research Division, Air Force Human Resources Laboratory.

Imhoff, D. L., & Levine, J. M. (1981). *Perceptual-motor and cognitive performance task battery for pilot selection* (AFHRL-TR-80-27). Brooks Air Force Base, TX: Manpower and Personnel Division, Air Force Human Resources Laboratory.

Ingram, D. L. (1968). Recent research in the selection and training of aircraft pilots for the Canadian armed forces. *Proceedings of the 10th Annual Meeting of the Military Testing Association.*

James, J. A. (1985). Canadian Automated Pilot Selection System. *Proceedings of the Third Symposium on Aviation Psychology,* 513–519.

Jessup, G. (1969). *The validity of the Eysenck Personality Inventory in pilot selection* (Memo No. 162). London: Science 4 (Royal Air Force), Ministry of Defence.

Jessup, G., & Jessup, H. (1971). Validity of the Eysenck Personality Inventory in pilot selection. *Occupational Psychology, 45,* 111–123.

Joaquin, J. B. (1980). *The Personality Research Form (PRF) and its utility in predicting undergraduate pilot training performance in the Canadian Forces* (Working Paper 80–12). Willowdale: Ontario: Canadian Forces Personnel Applied Research Unit.

Kells, P., & Joaquin, J. B. (1980). *Canadian automated pilot selection system (CAPSS) functional requirements* (Working Paper 80–15). Willowdale, Ontario: Canadian Forces Personnel Applied Research Unit.

Knight, S. (1978). *Validation of RAF pilot selection measures* (Note No. 7/78). London: Science 3 (Royal Air Force), Ministry of Defence.

Lane, G. G. (1947). Studies in pilot selection: I. The prediction of success in learning to fly light aircraft. *Psychological Monographs, 61,* 1–17.

LeMaster, W. D., & Gray, T. H. (1974). *Ground training devices in job sample approach to UPT selection and screening* (AFHRL-TR-74-86). Williams Air

Force Base, AZ: Flying Training Division, Air Force Human Resources Laboratory.

Leshowitz, B., Parkinson, S. P., & Waag, W. L. (1974). *Visual and auditory information processing in flying skill acquisition* (AFHRL-TR-74-103). Williams Air Force Base, AZ: Flying Training Division, Air Force Human Resources Laboratory.

Levine, A. S., & Tupes, E. C. (1952). Postwar research in pilot selection and classification. *Journal of Applied Psychology, 36,* 157–160.

Long, G., & Varney, N. (1975). *Automated pilot aptitude measurement system (APAMS)* (AFHRL-TR-75-58). Lackland Air Force Base, TX: Personnel Research Division, Air Force Human Resources Laboratory.

Marco, R. A., Bull, R. F., Vidman, R. L., & Shipley, B. D., Jr. (1979). *Rotary Wing Proficiency-Based Aviator Selection System (PASS)* (TR-79-A2). Alexandria, VA: U.S. Army Research Institute for the Behavioral and Social Sciences.

Mashburn, N. C. (1934a). The complex coordinator as a performance test in the selection of military flying personnel. *Journal of Aviation Medicine, 5,* 145–154.

_____ . (1934b) Mashburn automatic serial action apparatus for detecting flying Aptitude. *Journal of Aviation Medicine, 5,* 155–160.

McGrevy, D. F., & Valentine, L. D. (1974). *Validation of two aircrew psychomotor tests* (AFHRL-TR-74-4). Lackland Air Force Base, TX: Personnel Research Division, Air Force Human Resources Laboratory.

McLaurin, W. A., & Passey, G. E. (1967). *Critical behavioral functions and recommended tests for selection of aircrew members* (ER-8200). Marietta, GA: Lockheed-Georgia Corp.

McMullen, R. L., & Eastman, R. F. (1973). The current predictive validity of the flight aptitude selection tests. *Proceedings of the 17th Annual Meeting of the Military Testing Association.*

Melton, A. W. (Ed.) (1947). *Army Air Forces Aviation Psychology Research Reports: Apparatus Tests* (Report No. 4). Washington, DC: U.S. Government Printing Office.

Melton, R. S. (1954). Studies in the evaluation of the personality characteristics of successful Naval aviators. *Journal of Aviation Medicine, 25,* 600–604.

Miller, R. E. (1976). *Computer study of AFOQT and Navy Battery.* Unpublished manuscript. San Antonio: Air Force Human Resources Laboratory.

Mount, M. K., Muchinsky, P. M., & Hanser, L. M. (1977). The predictive validity of a work sample: a laboratory study. *Personnel Psychology, 30,* 637–645.

Mullins, C. J., & Cox, J. A. (1960). *Evaluation of the AFROTC flight instruction program* (WADD-TN-60-44). Lackland Air Force Base, TX: Personnal Laboratory, Wright Air Development Division.

Mullins, C. J., Keeth, J. B., & Riederich, L. D. (1968). *Selection of foreign students for training in the United States Air Force* (AFHRL-TR-68-111). Lackland Air Force Base, TX: Personnel Research Division, Air Force Human Resource Laboratory.

North, R. A., & Gopher, D. (1976). Measures of attention as predictors of flight performance. *Human Factors, 18,* 1–4.

Parry, J. B. (1947). The selection and classification of RAF aircrew. *Occupational Psychology*, 21, 158–167.

Passey, G. E., & McLaurin, W. A. (1966). *Perceptual-psychomotor tests in aircrew selection: Historical review and advanced concepts* (PRL-TR-66-4). Lackland Air Force Base, TX: Personnel Research Laboratory, Aerospace Medical Division.

Peterson, F. E., Booth, R. F., Lane, N. E., & Ambler, R. K. (1967). *Predicting success in Naval flight officer training* (NAMI-996). Pensacola, FL: Naval Aerospace Medical Center.

Rauch, M. (1980). Development of selection simulators in the German military aviation psychology. *Proceedings of the 22nd Annual Meeting of the Military Testing Association*.

Robertson, D. W. (1975). Prediction of naval aviator career motivation and job satisfaction from the Strong Vocational Interest Blank. *Dissertation Abstracts, 35* (8–B), 4244.

Rosenberg, N., & Izard, C. E. (1954). Vocational interests of naval aviation cadets. *Journal of Applied Psychology,* 38, 354–358.

Rossander, P. (1980). *Personality inventories and prediction of success in pilot training: the state of the art* (Working Paper 80–10). Willowdale, Ont.: Canadian Forces Personnel Applied Research Unit.

Roth, J. T. (1980). *Continuation of data collection on causes of attrition in initial entry rotary wing training* (Unnumbered Report). Valencia, PA: Applied Science Associates.

Sanders, J. H., Valentine, L. D., & McGrevy, D. F. (1971). *The development of equipment for psychomotor assessment* (AFHRL-TR-71-40). Lackland Air Force Base, TX: Personnel Research Division, Air Force Human Resources Laboratory.

Sells, S. B. (1955). Development of a personality test battery for psychiatric screening of flying personnel. *Journal of Aviation Medicine, 26,* 35–45.

———— . (1956). Further developments on adaptability screening of flying personnel. *Journal of Aviation Medicine, 27,* 440–451.

Sells, S. B., & Trites, D. K. (1957). Psychiatric screening of combat pilots: correction of the record. *U.S. Armed Forces Medical Journal, 8,* 1821–1824.

Sells, S. B., Trites, D. K., Templeton, R. C., & Seaquist, M. R. (1958). Adaptability screening of flying personnel: Cross validation of the personal history blank under field conditions. Washington, DC: *Proceedings of the 19th Annual Meeting of the Aero Medical Association*.

Siegel, A. I. (1978). Miniature job training and evaluation as a selection classification device. *Human Factors, 20,* 189–200.

Signori, E. I. (1949). The Arnprior Experiment: A study of World War II pilot selection procedures in the RCAF and RAF. *Canadian Journal of Psychology, 3,* 136–150.

Stoker, P. (1982). *The validity of the Swedish Defence Mechanism Test as a measure for the selection of Royal Air Force pilots* (Note 16/82). London: Science 3 (Royal Air Force), Ministry of Defence.

Stratton, G. M., McComas, H. C., Coover, J. E., & Bagby, E. (1920). Psychological tests for selecting aviators. *Journal of Experimental Psychology, 3,* 405–423.

Stricker, G. (1962). The construction and partial validation of an Objectively Scorable Apperception Test. *Journal of Personality, 30,* 51–62.

Taylor, C. W., Murray, S. L., Ellison, R. L., & Majesty, M. S. (1971). *Development of motivation assessment techniques for Air Force officer training and education programs: Motivation for pilot training* (AFHRL-TR-71-21). Brooks Air Force Base, TX: Professional Education Division, Air Force Human Resources Laboratory.

Trankell, A. (1959). The psychologist as an instrument of prediction. *Journal of Applied Psychology, 43,* 170–175.

Valentine, L. D., & McGrevy, D. F. (1971). Validation of a pilot psychomotor selection battery. *Proceedings of the 13th Annual Meeting of the Military Testing Association.*

Viteles, M. S. (1945). The aircraft pilot: 5 years of research. A summary of outcomes. *Psychological Bulletin, 42,* 489–526.

Voas, R. B. (1959). Vocational interests of naval aviation cadets: Final results. *Journal of Applied Psychology, 43,* 70–73.

Voas, R. B., Bair, J. T., & Ambler, R. K. (1956). Relationship between behavior in a stress situation and later separation from flight training with expressed anxiety toward flying. *Psychological Reports, 2,* 393–397.

Want, R. L. (1962). The validity of tests in the selection of Air Force pilots. *Australian Journal of Psychology, 14,* 133–139.

Williams, G. O. (1940). *Flying aptitude tests* (Report No. 152). London: Flying Personnel Research Committee, Royal Air Force, Ministry of Defence.

6

Evaluation of Individual Enlisted Performance

ROBERT VINEBERG and JOHN N. JOYNER

INTRODUCTION

The variety of methods used to evaluate individuals in the Armed Forces reflects the multidimensional character of military service. In the course of an enlisted person's career, the focus of evaluation shifts from the development of knowledge and skill in training to the maintenance and growth of technical proficiency in job assignments and the performance of general military duties. Throughout the career, evaluation is also concerned with adaptability to both the diversity and codification of military life.

In training, evaluation serves to show the type and amount of achievement that has occurred; variable instruction and remediation may follow. The quality of the training product can thereby be controlled, and the adequacy of instruction can be determined. On the job, evaluation is used to estimate performance levels and readiness for combat of both individuals and their units. Certification of technical proficiency is often a requirement for promotion. Evaluation of general military behavior and adjustment, like the evaluation of technical proficiency, contributes to estimates of the overall value and future performance of individuals.

It is appropriate at the outset to note several differences in evaluation methods that generate different kinds of evaluation information. In training, written tests of information and hands-on tests of performance are the methods generally used. In posttraining settings, supervisor ratings, certification of tasks performed, and written tests are most often used. Tests used to evaluate the proficiency of job incumbents are based on samples of more or less abstracted aspects of performance elicited during more or less artificial interventions. Ratings and certifications, on the other hand, are intended to be based on samples of performance either recalled or observed directly—performance in vivo, so to speak. Issues in the use of tests center on how best to sample and abstract content for particular purposes of evaluation. Issues in the use of performance ratings center on their reliability, susceptibility to bias, and whether they can be designed to differentiate among different aspects of performance.

This chapter first examines some of the difficulties of establishing criteria of individual military performance during peacetime when combat behavior is actually the performance of interest. This is followed by a brief description of methods used to evaluate technical performance in military training and of current and recent systems used to evaluate proficiency and general military performance in post-training, operational settings. These topics are followed by a discussion of selected methodological and research issues in military performance evaluation.

PEACETIME CRITERIA FOR COMBAT PERFORMANCE

Absence of Combat Measures

The criterion of performance in the military is success in combat. In the absence of this measure in peacetime, suitable performance must be defined, at least partially, in terms of readiness, the skills and knowledge considered prerequisite to success in battle. There is general recognition, however, that a given peacetime assignment will not necessarily reflect the skills and knowledge called for in combat and that evaluation of a person's peacetime performance alone is not sufficient.

In combat specialties in particular, there are marked differences between day-to-day peacetime activities and likely duties in battle. Samples of the actual peacetime activities of individuals in infantry combat specialties have confirmed what is perhaps a frequent impression, that the percentage of time spent in technical job activity is often quite low (Bialek, Zapf, & McGuire, 1977). The frequent rotation of military assignments is intended in part to compensate for the insufficiency of any assignment to prepare an individual for the range of requirements encountered in combat. To evaluate a person's ability to perform tasks not represented in daily duties, tests or test-like simulations must be introduced.

The absence of combat-related activity in the peacetime military, however, makes it difficult to define a criterion of acceptable performance even for a simulation. (In industrial settings, while the exact composition of an appropriate criterion may not be immediately obvious, a connection between daily activity and criteria such as production output or profit and loss can often be deduced, even if not directly measured [see Vineberg & Joyner, 1983].)

Surrogate Measures of Performance

An additional factor that appears related to the military's wide use of tests is the need for both initial and continuing training in many specialties. Individuals entering the military services often possess none of the skill and knowledge that are prerequisite to performance. Training must usually be provided, and proficiency testing is a natural adjunct to this training. Such training often continues beyond initial schooling into the job. Enlisted personnel in many occupations are actually considered to be in training for all of the noncombat portions of their careers. While the job of the industrial worker is to produce output, the job of many military personnel is to be trained. Thus there is ample justification for the use of tests to assess proficiency at virtually all career levels.

These factors are consistent with the high incidence of proficiency testing in the military,[1] a method of evaluation that indicates a person's potential, or capabilities, as distinct from how he or she may actually perform in a job situation. Tests, even those in which the administrator must make judgments about the completeness and correctness of samples of behavior, generally provide greater objectivity, standardization, and precision of measurement than reports of job performance via performance ratings. The preference for testing over rating in enlisted occupations has arisen in part by a concern that performance appraisal be demonstrably equitable — military service having been rightly perceived as a form of public employment well before the current focus on fairness in testing within the private sector.

Methods for gaining objectivity, however, often introduce weakness in coverage, such as criterion deficiency and contamination (Guion, 1965; P. C. Smith, 1976). Ratings, while they suffer the well-known shortcomings associated with subjectivity,[2] are often the only available means for evaluating day-to-day performance, especially when performance results in neither observable consequences nor tangible products or when for other reasons it cannot be easily captured in a test.

The extensive use of surrogate measures for actual combat performance leads to concern for the fidelity and reliability of the measures in representing the demands of the actual criterion. Even in constructing straightforward hands-on job sample tests, performance must be abstracted in some way, often by defining artificial boundaries for tasks. While the distortion of task requirements and the introduction of artificial cues to performance is obviously to be minimized, there are few guidelines for the test builder in how to do so. The impact of variations in fidelity of task simulation on measurement validity is largely unknown.

In summary, at least two reasons why individual evaluation in the military involves considerable testing are: (1) the focus on future performance and proficiency beyond current performance, and (2) the infrequency or absence of activity in peacetime that is the performance of ultimate interest, which leads to a need for surrogate measures and simulations. These requirements introduce special problems in identifying performance criteria and in constructing criterion measures.

TYPES OF MILITARY EVALUATION

There are two main types of individual evalution in the military services: evaluation of the performance of persons in training, referred to in this chapter as trainee evaluation; and periodic evaluation of the proficiency and performance of persons in posttraining assignments, generally for the purpose of screening or certifying individuals for promotion. Posttraining evaluation is generally accomplished annually or when an individual is to be transferred to a new assignment.

Trainee Evaluation

Written tests and hands-on tests are the two types of measures used most frequently to evaluate trainee achievement. Currently, each of the services encourages the use of hands-on tests when appropriate and feasible. Leniency in scoring hands-on tests, however, frequently limits their sensitivity to variability in trainee performance. Hands-on tests tend to be used more frequently in initial entry training, where the focus is on demonstrating fundamental military behavior and procedures, and in training for combat specialties, which emphasizes the acquisition of physical and motor skill.

Written tests are used more frequently in advanced forms of training, where technical information is to be assimilated during conventional academic instruction. Whether hands-on tests or written tests will be used in any given instance is sometimes decided more or less arbitrarily, either in accordance with a global policy or according to local preference. A third type of measure, instructor ratings of trainee performance, is used very rarely.

Trainee evaluation and information derived from it are used for several purposes. Most frequently, evaluation serves to show whether or not the training has been successful. Typical uses are to indicate (1) attainment of training objectives or completion of segments of training and thus fitness to advance to the next phase of training, and (2) completion of a training program and qualification for award of a particular occupational classification:

an Army or Marine Corps military occupational specialty, a Navy rating, an Air Force specialty code.

Certification tests are usually scored in a criterion-referenced manner and reveal attainment of particular objectives; less often, they may be norm-referenced, designating a level of performance relative to other trainees. In addition to being used in the administration of training and certification programs themselves, training performance data are also used as a surrogate for job performance data in validating selection and classification instruments. Two advantages of using training performance as a surrogate for job performance are that the longitudinal validation period is reduced from years to months and that training data are far easier and less expensive to obtain.

Another frequent purpose of trainee evaluation is diagnosis of learner needs, to guide remediation. Diagnostic testing also serves, less frequently, to place trainees within instruction, permitting individuals to bypass training content that may not be necessary for them. When evaluation is undertaken for diagnostic purposes it is, of course, being used in a criterion-referenced manner.

A third purpose of evaluation during training is to determine the comparative or absolute effectiveness of instruction itself. The systematic use of trainee performance data to monitor instructional effectiveness has been a cardinal tenet of service directives (e.g., Instructional System Development) for the design and quality control of training. There is evidence, however, that the use of information from trainee evaluation to adjust training content or method is in fact fairly rare (Vineberg and Joyner, 1980).

Periodic Evaluation

Posttraining evaluation methods parallel those used in training—written tests, hands-on tests, and ratings—but the order of frequency of use is different. Written tests, usually multiple-choice, remain the primary means of evaluating technical proficiency. Hands-on tests are used far less frequently than in training. One reason often cited for the infrequent use of hands-on tests is their high cost of development and administration. Another is the difficulty of maintaining uniform administration conditions and procedures and standardized scoring, when hands-on tests are administered by different persons in widely scattered locations. Control of procedures is more readily attainable in a restricted school setting. A major exception to the infrequent use of hands-on tests in periodic evaluation is the recently introduced Hands-on Component (HOC) of the Army's Skill Qualification Test program described later in this chapter.

One rating method that is used in several of the services in posttraining evaluation is certification of technical proficiency for particular tasks, skills, and knowledge. Supervisors confirm that they have observed performance in which the pertinent behavior has been displayed by endorsing a checklist or record. This procedure often depends on recall and is naturally subject to considerable variability in application from rater to rater.

Ratings, since they often represent the only feasible method for evaluating actual performance (apart from the evaluation of work products and recollected performance via checklists) play a much larger role in this phase of evaluation than in training. Supervisor rating instruments typically include scales for overall technical performance and such traits as leadership ability, military appearance, dependability, and conduct on and off duty.

During the early years after World War II, partially in response to directives from the Department of Defense, each of the services developed formal systems for periodic servicewide posttraining evaluation of enlisted personnel. In 1959 the Military Testing Association was established to meet annually for the purpose of exchanging information among the services about new developments and techniques in proficiency and performance evaluation. Although each service has in succeeding years refined the procedures used, the methods of evaluation have remained essentially the same and are similar across services. Since most persons to be evaluated are assigned to particular occupations or specialties, each system contains a component that is derived from and focuses on particular job requirements as well as a component that is directed at the evaluation of more universal military requirements. Achievement tests are used to evaluate technical proficiency, and supervisor ratings are used in summary evaluations of performance and personal attributes. The current evaluation instruments and systems particular to each of the major services are described in the next section.

EVALUATION SYSTEMS OF THE MILITARY SERVICES

Navy

Periodic evaluation of enlisted personnel in the Navy is undertaken for two major purposes: to assess the capabilities and readiness of units and to select individuals for promotion. In both contexts, checklists of task and knowledge requirements, developed primarily through occupational analysis, are completed by supervisors to certify whether or not incumbents meet job profiles. Personnel Qualification Standards (PQS) consisting of task statements pertinent to particular equipment and watch station requirements are used to certify individual competencies. These is turn provide a basis for assessing the overall readiness of the organizations to which the individuals belong. Personnel Advancement Requirements (PAR), comprising task statements and training requirements unique to particular rates,[3] are used to certify individuals as eligible for advancement.[4]

The task statements appearing on both types of checklist are generic statements derived from a much larger number of statements in the task inventories used in the original occupational analyses. In addition to tasks that emerge from analyses of actual performance, tasks that occur only in emergencies or combat must be placed on the certification lists. Thus a checklist represents a mix of empirically and rationally determined reqirements.

Examination for Advancement. The major measure of job proficiency in the Navy is a rating-specific, servicewide examination for advancement, a 150-item multiple-choice test of job information. Test items are based partly on the task statements contained in the PAR and in the task inventories. However, test developers also rely heavily on the experience of subject-matter experts with regard to occupational requirements. Test developers regard the generic task statements as too general for purposes of item construction and find the task statements from task inventories more useful, particularly the information about equipment used.[5]

Performance tests are used to establish qualifications for advancement in rate in a very limited number of occupational specialties: sending and receiving coded and plain text messages by flashing light and semaphore in Quartermaster and Signalman ratings, preparing a teletypewriter tape in the Radioman rating, typewriting in Disbursing Clerk, Postal Clerk, Yeoman, etc.

Performance Rating. Performance is appraised periodically using graphic rating scales. The personal and work characteristics to be rated depend on grade level: at lower grades, characteristics include responsiveness, reliability, and cooperation; at higher grades, resourcefulness, leadership, and verbal expression. Performance ratings are made by a ratee's immediate supervisor and then reviewed at intermediate and commanding-officer levels. Rating scales are contained in three separate instruments, for grades E1–E4, E5–E6, and E7–E9. The scale formats have been designed differently for each grade grouping in ways intended to reduce pile-up of ratings at the high end. This is of particular concern at higher pay grades. If the same instrument were used for evaluation of both middle- and senior-level personnel, for example, negatively skewed ratings could be rationalized for the latter group on the grounds that they are superior in performance relative to their subordinates. An additional feature of the scales is that their formats call for the typical ratee to be marked at the middle of each scale in an effort to induce normal distributions of evaluation marks.

Air Force

Skill Level Certification. The Air Force has established a system of performance standards for each occupational specialty and for each skill level within a specialty (training, apprentice, journeyman, supervisor). Requirements are specified for each skill level in the form of statements of task performance, task knowledge, and subject knowledge—referred to as Specialty Training Standards (STS). The STS also define hierarchical levels of application for the skill levels. For example, the four levels of task knowledge are (1) "Can name parts, tools, and simple facts about the task (nomenclature)," (2) "Can determine step-by-step procedures for doing the task (procedures)," (3) "Can explain why and when task must be done and why each step is needed (operating principles)," and (4) "Can predict, identify, and resolve problems about the task (complete theory)." The standards are incorporated into checklists used by supervisors to certify the skill level of their subordinates. Skill level certification is one of three major types of performance evaluation in the Air Force. It provides input to the the Weighted Airman Promotion System (WAPS), which is used to establish eligibility for promotion. The standards are also used in other Air Force programs such as course development for technical training and on-the-job training.

Written Knowledge Testing. Another major type of performance evaluation in the Air Force consists of written testing at various points in the airman's career. The Apprentice Knowledge Test (AKT) is used to assess the technical knowledge of persons with prior experience in an occupation, who apply for direct assignment into a specialty. The USAF 9 Skill Level Upgrade Examination is used to assess supervisory knowledge required at the superintendent level. Specialty Knowledge Tests (SKT) are administered to personnel in grades E4–E7 to assess technical knowledge, and the resulting scores are one of the elements contributing to the WAPS in establishing eligibility for promotion. Promotion Fitness Examinations (PFE), like SKTs, are also used in grades E4–E7, but to evaluate knowledge of training, supervisory, and managerial techniques and general military knowledge. Like SKT scores, the PFE is a component of the WAPS.[6] PFE scores have been demonstrated to be relatively independent of SKT scores (Gould and Shore, 1969). The USAF Supervisory Examination (USAFE) is used to assess the knowledge of master sergeants and senior master sergeants with regard to supervisory and managerial responsibilities.

The development of items for these knowledge tests, particularly the AKTs and SKTs, is accomplished by teams of subject-matter experts and psychologists. It begins with the preparation of an outline of job requirements based on the STS. Occupational survey data are used to refine decisions about test content and weighting. However, "the general wording of most STS paragraphs often does not provide the most exact or refined task statements that would be required in order to develop good test items," and task statements taken from an occupational survey are "sometimes too broad for use in outline development" (Welsh, 1980). Thus, as in the development of achievement tests in the Navy, interpretation of the implications of survey data for the identification of test content is heavily dependent on the judgment and experience of subject-matter experts.

Airman Performance Report. Reliance on the judgments of experts is a generally accepted tenet of proficiency test construction. As Guion (1965, 1979a) has indicated, the sampling of elements of job content to define a job domain is not a matter of random or representative sampling but should be based instead on judgments that are accepted by a panel of experts. Each of these written tests is intended to be used in evaluating knowledge that is general to performance in particular occupational specialty, not to performance that is specific to an assignment (billet) within the specialty. The overlapping requirements of different job situations within a specialty make it virtually impossible to develop separate tests for each billet. The instrument for evaluating performance in a particular situation is the third major type of performance evaluation used in the Air Force: the Airman Performance Report (APR). Like supervisor rating scales in the Navy, the APR is provided in three different forms, for grades E1–E3, E4–E6, and E7–E9. Unlike the Navy scales, the same format is used for all three levels: six 10-point graphic scales for the evaluation of particular characteristics and one 10-point scale for providing an overall evaluation. The characteristics to be evaluated vary somewhat: for example, the E1–E3 instrument includes Self-Improvement Efforts; E4–E6, Supervisor Ability; and E7–E9, Executive Ability. Each rated characteristic is endorsed by a second person, and the overall evaluation is endorsed by three additional persons.

Army

Army Enlisted Evaluation System. In the last 25 years, the Army has used two somewhat different systems of performance evaluation. Prior to about 1976, when Skill Qualification Testing was gradually introduced, the procedures for evaluating enlisted personnel took the same general form as those in the Navy and Air Force. Paper-and-pencil tests of job knowledge and information were administered to assess technical proficiency, and supervisor ratings were used to evaluate performance and personal attributes. Evaluation tests for each military occupational specialty were constructed at the Army Enlisted Evaluation Center, Ft. Benjamin Harrison, based on test material submitted by subject-matter experts located at Army schools. Like job knowledge tests in the other services, the MOS evaluation tests were directed toward general requirements of an entire specialty rather than toward particular tasks or assignments. The tests were administered annually, and the scores were used as one of two components comprising the Army Enlisted Evaluation System to determine a person's eligibility for proficiency pay. In the later years when the system was in effect, two levels of combined score were designated: MOS qualification and promotion qualification.

Information about the properties of tests that were assembled during this earlier period included correlations between test scores and performance ratings, measures of internal consistency, and measures of the stability of ratings of item criticality. For example, Shirkey and Urry (1965) described the procedures used to validate proficiency tests against peer ratings of job performance, and Willing (1969) described a method for the validation of proficiency test items based on consistency of ratings of criticality of test information. During this period the use of performance tests, as in the other services, was restricted to evaluation in selected specialties such as Bandsman, Radio Operator, Teletype Operator, Court Reporter, Stenographer, Clerk Typist, and Interrogator.

The second component of the Army Enlisted Evaluation System was supervisor performance ratings, called the Commander's Evaluation Report prior to 1968 and later the Enlisted Efficiency Report (EER). Over the years the number of scales in the rating instrument varied from 4 to 12, including scales for cooperativeness, reliability, job performance, job knowledge, adaptability, conduct, leadership, and so on (Bodi & Yellen, 1967; Burt et al., 1969). With continued use of the same instruments the ratings became increasingly inflated. In 1975, in an effort to counter this effect, the single EER for all grades was discontinued and two new forms for pay grades E3–E5 (Enlisted Evaluation Report) and E6–E9 (Senior Enlisted Evaluation Report) were introduced (Wance et al., 1976).

Skill Qualification Test. Also in 1975, the Army undertook a major change in the way it evaluated technical proficiency. The multiple-choice MOS evaluation test was replaced by the Skill Qualification Test (SQT), which was to be based on the performance of critical job-related skills. The intent of this change was to increase the relevance of the tests by making SQT hands-on demonstrations of performance insofar as possible. It was felt that the conventional paper-and-pencil tests previously used were not appropriate for assessing performance capabilities, particularly those requiring perceptual, motor, and other skills.

An entire task was made the unit of training and testing, since it was felt that evaluating only elements of task performance, like evaluation of only knowledge in a written test, did not provide a reliable index of performance capability. Whole-task testing also avoided the errors and distortions likely to be incorporated in attempting to analyze, extract, and test only the critical aspects of task performance. This practice of testing led in turn to the concept of scorable units: one or more scorable units would be assigned to a task, given equal weight in scoring, and scored in an all-or-none manner. Greater weight could then be given to particular tasks, such as those containing a large number of elements simply by devoting more than one scorable unit to them.

Where hands-on testing was not possible or desirable, performance-oriented knowledge tests, restricted to the evaluation of information that mediated task performance, were to be used. In such instances, as many test items as necessary to evaluate performance of a task could be assigned to one or more scorable units, and thereby the integrity of an entire task as the unit to be evaluated could be maintained.

The program for development of SQTs called for their gradual introduction into occupational specialties over a number of years. This evolution would begin with a mix of hands-on tests (Hands-On Component), paper-and-pencil tests (Written Component,[7] later misleadingly renamed Skill Component), and supervisor certifications of capabilities based on observed job behavior or job products (Performance Certification Component, later renamed Job Site Component). Supervisor certification was called for in instances where highly skilled behavior that precluded use of a written test could not be tested with a hands-on test because of administrative or other constraints. Ultimately the number of hands-on tests was to be maximized.

The difficulties inherent in attempting to introduce hands-on testing on a large scale in the Army soon became evident. These included not only higher costs and lack of availability of equipment needed to support testing but also problems in the development of tests and standardization of testing procedures—for example, selecting a suitable basis for sampling tasks from a job domain and controlling scorer bias. The SQT component making the greatest, and in some instances the only, contribution to total score variance remained the written tests. One unofficial Army source has indicated that the pass rate for scorable units from the Hands-On Component was about 80 percent or higher; for the Performance Certification/Job Site Component, about 100 percent; and for the Written/Skill Component, about 40-50 percent.[8]

In March 1982 the Army's SQT program was criticized by the U.S. General Accounting Office (GAO) on a varietiy of grounds, ranging from the complexity and lack of cost-effectiveness of the system to the practice of announcing test items prior to testing. Although a few of the comments in the GAO report are somewhat naive, such as faulting the SQT for sampling tasks rather than testing all tasks in an occupational specialty, many of the criticisms seem warranted. The Army has stated that it will continue to use written tests in conjunction with available common task tests for personnel actions while making a transition to a different system.

RESEARCH IN INDIVIDUAL EVALUATION

Issues of interest in individual evaluation in the military are concentrated around measuring on-going performance that is actually occurring in a job, not at the direction of an observer, and measuring performance via an intervention initiated by an observer and not a part of day-to-day work. (Measurement of the former can be accomplished either through analysis of the products of performance or through observation of the performance itself, supported by checklists or summarized in ratings.)

Where on-going job performance is measured, the validity of the content of the observation is not in question, and research has focused on improving the reliability of the major observation method: performance ratings. Where performance is measured via an intervention, the content and form of the intervention must be deliberately selected, and research has focused on how to identify, sample, abstract, and represent the content to be evaluated.[9]

DOD Performance Measurement Project

Before exploring these issues, it is worth noting the progress of an extensive project, which—although its ultimate goal is improved selection—has been the focal point of much military performance evaluation research in the 1980s. The Joint Service Performance Measurement and Enlisted Standards Project was initiated in 1980 by the Department of Defense to link enlistment standards to job performance. The aim of the project is to examine the relative costs and benefits of different entry standards and force-quality levels as they relate to outcomes in military performance.

Because a prerequisite to examining these relationships is the development of appropriate measures of the dependent variable, military performance, improving performance measurement is an integral part of the project's design. Early phases of the project were devoted in part to the development and study of hands-on and various prototype performance measurement techniques applied to a variety of occupational specialties in each service (Office of the Assistant Secretary of Defense, 1985). The prototype techniques are intended as potential surrogates for hands-on criterion tests. (Current project status for each of the services can be found in the 7th Annual Report [Office of the Assistant Secretary of Defense, 1988].)

Brief descriptions of the measurement techniques under examination in each of the major services are given in Table 6.1. We have categorized each of the techniques as (1) job-specific measurement via an intervention initiated by an observer and not part of day-to-day work; (2) job-specific measurement while performance is occurring in a job, rather than at the direction of an observer; (3) non-job-specific performance measurement. These categories are discussed in detail in the sections following; at this point we merely note that most of the performance measurement in the project involves an intervention and has thus been assigned to the first category.

Any further categorization of the measurement techniques according to the schema offered in Table 6.2 (direct work sample versus abstracted work sample, whole task versus task segment) awaits analysis of the details of the instruments themselves and the actual conditions of their administration as well as information about the intercorrelations among them.

Measurement of On-going Performance in a Job

The evaluation of on-going performance is, in concept, amenable to measurement in several ways, including summarization of observations by supervisors and peers during regular activity, evaluation of work products, and records of performance and administrative actions. In practice, however, each of these approaches has drawbacks.

Observation. Inferences about performance based on observation of performance as it is actually carried out by a job incumbent may be incorrect to the extent that the observation is intrusive and the motivations of the performer and possibly stresses produced by being observed differ from the conditions of regular unobserved daily performance. Evaluation of on-going performance usually suffers from a lack of standardized conditions for viewing preselected content as well as the distortions of various kinds of bias and selective recall. Unobtrusive techniques of observation in the military, other than product evaluation and analysis of records, are generally used only as part of experimental interventions.

Work Products. Work products, records, and other objective indices of performance, on the other hand, often do not provide adequate coverage of job requirements. Most military occupations do not generate products that can be clearly attributed to individuals, and standard conditions of production cannot be assumed. The job performance of individuals is not recorded frequently, and such records as are available pertain primarily to administrative actions that provide little or no information about proficiency. Although pleas have been made (Osborn, 1974) for greater use of work products in evaluation—presumably equally applicable to measurement of on-going job

Table 6.1
Measurement Techniques Categorized by Amount of Inference from Intervention to Job Performance

Job-specific measurement via intervention

> Hands-on performance tests of selected job tasks
> (Army, Navy, Air Force)
>
> Tests of performance of selected tasks on equipment simulators or training devices
> (Navy)
>
> Tests of oral descriptions (walk-through) of procedures of selected tasks by interview in job setting
> (Air Force)
>
> Pictorial paper-and-pencil and videodisc tests of knowledge of critical steps in representative job tasks
> (Navy)
>
> Paper-and-pencil tests of knowledge of critical steps in representative job tasks
> (Army)

Job-specific measurement while performance is occurring

> Ratings of task-level performance by supervisors, incumbents, or peers
> (Air Force)

Non-job-specific performance measurement

> Ratings of general performance/effectiveness by supervisors, incumbents, or peers
> (Army, Air Force)

Table 6.2
Intervention Alternatives for Inferring Task Performance on the Job

Direct Work Samples

Whole Task	Evaluate process or product of task
Complete segment(s) of task	Evaluate process or product of segment(s)
Isolated response element(s)	Evaluate process or product of element(s)

Abstracted Work Samples

Knowledge	Evaluate via selected response or constructed response items
Skill	Evaluate via abstracted process or abstracted product

performance and measurement of performance via intervention—there has been little, if any, research directed toward developing methods to reach this end.

Performance Ratings. Most military research on measurement of on-going performance in a job has centered on the development and application of performance ratings. Downey and Duffy (1978) reviewed peer-rating methodologies and concluded that they are highly reliable and have considerable potential for performance appraisal. Mitchell and De Nisi (1976) disagree about their value as operational criterion measures but suggest their effectiveness for validation and other research purposes. Downey, Duffy, and Shiflett (1979) compared ratings of peers, supervisors, and participant observers and obtained low correlations between peer ratings and the others, a finding generally interpreted as a consequence of different perspectives by persons at different organizational levels (Wiley, 1969; Borman, 1974).

Both peer and instructor ratings have been found relatively effective as predictors of success in military training and of subsequent job performance

(Flyer, 1963; Amir, Kovarsky, & Sharan, 1970). Vineberg and Joyner (1982), in a review of military performance prediction, report median correlations of aptitude, biographic, educational, and attitudinal variables with subsequent performance ranging from .12 to .17, and a median correlation of training performance with subsequent performance of .23. Wiley (1966, 1974; Wiley & Cagwin, 1968) has demonstrated both the usefulness of trait ratings as predictors of future performance and the importance of different traits in different Air Force jobs for making a prediction.

Performance ratings of separate tasks have been used to construct an overall job performance criterion and then examine its properties (Wiley, 1976; Wiley and Hahn, 1977). Considerable rater time is necessary to obtain task ratings, and it appears that the procedure may not be economical in all situations. However, evaluation at a task level has the potential advantage of providing both a more concrete focus for a rating and a basis upon which ratings can be related to job analysis information, such as task importance, difficulty, and frequency.

Several types of systematic error have frequently been observed in the use of performance ratings. These include pile-up of higher ratings with continuing use of a rating instrument and higher ratings for persons in higher pay grades even when grade is held constant (Wiley & Cagwin, 1968). For example, the Personnel Evaluation Report (PER), a seven-point rating scale introduced in the Unified Canadian Forces in 1968, was designed to produce a modal score of three. In 1971, "a validation study showed that level 'four' had become the most commonly used level for [corporals] . . . by 1977, the modal score for [corporals] had moved to level five . . . it is likely that some ranks will have a modal score of six in the near future." (*Evaluation of the Canadian forces other ranks personnel evaluation system*, 1982). The studies of Robertson, Royle, and James (1972) and Royle and Robertson (1974) are typical of those undertaken to deal with such problems. They designed rating instruments for operational use in the Navy that reduced pile-up at the upper end of performance by having superior performance marked in the center of scales. In an attempt to moderate stereotyped increase in ratings with increasing grade, they eliminated the comparability of scale formats and dimensions across pay-grade groupings.

In a series of studies, Ramsey-Klee and Richman (1976a, 1976b) developed techniques for classifying information in the narrative portions of Navy performance ratings (evaluation comments and justification comments). This type of analysis provided greater differentiation than the scale markings. The most discriminating factor in the protocols was the number of terms ("index terms") that raters used in describing ratees; this reflected the number of areas of performance selected for comment and provided an indication of the range of skills and abilities possessed by the ratee. Factors discriminating at the E7 level were number of index terms, descriptions of skill, professionalism, ability to communicate, and incidence of superlative adjectives and adverbs. At the E5–E6 level discriminating factors were descriptions of endurance and motivation. Ramsey-Klee and Richman cite the need for procedures to differentiate among incumbents; in the Navy some 14,000–20,000 promotion candidates are reviewed annually for two of the senior enlisted grades.

A difficulty often encountered in obtaining performance ratings is the scarcity of raters who have knowledge of the performance of the individuals to be evaluated. Wilson et al. (1954), Wiley (1975), and Mitchell and De Nisi (1976) report lack of familiarity of supervisors with the tasks their subordinates perform. Similar findings have been reported in the industrial literature (O'Reilly, 1973). The length of acquaintance required, however, at least for peer ratings, appears minimal; Urry (1963) reported that length of acquaintance beyond one month is not crucial.

Behavioral Scales. Recently, there has been a small amount of military research on development of behavioral expectation scales and the derivative behaviorally anchored scales and behavior observation scales (Borman, Hough, & Dunnette, 1976). This work is characterized by empirical derivation and scaling of performance dimensions for particular jobs based on analysis of behavior incidents reported by incumbents. The specificity of behavior-based scales sets them apart from the general graphic scales used widely in the services. Otherwise, few truly novel rating methodologies have been introduced in the military since the attempt to use forced-choice methods (Sisson, 1948; Gough, 1958; Wherry, 1959)—procedures that were not widely accepted, seemingly because raters are not comfortable with a method in which descriptors have been equated for desirability and the meanings of particular choices are not readily discernible. User acceptability and ease of administration are particularly important characteristics for any method intended to be adopted in the military.

Measurement of Performance Via Intervention

The totality of job requirements can rarely, if ever, be represented in any single specimen of performance. Measuring performance by means of an intervention in day-to-day work usually involves both selecting portions of the universe of job performance as the content of interest and sampling from those portions to avoid redundant measurement. As noted earlier, identifying and sampling job content are relevant both to measurement of on-going job performance and to measurement of performance via an intervention but are likely to be carried out for measurement of on-going performance only when tasks are preselected for measurement or when job content is analyzed to develop structured within-task performance checklists.

Selecting and Sampling a Performance Domain. The content of interest in a universe of individual performance is, as noted above, almost always purposely and selectively described and is said to define a particular *content domain*. All of the operations that could potentially be used in a test of the domain (i.e., all possible content that might be contained in a test, all formats that might be the vehicle for testing) have been referred to as a *test universe*. The particular test content and format that are actually used in a given application have been referred to as a *test domain* (Guion, 1979a), which consists of four major areas and a catch-all category.

OCCUPATIONAL ANALYSIS PROGRAMS: Each of the services has prescribed that the content of training and evaluation be identified through formal analysis of performance requirements (see, for example, Department of the Air Force, 1970, 1975; Branson et al., 1975). In seeking to implement these directives, training developers could avail themselves of a considerable body of information already available from military occupational analysis programs.

In 1958, for example, the Air Force established its Occupational Research Project which developed the Comprehensive Occupational Data Analysis Program, or CODAP, which would subsequently be used by each of the other services (Christal, 1974). Later the Navy established the Occupational Task Analysis Program (NOTAP), and recently the Army established the Occupational Survey Program (AOSP). The job analysis checklists used in such programs generate a wide variety of descriptive biographical data, task data (such as percent performing, difficulty of learning, consequences of inadequate performance, criticality of immediate performance), and equipment and tools data (frequency of operation, use, and repair).

Because the information from these occupational analysis programs is generally compiled and organized by task, it is natural that the task has become the unit of activity most often used as a starting point in analyzing the content of a performance universe to define a domain for evaluation. Several criteria for selecting tasks for training and evaluation have been proposed. Branson et al. (1975) list the following as major criteria, but leave the final choice to the user: percent of persons performing, percent of time spent in performing, probable consequences of inadequate performance, task learning difficulty, probability of deficient performance, length of time between job entry and task performance.

TASK SELECTION: The U.S. Army Training Support Center (1977), in its Guidelines for Development of Skill Qualification Tests, lists the following as possible bases for task selection: known performance deficiencies, tasks contributing to the operation or maintenance of critical combat systems, tasks related to deficiencies in crew/unit performance, tasks that have been revealed as important in prior evaluations, and proportional samples from different content or functional areas of performance. Again the final selection of a factor or combination of factors is left to the user. A handbook for constructing tests for use in the Navy (Ellis & Wulfeck, 1982) suggests that information be sampled based on importance if it varies on this dimension and sampled randomly within topics if it does not vary in importance.

In several current projects investigating the link between enlistment standards and job performance, tasks for the development of performance measures are selected by means of iterative sampling procedures based on task characteristics. In a large Army study,[10] the development of knowledge tests and hands-on job sample tests is based on selecting tasks according to frequency of performance and estimates of importance. In a Navy study alternate strategies for task selection are being compared.[11]

The authors cannot offer a comprehensive approach to task selection that organizes the entire range of methods that have been proposed. A certain degree of order can be imposed in this area, however, by considering how the strategy chosen for task selection can be related to the purpose for the evaluation.

TASK IMPORTANCE AND CRITICALITY: It is clear that a set of tasks that are candidates for selection should be identified primarily on the basis of the importance of the tasks in the context of a broader system within which the task is performed. An ideal way to identify important tasks would be to select those that have been shown to have the greatest impact on an operational system. However, system criteria and objective measures of their relation to the performance of particular tasks are rarely available. Instead, tasks usually must be identified by persons considered best able to judge their importance.

It should be noted at this point that concepts like criticality and importance appear subject to considerable variation in personal and situational definition, and judgments about task characteristics are sometimes unreliable (Smode, Gruber, & Ely, 1962; Mead, 1975). In efforts to increase reliability, characteristics like task importance have been defined in relation to particular scenarios, such as combat in Eastern Europe for tank crew tasks and aboard a particular class of ship for electronic repair tasks. It also seems reasonable to involve subject-matter experts themselves in the identification of task characteristics that might serve as reliable bases for sampling tasks. Such a practice is typically followed in identifying behavior dimensions for rating scales, but it is rarely if ever used in task sampling for test development.

BEHAVIORAL ANALYSIS: In addition to direct estimates of task importance, other types of task information often contribute to the specification of a domain. It is usually desirable, for example, to insure that all nontrivial dimensions of behavior are represented. A catalog of behavior dimensions for sampling can be developed through direct analysis of the elements of important tasks (e.g., differentiate sounds, read written material, decode visual signals, operate keyboard devices, position switches, use hand tools), or functional categories of performance can be used for sampling with the expectation that they are related to underlying types of behavior (e.g., operate wheel vehicles, operate track vehicles, perform checks and adjustments on communication equipment, troubleshoot ignition systems, troubleshoot radar systems).

While there is no certainty that sampling of tasks either by behavior dimensions or functional categories will insure adequate coverage (e.g., some relevant behavior dimensions may not have been identified, functional categories are imperfectly related to underlying behavior) sampling on the basis of behavior is usually preferable, since it focuses directly on the different behaviors intended for representation in the test.

OTHER TASK INFORMATION: After task importance and behavior representation have been taken into account, other types of task information may contribute to the sampling. Additional task characteristics that sometimes are introduced include frequency of performance, difficulty of learning or performing, and criticality of immediate performance. Characteristics such as generalizability of content and capacity to differentiate among performers may be considered in order to maximize efficiency of measurement.

The type of information that may be used to sample tasks, other than that related to importance and behavior representation, depends on the purpose of measurement. When a test is used to set selection criteria and matters of test fairness are of particular concern, for example, it may be desirable to give added weight to the factor of task importance. If tests are to be administered only to apprentices, and senior workers will be available to handle rarely performed, difficult tasks, perhaps task frequency will emerge as the sampling variable.

If measurement is intended to diagnose training achievement, task difficulty may be chosen as a basis for sampling. Information about the difficulty of learning or performing a task is usually based on expert judgment.

When measurement is used to evaluate job proficiency rather than more circumscribed training performance, greater attention may be given to generality of coverage. Generalizability refers to the extent to which performance on a given task is predictive of performance on another task or predictive of performance in a domain overall. Because empirical information about task intercorrelations is almost never available prior to the construction of a test through which such information can be generated, estimates of task generalizability must usually be based on a priori estimates of task similarity.

To estimate similarity, elements of tasks are defined and clustered into patterns. Performance elements may be defined in various ways, including job-oriented descriptions of activities and procedures, worker-oriented descriptions of behavior, descriptions of work products, and descriptions of job-related knowledge and skill (McCormick, 1976). Patterns of elements are then compared across tasks, and the generalizability of each task is estimated. It is assumed that the closer the match of patterns of elements, the greater the generalizability among tasks or between a task and a domain. An example of this procedure is given in Wheaton et al. (1978).

Representing a Performance Domain in an Intervention. A performance domain consists of four major areas.

INTERVENTION ALTERNATIVES: Only after the performance domain of interest has been identified and sampled is it appropriate to consider the content and format of the intervention itself. This is a matter of determining what behavior will provide an adequate basis from which to infer proficiency in those tasks or units of the performance domain to be examined. For some tasks, it may be judged that nothing less than acting out the entire task with real equipment and materials will support an inference about a performer's proficiency. For other tasks, it may be necessary only for the examinee to perform one or more segments of the task in the same fashion as the segment is performed on the job. In that case only the boundaries of the task being tested would be changed.

A third option, used especially but not exclusively in training, is to evaluate selected response elements of task performance in isolation from other responses that occur at the same time or in very close proximity to the tested response. Examples include typing sentences composed only of letters in a limited section of the keyboard, and demonstrating a parachute landing fall after jumping off a platform rather than as part of a complete jump. This category differs from the testing of a complete task segment in that it focuses on a much smaller element of behavior. Responses or conditions that would interfere with or distract from the main response of interest are deliberately not represented.

The first three measurement options—whole tasks, complete segments of tasks, and isolated response elements—can all be placed in that category which Guion (1979b) has referred to as a direct work sample, and they all have a "hands-on" appearance. The fourth option is to abstract some underlying component thought to contribute to proficiency: knowledge, motor skill, cognitive skill, and so on. Measures of separate components of either knowledge or skill have been referred to by Guion as abtracted work samples and often appear considerably different from performance seen on the job. Examples include multiple-choice tests of job information and soldering electronic parts on a "bread board" rather than on functioning equipment.

These options for measuring performance via an intervention have been summarized in Table 6.2. The order of the options indicates generally decreasing certainty that the intervention adequately represents task performance on the job. The greatest amount of inference from test performance would generally be required when an abstracted component of knowledge or skill is used to estimate job performance. Whether each option differs greatly from adjacent options may depend on the nature of the task. As Guion (1979b) has pointed out, in fact, even a job knowledge test, usually classified as an abstracted work sample, could be considered a direct work sample if it were harder to acquire the knowledge needed to perform the task than to carry out the actions that use the knowledge.

DIRECT WORK SAMPLES: Using an entire task as the focus of measurement can avoid many errors of analysis, possible distortions of stimulus conditions, and omission of important behavior that can occur when constructing tests of task segments, isolated response elements, or abstracted components. Nevertheless, at least the cues that initiate task performance must be artificially supplied, even in whole-task measurement, and many minor cues, distractions, and other conditions that are part of job task performance will inevitably be lost. In addition, whole-task measurement is also subject to the potential shortcomings that are consequences of any intrusive intervention: test subject anxiety, misunderstood instructions, unintentional cuing, modifications introduced to permit observation or scoring, and so forth. Additional drawbacks of whole-task measurement are cost and reduced coverage of the range of job tasks.

Some of these drawbacks were among the problems that arose in the Army's Skill Qualification Test program. The Army initially made entire tasks the unit of training and testing and attempted to make the SQT a completely hands-on test. This was sometimes done even where it was arguable that demonstrating a procedure, as distinct from displaying knowledge of the procedure, was necessary for inferring a capability to perform. The prohibitive expense of developing and using hands-on tests on a very large scale, the limited number of tasks for which tests were actually constructed and administered, and the difficulty of achieving controlled, reliable scoring led the Army to shift to a mix of knowledge tests and hands-on tests.

Measurement of segments of a task or isolated response elements is further removed from daily performance and, of course, introduces a larger presupposition about actual performance than an inference based on whole-task measurement. Any modifications made to part of a task in order to present it in a test may generate cues that induce performance that would otherwise not occur. Conversely, the absence of cues from parts of performance deleted to create the test may inhibit performance that would otherwise occur.

ABSTRACTED WORK SAMPLES: Measurement of abstracted components of knowledge or skill generally requires the largest inference about task performance. When abstracted knowledge or skill is the basis for estimating performance, error may be attributable to requirements of either type that have intentionally or unintentionally been omitted and requirements that have been artificially added. Performance requirements are probably most frequently omitted from measurement when inappropriate formats are used to measure abstracted knowledge. While there are some situations where multiple-choice, true/false, and other types of selected response items can be used, they are usually inappropriate because they measure the recognition of knowledge when most performance calls for its recall. Even a test that gives the appearance of covering all of task performance may remain a knowledge test with an inappropriate format. Shriver, Hayes, and Hufhand (1974) had test subjects identify correct and incorrect performance in video portrayals of electronic maintenance tasks (e.g., removing and replacing components, performing alignment and adjustment tests). Even though innovative video simulations of performance were used rather than conventional multiple-choice tests, the passivity of the subjects' role made for tests of knowledge recognition rather than recall.

Where knowledge mediates performance of a procedure that is done the same way each time, a single test item will often suffice for measurement of an element of knowledge. When, however, knowledge is to be applied to new situations as in the use of rules and principles to make decisions and solve problems, two or more items are necessary to demonstrate that the user is able to generalize the information. Procedures for analyzing the knowledge requirements of different types of performance and methods for checking the adequacy of test formats for measurement of knowledge are available in a series of reports by Ellis and Wulfeck and their co-workers (Wulfeck et al., 1978; Ellis, Wulfeck, & Fredericks, 1979; Fredericks, 1980; Ellis & Wulfeck, 1982).

All forms of abstracted work samples involve the explicit selection of content to be covered in the measurement and provide an opportunity for both intentional and unintentional additions, modifications, and omissions of task requirements. When requirements beyond those present in actual job performance occur in a test, it is usually as a direct consequence of the test format. The added reading requirements that written tests may impose are, of course, well known. A study reported by Osborn (1974) provides an example of response-related requirements that were unintentionally added. He compared performance on four different types of knowledge tests with hands-on performance for manual procedural tasks. Average correlations between the hands-on tests, multiple-choice tests, and pictorial knowledge tests in which procedure steps and errors were to be identified were in the .80s. Average correlations dropped to .58 between hands-on tests and pictorial tests in which pictures were to be arranged to demonstrate a correct sequence of steps. The latter type of test required persons first to form a mental image of the entire procedure and then to arrange the pictures in accordance with this mental image. It is unlikely that these processes intervene when the tasks are actually carried out. Lower-aptitude persons had the lowest scores with this test format.

Omissions and modifications of performance requirements often occur in abstracted samples because some stimulus requirements are difficult to represent, artificial cues to performance are provided, or the abstracted situation encourages or permits behavior that is not likely to occur in actual performance. Shriver and Foley (1974) have pointed out, for example, that the "main line" of electronic troubleshooting contains subprocedures and distracting factors such as a need to set up test equipment and obtain error-free information that in actual performance often interferes with problem identification. Abstracted tests of troubleshooting that omit these real-life requirements are not likely to correlate well with a full hands-on test.

Nonprocedural tasks such as problem solving, troubleshooting, and decision making are particularly prone to distortion when the processes are represented in an abstracted work sample. In these tasks, relevant facts, response options, and solution criteria are not usually explicit in the situation but must be identified and then selected by the performer. The troubleshooter needs to devise an overall strategy and draw inferences from the results of the checks he or she elects to perform. The decision maker must often both establish limits to the search for the anticipated consequences of alternate courses of actions and select a basis for making the choice. When any of these elements of performance is made explicit in an abstracted test, a critical aspect of actual performance is likely to be lost.

An example of the difficulty of preserving actual task requirements—even in an innovative measure—is the Tab Test (Glaser, Damrin, & Gardner, 1952; Cornell et al., 1954). When the test is used to simulate electronic troubleshooting, the performer obtains test "readings" by lifting tabs, erasing opaque coverings, and so on. Steinemann (1966) demonstrated that the behaviors exhibited in such a simulation are quite different from those in troubleshooting actual electronic equipment. Correlations between a hands-on performance test and the Tab Test ranged from − .50 to + .14. One clear difference between the two measures is that the Tab Test required no effort in setting up test equipment and no skill in using it. Another notable factor is that the Tab Test provides considerable structure to a task that in real life is often ambiguous. It clearly suggests the response options to the subject.

In measuring troubleshooting or decision-making skill, the focus is on a generalized process, rather than particular problems used to represent the process. Thus, attempts to measure such processes as abstractions apart from the particulars of a given situation are readily understandable. Nevertheless, the fact that these kinds of tasks are loosely structured, and their structure poorly understood, readily permits abstractions to be designed that omit major requirements of "actual" or typical performance. When evaluation is undertaken for criterion purposes, measurement of unstructured tasks via abstracted models may often be invalid. Procedural tasks and other types of structured tasks, in which departures from typical requirements are likely to be obvious, are more likely to be reliable objects for abstracted measurement.

SYNTHETIC TESTS: Osborn (1970) has suggested a scheme for constructing "synthetic" tests for procedural tasks by which the fidelity of different task components is progressively reduced to explore their contribution to variability of performance. For example, in a binocular ranging task, targets could be represented in successive stages of simulation as photographs mounted at a distance, target pictures printed in a test booklet, and so on, while the fidelity of other task components is left the same. Osborn suggests that considerable savings in measurement costs might often be achieved with relatively slight loss in behavioral coverage by selecting a simulation in the middle of a range of simulation options. Since the dimensions of simulation are largely unknown, however, he acknowledges that the plan is not a procedure for developing an optimal test, but rather a plea for being analytic, resourceful, and imaginative in test construction.

The promise of any synthetic approach to performance testing is based on the not unreasonable assumption that the components of many procedural tasks are largely independent of one another. Nevertheless, since the effects of any changes in task requirements and response-induced cues that may be introduced in synthetic and other hands-on-like simulations cannot generally be anticipated, it seems appropriate to consider such tests as being closer to hands-on demonstrations of knowledge than hands-on demonstrations of performance. Such tests may have their greatest virtue in avoiding the verbal descriptions, literacy requirements, and content omissions of conventional knowledge tests. Their principal shortcoming may possibly be a tendency to produce false negatives, persons who can perform a task on the job but who fail when faced with a simulation that may introduce other symbolic requirements in order to represent a task.

As was indicated in Table 6.1, evaluating the product of performance is a technique applicable to any of the major classes of measurement content. That is, work products can be used in evaluating both job performance as it occurs and various kinds of performance in an intervention: whole task, task segment, isolated response element, or abstracted component of knowledge or skill. In some jobs, of course, task products may not be revealing of significant aspects of task performance and may be unavailable for some or all tasks. The advantages and disadvantages of product measurement in comparison to process measurement have been discussed elsewhere (see, for example, Osborn, 1974) and will not be repeated here. In general, product measurement can often provide for somewhat greater objectivity than process measurement. The relative advantages and disadvantages of the two methods do not appear to differ for any of the classes of measurement content discussed here.

Representing the Performance Domain: Summary. Since it is rarely, if ever, possible to measure the totality of job performance or technical performance, evaluation begins with identification of the domain to be evaluated. This domain can be defined in a variety of ways depending on the purposes of evaluation. Often it amounts to identification of those areas of performance where human errors occur and have a significant impact on a larger system within which the performance takes place. Occasionally the domain of interest may be defined in terms of performance requirements viewed as important for reasons such as criticality or frequency, even if errors are infrequent.

The domain that has been selected for evaluation is then sampled to arrive at a set of tasks or other class of performance requirements that can be evaluated. The question that must then be met is what kind of test performance will be taken as evidence of proficiency with regard to the performance of interest: what will be the content and form of the test?

There are few certain prescriptions that can be offered in deciding what type of behavior will suffice. Rather, there are three questions to be asked in guiding the decision:

1. How complete a representation of a task is likely to be adequate for estimating task proficiency: whole task, task segment, isolated response element, abstracted component of knowledge or skill?

2. If a task segment, response element, or abstracted component is judged to be sufficient, can the appropriate part be picked out, and is it sufficiently independent of other task parts that are not represented to permit its extraction from the task?

3. If a task segment, element, or abstracted component is to be used, what evaluation format is essential to maintain the response requirements that characterize the performance of interest?

Using an entire task avoids errors attendant upon breaking the task into smaller elements and to that extent reduces the opportunity for criterion contamination and deficiency, but it is less efficient and more costly than the various part-task and abstracted component alternatives. Thus, the fact that increasing inference is required in estimating proficiency when other than whole-task evaluation is undertaken is not sufficient reason to restrict proficiency measurement to whole-task, hands-on tests. Understanding which situations are amenable to the use of part-task and abstracted component testing is likely to come about only in the course of studies that deliberately compare these alternatives. Such comparative studies are, at present, rare.

NOTES

1. Military research publications reflect a greater emphasis on tests than other forms of evaluation, although other factors—for example, a general disenchantment with and diminution of research on ratings—undoubtedly contribute to this occurrence. For example, *Proceedings of the Military Testing Association* for 1980 through 1982 contain 38 articles concerned with achievement and proficiency testing of military personnel and 4 articles concerned with summary ratings of performance.

2. The common errors and sources of bias in rating procedures have been described repeatedly in the industrial psychology literature—such as P. C. Smith (1976)—and will not be discussed here.

3. Rate refers to a particular rank, corresponding to pay grade, within an occupational specialty. Rating is the basic title for Navy occupational specialties.

4. Attainment of prerequisite time in service and time in rate is also a requirement of promotion eligibility.

5. David Robertson, Navy Personnel Research and Development Center, San Diego, personal communication.

6. The other elements that contribute to the WAPS are time in service, time in grade, decorations received, and Airman Performance Reports.

7. The written component included two types of items: (1) performance-based items, which focus on information that mediates performance, and (2) written-performance items, which focus on tasks that involve written operations or calculations such as completing a requisition form. In later years of SQT development, an Alternate Hands-on Component (AHOC) was introduced, consisting of written items supported by illustrations.

8. U.S. Army Training Support Center, personal communication.

9. Prior identification and sampling of job content are, of course, relevant both to measurement of on-going job performance and to measurement of performance via an intervention. Much, if not most, measurement of on-going performance, however, focuses on the general character of the performance and does not call for partitioning and sampling performance at the level of the task or similar element. Sampling is more likely to be an issue in those instances where structured rating instruments or performance checklists are used to support the observations.

10. U.S. Army Research Institute for the Behavioral and Social Sciences project: Development and Validation of Army Selection and Classification Measures (Contract MDA 903-82-C-0531).

11. Navy Personnel Research and Development Center project: Development of Procedures to Identify Critical Job Tasks for Measuring Maintainer and Operator Performance (Contract N66001-83-D-0341).

REFERENCES

Amir, Y., Kovarsky, Y., & Sharan, S. (1970). Peer nominations as a predictor of multi-stage promotions in a ramified organization. *Journal of Applied Psychology, 54*(5), 462–469.

Bialek, H. M., Zapf, D., & McGuire, W. (1977). Personnel turbulence and time utilization in an infantry division. *Proceedings of the 19th Annual Conference of the Military Testing Association*, 461–475.

Bodi, M. J., & Yellen, T.M.I. (1967). The methodology underlying the development of a revised commander's evaluation report (CER). *Proceedings of the 9th Annual Conference of the Military Testing Association*, 104–114.

Borman, W. C. (1974). The rating of individuals in organizations: An alternate approach. *Organization Behavior of Human Performance, 12*, 105–214.

Borman, W. C., Hough, L. M., & Dunnette, M. D. (1976, February). *Development of behaviorally based rating scales for evaluating the performance of U.S. Navy recruiters* (NPRDC Technical Report 76-31). San Diego: Navy Personnel Research and Development Center.

Branson, R. K., Rayner, G. T., Cox, J. L., Furman, J. P., King, F. J., & Hannum, W. H. (1975, August). *Interservice Procedures for Instructional Systems Development* (5 vols.) (TRADOC Pam 350-30). Ft. Monroe, VA: U.S. Army Training and Doctrine Command.

Burt, J. A., Corts, D. B., Yellen, T.M.I., & Waldkoetter, R. O. (1969). Redesign of the enlisted efficiency report. *Proceedings of the 11th Annual Military Association*, 330–336.

Christal, R. E. (1974, January). *The United States Air Force occupational research project* (AFHRL-TR-73-75). Brooks Air Force Base, TX: Occupational Research Division, Air Force Human Resources Laboratory.

Cornell, F. G., Damrin, D. E., Saupe, J. L., & Crowder, N. A. (1954). *Proficiency of Q-24 radar mechanics: III. The Tab Test—a group test of trouble-shooting proficiency* (AFPTRC-TR-54-52). Lackland Air Force Base, TX.

Department of the Air Force. (1970, December; rev. 1975). *Instructional Systems Development* (Air Force Manual 50-2). Washington, D.C.: Author.

Downey, R. G., & Duffy, P. J. (1978, October). *Review of peer evaluation research* (TP 342). Alexandria, VA: Army Research Institute for the Behavioral and Social Sciences.

Downey, R. G., Duffy, P. J., & Shiflett, S. (1979, June). *Construct validity of leader effectiveness criteria* (Technical Paper 368). Alexandria, VA: Army Research Institute for the Behavioral and Social Sciences.

Ellis, J. A., & Wulfeck, W. H., II. (1982, October). *Handbook for testing in Navy schools* (NPRDC Special Report 83-2). San Diego: Navy Personnel Research and Development Center.

Ellis, J. A., Wulfeck, W. H., II. & Fredericks, P. S. (1979, August). *The instructional quality inventory: II. User's manual* (NPRDC Special Report 79-24). San Diego: Navy Personnel Research and Development Center.

Evaluation of the Canadian forces other ranks personnel evaluation system (1982, March). (Vol. 1, Main Report. DPCAOR 5788-20-2). Ottawa: Author.

Flyer, E. S. (1963, June). *Prediction of unsuitability among first-term airmen from aptitude indexes, high school reference data, and basic training evaluations* (PRL-TDR-63-17, DDC Document AD-420 530) (OTS). Lackland Air Force Base, TX: Personnel Research Laboratory, Officers Training School.

Fredericks, P. S. (1980, July). *The instructional quality inventory: III. Training workbook* (NPRDC Special Report 80-25). San Diego: Navy Personnel Research and Development Center.

Glaser, R., Damrin, D. E., & Gardner, F. M. (1952, June). *The tab item: A technique for the measurement of proficiency in diagnostic problem-solving tasks.* Unpublished study, Bureau of Research & Services, College of Education, University of Illinois, Urbana.

Gough, H. G. (1958). *An assessment study of Air Force officers: IV. Predictability of a composite criterion of officer effectiveness.* United States Air Force, Wright Air Development Command Technical Report, 58-91.

Gould, R. B., & Shore, W. C. (1969). Evaluation of the promotion fitness examination as a factor in the weighted airman promotion system. *Proceedings of the 11th Annual Conference of the Military Testing Association*, 222–232.

Guion, R. M. *Personnel Testing.* (1965). New York: McGraw-Hill.

———. (1979a). *Principles of work sample testing: II. Evaluation of personnel testing programs* (TR-79-A9). Alexandria, VA: Army Research Institute for the Behavioral and Social Sciences.

———. (1979b). *Principles of work sample testing: III. Construction and evaluation of work sample tests* (TR-79-A10). Alexandria, VA: Army Research Institute for the Behavioral and Social Sciences.

Guion, R. M., & Ironson, G. H. (1979, April). *Principles of work sample testing: IV. Generalizability* (TR-79-A11). Alexandria, VA: Army Research Institute for the Behavioral and Social Sciences.

Mead, D. F. (1975). Determining training priorities for job tasks. *Proceedings of the 17th Annual Conference of the Military Testing Association.*

McCormick, E. J. (1976). Job and task analysis. In M. D. Dunnette, ed., *Handbook of industrial and organizational psychology.* Chicago: Rand McNally.

Mitchell, J. L., & De Nisi, A. (1976). Another look at the ratings. *Proceedings of the 18th Annual Conference of the Military Testing Association*, 150–165.

Office of the Assistant Secretary of Defense (Force Management & Personnel). (1985). *Fourth annual report to the House Committee on Appropriations: Joint service efforts to link enlistment standards to job performance.* Washington, D.C.: Author.

———. (1988) *Seventh annual report to the House Committee on Appropriations: Joint service efforts to link enlistment standards to job performance.* Washington, D. C.: Author.

O'Reilly, A. P. (1973). Skill requirements: Supervisor-subordinate conflict. *Personnel Psychology, 26,* 75–80.

Osborn, W. C. (1970, December). *An approach to the development of synthetic performance tests for use in training evaluation* (HumRRO Professional Paper 30-70). Alexandria, VA: Human Resources Research Organization.

_____ . (1974, October). *Process versus product measures in performance testing* (HumRRO Professional Paper 16-74). Alexandria, VA: Human Resources Research Organization.

Osborn, W., & Ford, P. (1977). Knowledge tests of manual task procedures. *Proceedings of the Annual Conference of the Military Testing Association*, 634–649.

Ramsey-Klee, D. M., & Richman, V. (1976a, February). *Final studies of content analytic techniques for extracting the differentiating information contained in the narrative sections of performance evaluations for Navy enlisted personnel* (Technical Report 76-1). Personnel and Training Research Programs, Psychological Sciences Division, Office of Naval Research.

_____ . (1976b, February). Content analytic techniques for extracting the differentiating information contained in the narrative sections of performance evaluations for Navy enlisted personnel (Technical Report 76-2). Personnel and Training Research Programs, Psychological Sciences Division, Office of Naval Research.

Robertson, D. W., Royle, M. H., & James, J. (1972, November). *Design and fleet trial of automated performance evaluation forms for two pay grade groups: E5–E6 and E1–E4* (Research Report SRR 73-11). San Diego: Naval Personnel and Training Research Laboratory.

Royle, M. H., & Robertson, D. W. (1974). Scaling techniques to reduce rater leniency for Navy enlisted performance evaluation forms. *Proceedings of the 16th Annual Conference of the Military Testing Association*, 616–631.

Shirkey, E. C., & Urry, V. W. (1965). The effect of length of acquaintance on reliability of peer ratings. *Proceedings of the 7th Annual Conference of the Military Testing Association*, 28–31.

Shriver, E. L., & Foley, J. P. (1974, November). *Evaluating maintenance performance: The development of graphic symbolic substitutes for criterion-referenced job task performance tests for electronic maintenance* (AFHRL-TR-74-57(III). Brooks Air Force Base, TX: Air Force Systems Command, Air Force Human Resources Laboratory.

Shriver, E. L., Hayes, J. F., & Hufhand W. R. (1974, July). *Evaluating maintenance performance: A video approach to symbolic testing of electronics maintenance tasks* (AFHRL-TR-74-57 (IV)). Brooks Air Force Base, TX: Air Force System Command, Air Force Human Resources Laboratory.

Sisson, E. D. (1948). Forced-choice: The new Army rating. *Personnel Psychology, 1*, 365–381.

Smith, P. C. (1976). Behaviors, results, and organizational effectiveness: The problem of criteria. *Handbook of Industrial and Organizational Psychology*, Dunnette, M.D. (Ed.). Chicago: Rand McNally.

Smode, A. F., Gruber, A., & Ely, J. H. (1962, February). *The measurement of advanced flight vehicle crew proficiency in synthetic ground environments* (MRL-TDR-62-2). Wright-Patterson Air Force Base, OH: Behavioral Sciences Laboratory.

Steinemann, J. H. (1966, July). *Comparison of performance on analogous simulated and actual troubleshooting tasks* (RM SRM 67-1). San Diego: U.S. Naval Personnel Research Activity.

Urry, V. W. (1963). *Effect of rater-ratee acquaintance period on CER ratings*. Fort Benjamin Harrison, IN: U.S. Army Enlisted Evaluation Center (Research Study No. 5).

U.S. Army Training Support Center, Individual Training and Evaluation Directorate. (1977, December). *Guidelines for development of skill qualification tests*. Ft. Eustis, VA: Author.

U.S. General Accounting Office. (1982, March). *Report to the Secretary of the Army: The Army needs to modify its system for measuring individual soldier proficiency* (FPCD-82-28). Washington, D.C.: Author.

Vineberg, R., & Joyner, J. N. (1980, January). *Instructional system development (ISD) in the armed services: Methodology and application* (HumRRO Technical Report 80-1). Alexandria, VA: Human Resources Research Organization.

_____ . (1982, March). *Prediction of job performance: Review of military studies* (NPRDC Technical Report 82-37). San Diego: Navy Personnel Research and Development Center.

_____ . (1983). Performance measurement in the military services. In F. Landy, S. Zedeck, & J. Cleveland (Eds.), *Performance Measurement and Theory*. Hillsdale, NJ: Lawrence Erlbaum Associates, 1983.

Wance, W. W., Hermansen, A. G., Mahnen, H. A., & Brittain, C. V. (1976, March). *Revision of the enlisted evaluation report* (Technical Memorandum 39). Ft. Benjamin Harrison, IN: U.S. Army Enlisted Record and Evaluation Center.

Welsh, J. R. (1980). Criteria definition and measurement in the U.S. promotion system. *Proceedings of the 22nd Annual Conference of the Military Testing Association, 2.*

Wheaton, G. R., Fingerman, P. W., & Boycan, G. G. (1978). *Development of a model tank gunnery test* (Technical Report 78-A24). Alexandria, VA: U.S. Army Research Institute for the Behavioral and Social Sciences.

Wherry, R. J., Jr. (1959). An evaluative and diagnostic forced-choice rating scale for servicemen. *Personnel Psychology, 12,* 227–236.

Wiley, L. N. (1966, November). *Describing airman performance in the administrative career ladder by identifying patterns of trait ratings*. (PRL-TR-66-13). Lackland Air Force Base, TX: Personnel Research Laboratory, Aerospace Medical Division, Air Force Systems Command.

_____ . (1969, August-September). *Analyzing supervisor ratings of performance of job type members*. Paper presented at the meeting of the American Psychological Association, Washington, DC.

_____ . (1974, July). *Across-time prediction of the performance of airman administrators and mechanics* (AFHRL-TR-74-53, AD-786 409). Lackland Air Force Base, TX: Occupational Research Division.

_____ . (1975, June). *Familiarity with subordinates' jobs: Immediate versus secondary supervisors* (AFHRL-TR-75-7). Lackland Air Force Base, TX: Occupational and Manpower Research Division.

_____ . (1976, October). Airman job performance estimated from task performance ratings (AFHRL-TR-76-64). Lackland Air Force Base, TX: Occupational and Manpower Research Division.

Wiley, L. N., & Cagwin, L. P. (1968, October). *Comparing prediction of job performance trait ratings for aircraft mechanics and administrative airmen* (AFHRL-TR-68-108). Lackland Air Force Base, TX: Personnel Research Division, Air Force Human Resources Laboratory, Air Force Systems Command.

Wiley, L. N., & Hahn, C. P. (1977, December). *Task-level job performance criteria development* (HRL-TR-77-75). Brooks Air Force Base, TX: Air Force Human Resources Laboratory, Air Force Systems Command.

Willing, R. C. (1969). Using content validity to improve military occupational specialty proficiency test. *Proceedings of the 11th Annual Conference of the Military Testing Association*, 100–105.

Wilson, C. L., Mackie, R. R., & Buckner, D. N. (1954, February). *Research on the development of shipboard and performance measures. Part III. The use of performance check lists in the measurement of shipboard performance of enlisted Naval personnel*. Washington, D. C.: Personnel and Training Branch Office of Naval Research, Department of the Navy.

Wulfeck, W. H., Ellis, J. A., Richards, R. E., Wood, N. D., & Merrill, M. D. (1978, November). *The instructional quality inventory: I. Introduction and overview* (NPRDC Special Report 79-3). San Diego: Navy Personnel Research and Development Center, November 1978.

Index

Ackerman, T. A., 12
Air Force: classification procedures of, 48–49; enlisted testing of, 30–32; evaluation systems of, 176–177; officer aptitude selection measures of, 112–115; officer candidate programs of, 98–100
Air Force Academy (USAFA), 98; selection for, 112
Air Force Human Resources Laboratory (AFHRL), 121, 147
Air Force Officer Qualifying Test (AFOQT), 113–115, 119–121
Air Force Officer Training School, 115
Air Force Reserve Officer Training (AFROTC), 112–115
Air Force Specialty Code (AFSC), 48–49
Airman Performance Report (APR), 177
Alf, E. F., Jr., 58, 61
Algorithms: discriminant function approaches, 61; near optimal solutions, 60; optimal assignment, 60; performance, 61
Allocation systems: discriminant analysis models, 58–59; fill policies, 52–54; fit/fill policies, 54–57; miscellaneous, 59–60; multiple

criterion models, 57–58; profile matching models, 59; research in, 64–65; sequential assignment, 54; single criterion models, 57
All Volunteer Force (AVF), 46
Ambler, R. K., 155
Armed Forces Qualification Test (AFQT), 2–4
Armed Services Vocational Aptitude Battery (ASVAB), 3–7, 15–16
Army: classification procedures of, 47; enlisted testing of, 29–30; evaluation systems of, 177–180; officer aptitude selection measures of, 102–107; officer candidate programs of, 98–100; officer selection battery, 115–117; Training Support Center, 186–187
Army Education Information System (AREIS), 83–86; evaluation of, 86; subsystems of, 85
Army General Classification Test (AGCT), 2
ASCAL program, 14
Assignment, 41–42, 44–50; history of, 44–47; optimal, 41n
Automated Guidance for Enlisted Navy Applicants (AGENA), 81–83
Aviation Officer Candidate School (Navy), 109–111

Aviator selection, 129–161; light-plane
    and job-sample tests, 154–158;
    paper-and-pencil cognitive ability
    tests, 131–136; personality, interest,
    and background information tests,
    137–144; psychomotor and
    information-processing tests,
    145–154

Baker, H. G., 80
Bale, R. M., 142
Barnes, V., 65
Bartlett, F. C., 132
Baum, D. R., 156
Beach, L. R., 65
Behavioral analysis, 187–188
Behavioral scales, 185
Berkshire, J. R., 155
Bigbee, L. R., 155
BILOG program, 14
Bolanovich, D. J., 3
Borack, J., 46
Boyle, D. J., 155
Brandon, R. K., 186
Brogden, H. E., 43
Brown, W. R., 133
Bucky, S. F., 139–140
Burke, E. F., 143, 147

Campbell, J. P., 29
Canadian Forces Career Information
    System (CFCIS), 87–89
Cardinet, J., 59
Career Advisement and Personnel
    System (CAPS), 65
CAT-ASVAB Technical Manual, 26–27
Charnes, A., 58
Christal, R. E., 31
Classification: the criterion problem,
    52; history of, 42–44; models for,
    50–57
Classification and Assignment Within
    PRIDE (CLASP), 55–56, 64
Classification procedures: Air Force,
    48–49; Army, 47; Marine Corps,
    47–48; Navy, 49–50

Cleff, S. H., 59
Combat performance, peacetime cri-
    teria for, 170–172
Computer Assisted Assignment System
    (COMPASS), 49, 53
Computer-based psychomotor tests,
    147–149
Computer Based Recruit Assignment
    (COBRA), 48, 53
Computerized Adaptive Screening
    Test (CAST), 21, 83
Computerized adaptive testing (CAT),
    18–28; concept of, 18–20; current
    programs, 22–28; motivation for,
    20–22
Computerized vocational guidance
    (CVG), 75–92; civilian approxima-
    tions of, 76–78; components of,
    78–80; current U.S. Navy programs,
    90–91; military approximations of,
    80–90; requirements for, 75–76
Cook, L. L., 11
Cox, J. A., 155
Criterion problem, the, 52
Cronbach, L. J., 58

Dailey, J. T., 43
Damos, D. L., 150–151
Defense Mechanism Test (DMT),
    142–144
DeVries, P. B., 141
Dockeray, F. C., 131
DOD Performance Measurement Pro-
    ject, 180–181
Dorfman, D. D., 58
Dow, A. N., 49
DuBois, P. H., 2
Dwyer, P. S., 43

Eastman, R. F., 133
Enlisted Efficiency Report, (EER), 178
Enlisted performance, 169–195
Enlisted Personnel Allocation System
    (EPAS), 56, 64
Enlisted testing: the AFQT, 3–4; Air
    Force efforts, 30–32; Army efforts,

29–30; the ASVAB, 4–7; expanding
domain of, 28–33; history of, 2–8;
item response theory, 8–13; Navy
efforts, 32–33; new directions in, 8;
the 1944 Metric, 2–3; progress in,
7–8; World War I and II, 2
Evaluation, 169–195; Air Force Systems, 176–177; Army systems,
177–180; Navy systems, 174–175;
peacetime criteria for combat performance, 170–172; periodic,
173–174; research in, 180–195;
trainee, 172–173
Examination for advancement, 175

Fiske, D. W., 131–132, 137
Fit, goodness of, 61–62
Fitts, P. M., 145
Flanagan, J. C., 131
Fleischman, H. L., 141
Fleishman, E. A., 133
Flyer, E. S., 155
Folchi, J. S., 28
Foley, J. P., 192
Fowler, B., 151

Gade, P. A., 22–23
Geldard, F. A., 132, 145
Gleser, B. C., 58
Goebel, R. A., 156
Gopher, D., 149–151
Gordan, T., 138
Govindan, M., 46
Grabowski, B. T., 76
Green, B. F., 11–12
Guilford, J. P., 2
Guinn, N., 141
Guion, R. M., 189–190

Hagin, W. V., 155–156
Hambleton, R. K., 11–12
Harris-Bowlsbey, J., 76
Harris, C. W., 132, 145
Harris, J. E., 77
Hattie, J., 12
Hayes, J. F., 191

Hecht, R. M., 59
Hendrix, W. H., 55
Henmon, V.A.C., 145
Hertli, P., 133
Hewlett Packard (HP), 27–28
Hill, J. W., 156
Holtzman, W. H., 138
Hook, M. E., 59
Hopkins, P., 132, 137, 145
Horst, P., 52, 60
Hufhand, W. R., 191
Human Resources Information Sys-
tem (HRIS), 59–60
Hunt, E., 32

Information-processing tests, 149–151
Ingram, D. L., 155–156
Isaacs, S., 131
Item response theory (IRT), 8–13;
advantages of, 9–10; assumptions of,
10–13; calibration methods, 13; and
CAT, 18–19; item parameters, 14–16;
practical applications of, 16–18
Izard, C. E., 140

Jacobson, M. D., 76
Jessup, G., 142
Jessup, H., 142
Joaquin, J. B., 142
Johnson, R. M., 23
Joint Optical Information Network
(JOIN), 22–23, 89–90
Jones-James, G., 27

Kahneman, D., 149
Keeth, J. B., 133
Kingsbury, G. G., 19–20
King, W. R., 58–59
Knapp, D. J., 23–24
Knight, S., 146–147
Kuder, F., 65
Kyllonen, P. C., 31–32

Lacey, J. I., 2
Learning Abilities Measurement Program (LAMP), 30–31

Levine, A. S., 132–133, 137
Light-plane tests, 155–156
Lintern, G., 150–151
LOGIST program, 13
Long, G., 157
Lord, F. M., 11–13, 20, 43

Marine Corps: classification procedures
    of, 47–48; officer aptitude selection
    measures of, 111–112, 117–119; of-
    ficer candidate programs of,
    98–100; payoff functions, 63
Mashburn, N. C., 145
McGrevy, D. F., 147
McHenry, J. J., 30
McLaurin, W. A., 147
McMullin, R. L., 133
Melton, A. W., 2, 131
Melton, R. S., 138
Military Academy (USMA), 98; selec-
    tion into, 102–103
Military Entrance Processing Station
    (MEPS), 27–28
Miller, R. E., 134
Mislevy, R. J., 16
Monitoring: personal, 78; system, 77
Morgan, F., 46
Mullins, C. J., 133, 155
MULTILOG program, 14

National Opinion Research Center
    (NORC), 5
Naval Academy (USNA), 98; selection
    into, 107–108
Navy: classification procedures of,
    49–50; current CVG programs of,
    90–91; enlisted testing of, 32–33;
    evaluation systems of, 174–175; of-
    ficer aptitude selection measures of,
    107–111, 117–119; officer candidate
    programs of, 98–100
Navy General Classification Test
    (NGCT), 2
Navy Occupational Task Analysis
    Program (NOTAP), 58

Navy Personnel Research and Develop-
    ment Center (NPRDC), 10, 28, 81
Navy Reserve Officer Training Corps
    (NROTC), 108–109
Navy Vocational Information System
    (NVIS), 81
1944 Metric, the, 2–3
North, R. A., 150

Occupational Analysis Programs, 186
Officer aptitude selection measures,
    97–125
Officer candidate programs: for college
    graduates, 99–100; for college
    students, 98–99
Officer Candidate School (Army),
    105–107
Officer Candidate School (Navy),
    109–111
Officer Career Information and Plan-
    ning System (OCIPS), 86–87
Officer selection tests: Air Force,
    113–115, 119–121; Army, 115–117;
    Navy and Marine Corps, 117–119
Osborn, W., 191–193
Owen, R. J., 19

Parry, J. B., 132
Passey, G. E., 147
Payoff values, 52, 62–64
Performance domain: abstracted work
    samples, 191–193; direct work
    samples, 190–191; intervention alter-
    natives, 189–191; synthetic tests,
    193–194
Performance measurement, 181–185;
    via intervention, 185–195
Performance rating, 175, 183–185
Periodic evaluation, 173–174
Personalized Reservation for Immedi-
    ate and Delayed Enlistment
    (PRIDE) system, 49
Person-job matching, 61–64
Personnel classification models, 50–57
Peterson, N., 29–30

Pilot training, cost of, 130
Pliske, R. M., 23–24
Procurement Management Information System (PROMIS), 49, 54–55, 64
Programs (computer): ASCAL, 14; BILOG, 14; LOGIST, 13; MULTILOG, 14
Psychometric Decision List, 26
Psychometrika, 43
Psychomotor tests, 145–149

Rafacz, B. A., 23, 27
Ramsey-Klee, D. M., 184–185
Rayman, J. R., 76
Research: in allocation systems, 64–65; in individual evaluation; 180–195; on paper-and-pencil cognitive tests, 131–136; on personality, interest, and background information tests, 137–144
Reserve Officer Training Corps (ROTC), 98–99; selection into, 103–105
Richman, V., 184–185
Riederich, L., 133
Robertson, D., 141
Roseen, D., 46
Rosenberg, N., 140
Roth, J. T., 142
Rovinelli, R. J., 12

Sanders, J. H., 147
Sands, W. A., 22–23
Schmitz, E. J., 65
Sells, S. B., 138–139
Sequential assignment, 54
Sequential Classification Module (SCM), 56
Shriver, E. L., 191–192
Signori, E. I., 132, 137, 145, 155
Simulator-based testing, 156–158
Skill level certification, 176
Skill Qualification Test (SQT), 178–180
Sorenson, R. C., 52, 60
Spielberger, C. D., 139–140

Steinemann, J. H., 192
Stoker, P., 143
Super, D. E., 86
Swanson, L., 49

Task selection, 186–87
Taylor, C. W., 140–141
Tests: enlisted, *see* enlisted testing; light-plane and job-sample, 154–158; officer selection, *see* officer selection tests; paper-and-pencil cognitive ability, 131–136; personality, interest, and background information, 137–144; psychomotor and information-processing, 145–154; synthetic, 193–194; *see also* evaluation
Thissen, David, 14
Thompson, N. A., 134, 141, 148, 157
Thorndike, R. L., 43
Trade and Lifestyle Videotapes (TLVs), 88
Trainee evaluation, 172–173
Trandell, A., 146
Tupes, E. C., 132–133, 137

Uhlaner, J. E., 3
United States Military Entrance Processing Command, 3–4

Vale, C. D., 15
Valentine, L. D., 147
Varney, N., 157
Viteles, M. S., 131, 137, 145
Voas, R. B., 139–140
Vocational Interest for Career Enhancement (VOICE), 64
Votaw, D. F., Jr., 43, 51

Waldeisen, L. E., 142
Want, R. L., 133
Ward, J. H., Jr., 43–44, 55, 59, 63
Weighted Airman Promotion System (WAPS), 176
Weiss, D. J., 19–20

West Point, *see* Military Academy
Wild, C. L., 17
Willing, R. C., 178
Wingersky, Marilyn, 13
Wolfe, J. H., 32–33
Women, opportunities for, 46–47
Work samples: abstracted, 191–193;
    direct, 190–191

Wright, Orville, 129
Wright, Wilbur, 129
Written knowledge testing, 176

Yen, W. M., 17
Yerkes, Robert M., 2

About the Editors
and Contributors

MARTIN F. WISKOFF is a Senior Scientist at the Defense Personnel Security Research and Education Center (PERSEREC), Monterey, California. At PERSEREC he is responsible for managing a Department of Defense research program addressing the screening of personnel for security clearances. He was formerly the Director of the Manpower and Personnel Laboratory at the Navy Personnel Research and Development Center, San Diego, a visiting professor at the Naval Postgraduate School, Monterey, and the Head of the Psychological Research Branch of the Bureau of Naval Personnel, Washington, DC. He received his M.A. and Ph.D. in industrial psychology from the University of Maryland. Dr. Wiskoff has numerous publications and is affiliated with several professional organizations, including the American Psychological Association (Fellow and Past President, Division of Military Psychology), and the Military Testing Association (Board of Directors). He is the founder and editor of *Military Psychology*, a journal of the Division of Military Psychology of the American Psychological Association. Wiskoff is listed in *Who's Who in Government*, *Who's Who in the West*, *American Men and Women of Science*, *Personalities of America*, and other honorary societies.

GLENN M. RAMPTON, C.D., B.Sc., M.Sc., Ph.D., is currently Assistant Vice-President (Human Resources) for York University in Toronto, Canada. Earlier in his career, he gained broad professional experience in personnel selection, assessment, development, and management through a variety of "hands-on" practitioner and research roles. Subsequently, he spent three years as an Associate Professor of Leadership and Management at the Royal Military College of Canada. He was then promoted to assume the position of Commanding Officer of the Canadian Forces Personnel Applied Research

Unit in Toronto. He next served as chief military psychologist at National Defence Headquarters where he was responsible for directing the research and applied services provided to the Canadian Forces by military human resource professionals located throughout Canada and in Europe.

On retiring from the Canadian Forces in 1983, Dr. Rampton became Director of Human Resources Planning and Development for the Canadian Post Office. Just prior to joining York University, he spent two years as Director of Human Resources for the Pulp and Paper Research Institute of Canada.

A past President of the Military Testing Association, Rampton has been active in various professional associations at both the national and international level. He has more than 50 publications as book chapters, in refereed journals, or as technical reports, and he recently served as one of five members of a select committee to draft new Educational and Psychological Testing Guidelines for the Canadian Psychological Association.

HERBERT GEORGE BAKER is a Research Psychologist in the Personnel Systems Department at the Navy Personnel Research and Development Center. His research there is in the areas of performance assessment, vocational interests, and computerized vocational guidance and occupational information systems. Dr. Baker's previous research activities have ranged from enlisted career development to antiterrorism research data base design. Currently, he is Deputy Research Program Manager for the Navy Job Performance Measurement Program. Dr. Baker received his doctorate from the United States International University (USIU) and is affiliated with a number of professional organizations. He has taught at several colleges and universities and now serves on the faculty of USIU. He is Past President of Division 14, International Imagery Association. His extensive list of professional publications reflects his interests and expertise in several areas of human behavior research and application.

DIANNE C. BROWN is a Research Psychologist with Edison Electric Institute (EEI) where she designs and conducts research in support of EEI's Industry Testing Program. Prior to this Ms. Brown was a Research Associate with the Human Resources Research Organization (HumRRO). Under HumRRO's Manpower Analysis Program for over three years, she was involved with a study of the enlistment and utilization of high-aptitude military personnel, a test-equating study to provide reading grade levels for the Armed Services Vocational Aptitude Battery, and a project to develop selection instruments for Army civilian first-line supervisors. Her research on military officers originated from the study of high-aptitude personnel. In addition to documenting the various commissioning sources and selection criteria, she has analyzed officer performance data in relation to aptitude test scores. Ms. Brown is completing her M.A. in industrial/organizational psychology at George Mason University.

REGINALD T. ELLIS is a consultant specializing in personnel assessment and the development of personnel selection systems. He has held a variety of appointments with the Canadian Department of National Defense as a Personnel Research Specialist. Prior to entering private practice, he occupied a senior management position in charge of selection systems development for Canadian National Railways. Ellis's work has involved the development and evaluation of all types of selection measures, including management assessment centers and computerized vocational guidance systems. He received his doctorate in Industrial/Organizational Psychology from the University of Waterloo in 1986. Dr. Ellis is a member of the Canadian Psychological Association and is registered as an Industrial Psychologist with the Corporation Professionnelle de Psychologue du Quebec.

DAVID R. HUNTER is a Research Psychologist with the Army Research Institute element located at the Army Aviation Systems Command, St. Louis. He received his doctorate in educational psychology from the University of Texas at Austin. Formerly, he was employed with the Air Force Human Resources Laboratory, San Antonio, and has also served for two years with the Ministry of Defence in London as an exchange scientist. While with the Air Force he was engaged in the development of aircrew selection measures, particularly those dealing with computer-based cognitive and psychomotor assessment. During his exchange assignment with the Ministry of Defence he developed an extensive battery of computer-based tests that is now being used for aircraft controller and pilot selection. His current research interests are in the areas of man-machine interface, measurement and evaluation of human performance, and organizational development. Dr. Hunter is a member of the American Psychological Association and is a frequent contributor to the professional literature on aircrew selection.

JOHN N. JOYNER served as a Senior Scientist with the Human Resources Research Organization until 1986 and was formerly the director of the functional literacy training program at Fort Ord, California. At HumRRO his work included developing and evaluating literacy training, developing task-related measures of job reading requirements, evaluating Instructional System Development methodologies, analyzing alternative instruction media for nonresident professional education, developing individualized professional training, analyzing the job performance of enlisted personnel in different mental aptitude categories, and analyzing predictors and criteria of performance in technical training schools. Joyner holds a degree in English from Yale University and is currently developing computer hardware and software documentation and consulting on documentation development methods.

LEONARD P. KROEKER is a Research Psychologist in the Personnel Systems Department at the Navy Personnel Research and Development Center. At the Center he has conducted personnel selection and classification research that led to the development of CLASP, the Navy's automated classification system. His research interests also include policy-capturing, utility theory, and individual and organizational decision making. Dr. Kroeker holds a Ph.D. in psychometrics and statistics from the University of Wisconsin. From 1971 to 1976 he was a faculty member at the University of Illinois, Chicago, and was active in the business community as an industrial/organizational consultant. During the last decade he has taught regularly at San Diego State University. He is presently Research and Technical Issues Coordinator in the Center's Job Performance Measurement Program.

MALCOLM JAMES REE is an adjunct faculty member at the graduate school of St. Mary's University of Texas, where he teaches research methods and advanced statistics. He is the Senior Scientist for the Force Acquisition Branch of the Manpower and Personnel Division of the Air Force Human Resources Laboratory. In this role he has bridged the tradition from the World War II generation to the present. Dr. Ree chairs the Joint Services Selection and Classification Technical Task Group, which provides the technical direction for the Armed Services Vocational Aptitude Battery that is administered more than 2 million times annually. A frequent contributor to the literature of tests and measurements, he received his doctorate at the University of Pennsylvania.

MARY K. SCHRATZ is an Associate Professor of Industrial/Organizational Psychology at California State University, Long Beach. In earlier associations she was a Personnel Research Psychologist at the Navy Personnel Research and Development Center, an educational research psychologist at The Psychological Corporation, a psychometric research fellow at Fordham University, a lecturer of graduate education at the University of San Diego, and an instructor in psychology at Fordham University. Dr. Schratz received her doctorate and master's degrees in psychometrics from Fordham University and her B.S. in psychology from Fordham College.

Her current research interests include the development and application of psychometric techniques in personnel and educational measurement. Dr. Schratz is a member of the American Psychological Association, National Council on California Educational Research Association, Sigma Xi, and Phi Kappa Phi. She is a frequent contributor to the professional literature in personnel/educational measurement.

ROBERT VINEBERG is a former Research Manager of the Human Resources Research Organization, where he directed research focusing on the measurement of individual military performance. His work included analysis of aptitude and work experience as determinants of job performance, development of models for estimating psychological attrition in conventional and nuclear combat, and experimental evaluation of the retention of job skills. He has conducted studies for the U.S. Army, U.S. Air Force Human Resources Laboratory, Navy Personnel Research and Development Center, and Office of Naval Research. Dr. Vineberg has been a consultant to several agencies within the Department of Defense, most recently to the Defense Nuclear Agency. He received a doctorate in experimental psychology from New York University. He is a contributor to several books and has authored over 70 professional papers, and is a fellow of the American Psychological Association.